When All Hell Breaks Loose

WHEN ALL HELL BREAKS LOOSE

YOU MAY BE DOING SOMETHING RIGHT
Surprising insights from the life of Job

STEVEN J. LAWSON

NAVPRESS
BRINGING TRUTH TO LIFE
NavPress Publishing Group
P.O. Box 35001, Colorado Springs, Colorado 80935

The Navigators is an international Christian organization.
Jesus Christ gave His followers the Great Commission
to go and make disciples (Matthew 28:19). The aim of
The Navigators is to help fulfill that commission by
multiplying laborers for Christ in every nation.

NavPress is the publishing ministry of The Navigators.
NavPress publications are tools to help Christians grow.
Although publications alone cannot make disciples
or change lives, they can help believers learn biblical
discipleship, and apply what they learn to their lives and
ministries.

© 1993 by Steven J. Lawson
All rights reserved. No part of this publication may be
    reproduced in any form without written permission
    from NavPress, P.O. Box 35001, Colorado Springs,
    CO 80935.
Library of Congress Catalog Card Number:
    93-24957
ISBN 08910-97325

Second printing, 1993

Cover photograph: © 1993 The Stock
Market/Tom Ives

Some of the anecdotal illustrations in this book are
true to life and are included with the permission of the
persons involved. All other illustrations are composites
of real situations, and any resemblance to people living
or dead is coincidental.

Unless otherwise identified, all Scripture quotations in
this publication are taken from the *New American Standard Bible* (NASB), © The Lockman Foundation 1960,
1962, 1963, 1968, 1971, 1972, 1973, 1975, 1977.

Lawson, Steven J.
    When all hell breaks loose, you may be doing
something right / Steven J. Lawson.
        p.   cm.
    ISBN 0-89109-732-5
    1. Bible. O.T. Job—Criticism, interpretation, etc. 2.
Suffering—Religious aspects—Christianity.   I. Title.
BS1415.2.L36   1993
231′.8—dc20   93-24957
                                                  CIP

Printed in the United States of America

FOR A FREE CATALOG OF
NAVPRESS BOOKS & BIBLE STUDIES,
CALL 1-800-366-7788 (USA)
or 1-416-499-4615 (CANADA)

CONTENTS

Foreword   9

Chapter 1
LIGHTNING ROD IN THE STORM   11

Chapter 2
THE INVISIBLE WAR   27

Chapter 3
LIVING HELL   45

Chapter 4
I JUST WANT TO LIE DOWN AND DIE   57

Chapter 5
WITH FRIENDS LIKE THESE   71

Chapter 6
THE FOUR SPIRITUAL FLAWS   91

Chapter 7
I NEED YOU ON MY TEAM, NOT ON MY BACK   111

Chapter 8
THERE'S HOPE AT THE END OF YOUR ROPE   131

Chapter 9
COME IN OUT OF THE PAIN   155

Chapter 10
IT'S TIME TO TAKE INVENTORY   177

Chapter 11
PUTTING THE PIECES BACK TOGETHER   199

Chapter 12
SPEECHLESS, SPITLESS, AND ALL SHOOK UP   221

Chapter 13
NOWHERE TO LOOK BUT UP   243

To Dr. Carl E. Wenger—

a man whom God has greatly used in my life

Mentor. Friend. Encourager. Intercessor.

A gray head is a crown of glory;
It is found in the way of righteousness.
PROVERBS 16:31

ACKNOWLEDGMENTS

▼

A special thanks to the following people:

Steve Webb, my editor, who helped shape this manuscript and encouraged me in the process.

Steve Eames, NavPress, who designed the jacket for this book. I believe you can judge *this* book by its cover.

Dr. R.C. Sproul, who has greatly influenced my life and whom God used to help put the passion back in my ministry. And for taking the time out of a very busy schedule to write the foreword for this book.

Todd Murray, who first encouraged me to put these truths into a book and offered countless other ideas found herein. Jeff Kinley, who provided a wealth of creative brainstorming for this book when these chapters were first preached as sermons on Sunday evenings. Curtis Thomas, who bears much of my pastoral and administrative load so that I can be freed up to communicate God's Word.

Sherry Humphres, my secretary, who typed and retyped this manuscript. Thank you for your long hours of tireless work.

Roger Yancey, who reviewed and helped edit this manuscript here in Little Rock. Betty Lawson, my mother, and Monavee Kiesow, my aunt, who carefully proofread this manuscript.

Dr. Adrian Rogers, my former pastor, who first modeled biblical exposition for me. Twenty years later, I write this book still under the powerful influence of his ministry.

Anne, my wife, who endured much "hell" with me as I wrote this book. Unlike Job's wife, my faithful wife encouraged me to remain true to the Lord in all my trials. I am unworthy of such love.

FOREWORD

Life is full of suffering. In this fallen world, marred by sin and plagued by Satan, suffering is par for the course. The effects of the curse are everywhere.

How we respond to our suffering says so much about us. Perhaps it reflects *everything* about us. Our response to suffering, we could say, is an accurate barometer of our soul.

Too often, Christians attempt to mask their pain in a fraudulent piety. But we need not be stoic. Neither should we retreat into a fantasy world that denies the reality of suffering. We must acknowledge that suffering is real. To suffer as a Christian is no shame; it is part and parcel of life. Tragedy is a universal traveler, calling upon both the Christian and nonChristian.

Suffering is a part of the sovereign will of God. Our Savior was a suffering Savior. He went before us into the uncharted land of agony and death. As we take up our cross and follow Him, the narrow path we take is paved with pain and sorrow. In the midst of suffering, our souls ache for explanations to soothe our wounds and hurts. Why the trouble in my job? Why the pain in my marriage? Why the loss of health? Why?

Heaven is often silent. In such times, the only answer God gives is a deeper revelation of Himself. We learn that *He* is the answer we seek. Ultimately, we must not trust a plan, but a Person. In the face of chaos and confusion, we trust a personal God who is sovereign, wise, and good. In these times, God invites us to learn who He is.

Only in knowing Him do we find the adequate resources to endure and conquer.

God calls us to faith in Himself. He calls us not to blind faith, but to an implicit faith based upon the knowledge of His character. God never requires a foolish leap into the darkness, but a step of faith into the light of His glorious countenance.

Admittedly, our faith is never constant. It vacillates between moments of resolute confidence in God and sinking spells of discouragement. God knows our limits. When pushed to the edge of despair, we find the strength we need through our faith in Him that makes it possible to stand up under life's greatest pressures.

That's why the suffering of Job is so captivating. His story is a case study in human suffering. It records the real-life drama of a righteous man who underwent extreme misery and pain.

Job's faith wavered. He mourned. He cried. He protested. He questioned. He even cursed the day of his birth. But he never cursed God. In the face of adversity, he remained firm in his only hope—God. While God never disclosed His secret counsel to Job, He did reveal His character. Such divine revelation is sufficient in the absence of explanations to carry us through every severe heartbreak.

This is why I strongly recommend *When All Hell Breaks Loose*. It is a popular exposition of the oldest book in the Bible—the story of Job.

Steve Lawson is a former student of mine at Reformed Theological Seminary. I remember well our time together in the classroom, especially the class I teach on communication. I encourage my seminary students to teach the often neglected narratives of the Bible. People love to hear a story. They remember a story. Jesus taught by telling stories. Steve Lawson has taken my admonition to heart. Here is a retelling of one of the most memorable and profound stories in all literature—the story of Job's sufferings. This book is a lucid, pithy, carefully developed exposition of the book of Job, full of practical application and memorable illustrations.

As you read this book, do not be surprised if God tests your faith. Truth learned always brings a greater responsibility to act accordingly. So, as you learn about Job's faith in the midst of his suffering, prepare to have your faith challenged.

R. C. SPROUL
Orlando, Florida

CHAPTER 1

LIGHTNING ROD IN THE STORM

▼

There comes a time in every life when all hell breaks loose. Suddenly. Unexpectedly. Cataclysmically. All hell breaks loose.

One day, life is sunny. Calm. Clear. Placid. Predictable. Your job is secure. Your children behave. Your health is good. Then, out of the blue, like a violent, angry thunderstorm blowing across your landscape, tragedy strikes. You're hit hard. All hell breaks loose.

Suddenly, your life is stormy. Dark. Overcast. Turbulent. Threatening. Boiling. Swirling. Out of control. Lightning strikes your life and you go up in flames. All hell breaks loose.

It's never pretty. Never. A business goes sour. A marriage dissolves. A child rebels. A loved one is diagnosed with cancer. Your daughter miscarries. All hell breaks loose.

Your life becomes engulfed in the fire. Your soul is torched. Your faith scorched. Your heart is singed and seared. You have been inhaled into life's back draft. Permanent scars begin to form. All hell breaks loose.

"Am I ever going to pass through the flames?" your heart aches. "Will I survive life's inferno?"

It happens to all of us. Your teenage daughter is hit by a drunk driver and killed. Instantly. Or Friday comes and your pay envelope includes a terse termination notice. Or your doctor sits down on the edge of your bed, clears his throat, and then breaks the grim news: "The reports don't look good. We'll have to operate in the morning."

You leave your toddler son with a baby-sitter, and while she is talking on the phone with a friend, he falls into your swimming pool and drowns. Tragedy. Despair.

Your husband is suddenly tired of being married and leaves you for his secretary. This could never happen to you. But it just did.

Life is playing hardball. And you don't have a glove. Life is now bigger than life.

All that you cherish most is painfully ripped from your life. Gone. In a heartbeat. You are left behind in a heap of smoldering ashes, scorched by the hellish heat of fiery trials. Blistered. Blasted. All hell has broken loose.

It happens to all of us. No one is exempt. One way or another, tragedy strikes every life. One day, life is fine. Then, like a deadly arsonist on a midnight prowl, tragedy strikes without warning, igniting its destructive fires, consuming its unsuspecting victims. You are shaken to your very core. You can feel the gnawing fear in the pit of your stomach. The knot in your throat. You're in shock. Too numb to even respond. All hell breaks loose.

You long to wake up from this nightmare, but you can't. You have never been more awake. Your aching heart cries out for relief, but there is none to be found. All hell breaks loose.

Just as suddenly, just as unexpectedly, the doubt begins. The questions gush forth. Why is this happening to *me*? What have *I* done to deserve this? Why do I feel guilty? God, what's wrong with me? God, do you still love me?

On the surface, it seems tragedy does strike indiscriminately. It appears to work blindfolded. Like a misguided missile, it often seems to strike the wrong target. Why *do* bad things happen to good people? Why does tragedy visit those who love God the most?

Really, how do you explain that?

How do you explain a couple, who would be exemplary parents, waiting ten years to finally have a baby—only to lose their child at birth?

How do you explain when a Christian businessman, who is hardworking, honest, and the only spiritual witness in the office, is dismissed and loses his job? The good worker is fired, mind you, not someone whose productivity is far below his.

How do you explain a Christian housewife who gives her life to Christ, only to become alienated from her unbelieving husband and asked to leave?

How do you explain when a single father, the only Christian influence on his daughter, is the one who comes down with cancer—and not his unbelieving wife, who is left to raise their daughter?

These are all real questions I have had to wrestle with as a pastor. In fact, I had to deal with all these recently. I would be willing to wager that you have had to wrestle with at least some of these dilemmas as well.

Why do the righteous suffer? Why do bad things happen to good people? Why do the good die young? These difficult universal questions clog our souls and incapacitate our thinking.

Our mind runs quickly to certain inescapable conclusions. How can a good God allow tragedy to fall upon His own children? If you were a loving parent, wouldn't you shield your children from disaster if you could? Is God loving, but inept or powerless—unable to overturn some hidden ironclad hand of fate and prevent our tragedies? Conversely, is God all-powerful, but hardhearted and uncaring toward the plight of His beloved children? Is God guilty of child abuse?

Either way, the choices don't look good. Not for God, nor for us. Either God is loving but impotent or powerful but indifferent. Or is He both—impotent and indifferent?

Before we jump to conclusions, I want to suggest a fourth option. Another possibility. First, let's suppose God is as He is described in the Bible—loving, sovereign, and all-powerful. Then, could not God, who is both loving and sovereign, have higher purposes for trials in our lives—purposes both for our good and His glory? Could not God both love us deeply and still claim absolute sovereignty, yet have reasons far beyond our understanding for allowing tragedy to come into our lives?

That's my belief, but then I write from the evangelical, Protestant, Reformed traditions. Let me explain more of this belief and along the way I'll try to show you how it worked out in one man's life long ago to help you see that the truth one man experienced is still to be discovered today. There are many today, we'll see, who have had similar encounters.

In the absence of a clear explanation from God, I want you to consider one strategic assumption: We must accept that God plays in a higher league than we do. His ways are far above our ways. God is greater in intellect, power, and knowledge than we are. So, His ways are usually past our finding out.

So often, God never explains why. There are no "behind-the-scenes" reports sent from Heaven. Not even a fax. If we could just know why, it probably would give us some hope and staying power. But, in the midst of tragedy when we need them the most, there are no divine answers. No hints. No clues. Only silence from above. And the silence is deafening.

There is something about our inquisitive minds that longs for answers. If we only knew why, we reason, then we could handle the pain. But in the absence of our understanding, the trials become unbearable.

But, let's face it, even if God were to explain to us all the whys, we couldn't understand it. Placing His infinite wisdom into our finite brains would be like trying to pour the Atlantic Ocean into a Dixie Cup. It just wouldn't fit. It's too vast and deep.

How could we possibly grasp the inscrutable wisdom of God? The lines of providence intersect far above our heads. Nevertheless, what is darkness to my mind can be sunshine to my heart.

Consider a tapestry. On one side, we find countless threads interwoven, with no apparent design or connection. It appears all so disjointed. There are hundreds of different colored threads connecting to the other unseen side—some muted, some bright—all merging together. There is no pattern or design. Only confusion.

But, turn the tapestry over and a beautiful pattern appears. All the different colored threads come together perfectly to form a masterful work of art. What is confusion and disorder on one side is beauty and precision on the other. What a striking contrast!

So it is in life. There is our side—our perspective—and there is God's side, or Heaven's perspective. So often, tragedy strikes and all the threads seem so confusing and disjointed. No plan. No big picture. But, from God's perspective, there is striking symmetry. A perfect picture. A beautiful masterpiece. All designed for His glory and our good.

Here is our problem: *We can't see the other side of the tapestry.* All we can see are the various threads that don't seem to fit together. Faith in God is trusting that His side of the tapestry presents a beautiful heirloom.

Can I find comfort for my devastated and confused heart in viewing God's side of the tapestry? When it seems I can see only disjointed threads and no apparent purpose, is there hope?

I believe the answer is affirmative. Yes, there is comfort for our broken hearts when there are no answers to be found. True comfort comes not in seeing the other side of the tapestry, but in seeing the One who designs and weaves the tapestry. True comfort comes in knowing God. True comfort comes not in knowing why. True comfort comes in knowing *who*. It comes in knowing God. In trusting God. In worshiping God.

When our world falls apart unexplainably, we must not dwell upon *why*, but upon *who*. When our life falls apart and tragedy strikes, strength and comfort come, ultimately, from a personal knowledge of God.

Maybe you have been trying to untangle the mysteries behind your suffering. Maybe the storms of life have left you confused and disoriented. Neither you nor I may ever understand why. We may never see the other side of the tapestry. So, let's not focus our lives and energies on the pursuit of something that may be unknowable. In the absence of understanding, we must pursue knowing God. In an attempt to handle our trials, we must look beyond ourselves to God for answers.

A MAN WHO KNEW GOD

To best learn this critical life lesson, I want us to consider a man who experienced one of the greatest storms anyone has ever undergone. Storm may be an understatement. Typhoon perhaps. Hurricane. Tornado. A man who had everything and then lost it all. With no explanation from God. Not a clue. A man who eventually weakened, but who grew stronger and closer to God in the process.

Let's consider a man named Job.

Few people have ever suffered like Job. In a single day, Job had his family and wealth instantly taken from his life. Then, in a second wave of hellish attack, Job had his health removed as well. All that remained were his life and his wife. He was given no warning. No explanations. No options.

All hell broke loose.

This man was then left to pick up the broken pieces of a shattered life and try to make sense of it. How did he cope? Where did he find strength? How did he fail?

Strange as it sounds, I think you'll find that the life of Job is a great encouragement. Why? Because when all hell breaks loose, it may not mean there is anything *wrong* in your life. To the contrary, it may mean there is everything *right* in your life. That was the case with Job. And it may be the case with you.

Incredibly, throughout Job's storm, God never did tell him why such a hellish torrent had crushed his life. Not one word of explanation. Instead, all God ever revealed to Job was Himself. But Job discovered that a deeper knowledge of God was substantial.

For Job there were no simple answers. He was God's lightning rod, the tallest tree in the forest of his day. Unknown to Job, he stood as the leading candidate to draw the Devil's fire.

God chose to reveal only Himself to His trusted servant. Job found comfort, not in answers, but in God Himself. Not in divine mysteries untangled, but in God Himself unveiled. He discovered that the knowledge of God alone ultimately brings peace and strength. Only the knowledge of God can comfort the troubled heart.

It is the same with you and me.

There are times when all hell breaks loose. Sometime. Somewhere. Someplace. All hell breaks loose. If not yesterday, today. If not today, tomorrow. But be assured, all hell *will* break loose.

This book is all about withstanding life's heat when the fire falls. Yes, there is hope for those who have been admitted to life's burn center. There is an ointment of healing for those blistered by life's trials. It is found in the soothing salve of knowing God. Mere reasons and explanations are impotent balms. Only God's revelation of Himself is strong enough to heal the heart and relieve the pain.

A MOST UNLIKELY CANDIDATE FOR HERO

Let me now introduce you to the protagonist. Perhaps you have met Job. Perhaps not. Regardless, you will benefit greatly from knowing him, because each of us has so much in common with him. Sooner or later, we all identify with Job because suffering is part and parcel of life. We are bonded to Job through our common experience of pain.

Probably no person is more misunderstood than Job. Few people have been shrouded with greater mystery than this man who has become a timeless symbol of suffering.

Recently I was in Orlando, Florida, talking to my publishers about writing this book. I awoke early one morning in my hotel, too anxious to go back to sleep. So, I went down in the wee hours of the morning to the vacant lobby to read my Bible—the book of Job—and to pray.

Alone and pacing, I came upon a shoeshine stand in a remote corner of the lower convention level. A dear black woman was sitting there reading a book, preparing for a long day.

I hopped up in her chair to get my shoes shined. As I looked around, I discovered she was reading her Bible. Hmmmm. "What are you reading?" I inquired.

"The Bible, sir," she replied, looking into my eyes.

"What part of the Bible are you reading?" I followed up.

"Job. I'm reading the book of Job," she answered.

"Really? What do you think of it?" I asked, beginning to suspect the "coincidence" of the meeting might be a divine appointment, orchestrated by God.

"I don't understand it," she said sincerely. "I wish someone would explain it to me."

As she worked over my shoes, we enjoyed the moments together as I walked her through the pages of Job. I attempted to crystallize the main truths and weave the parts together into one—er, well—tapestry.

This shoeshine woman thanked me because the book of Job had always been a mystery to her. But now she understood it and was blessed.

I consider that "chance" encounter, insignificant as it may seem, a providential meeting. I believe that wonderful woman was placed there by God to encourage me to write this book. Job, so profound and yet so mysterious, is a book that requires some careful explanation.

So, who was Job?

Job was a man—a *real* man—who lived over 4,500 years ago. He's not a myth. Nor an ancient allegory. Job was a *real* man who lived in a *real* place, who was attacked by a *real* enemy, who was confronted with *real* problems, who experienced *real* pain, and who experienced *real* comfort from a *real* God. *Really!*

Incidentally, his enemy was a *real* devil. Satan. Lucifer. The prince of darkness. A person so evil he makes our modern tales of Dracula pale in comparison. *Really.*

Job lived in a land called Uz, which was southeast of Palestine near modern-day Jordan, and was probably a contemporary of Abraham.

Interestingly, Job was probably the first book actually written in the Bible. He predated Moses, who wrote the first five books of the

Bible. What's my point? The first divinely inspired book written deals with humanity's age-long mystery—"Why do the 'good people' suffer?" Some things never change.

As we begin our look at Job, we see the calm before the storm.

> There was a man in the land of Uz, whose name was Job, and
> that man was blameless, upright, fearing God, and turning away
> from evil. And seven sons and three daughters were born to
> him. His possessions also were 7,000 sheep, 3,000 camels, 500
> yoke of oxen, 500 female donkeys, and very many servants; and
> that man was the greatest of all the men of the east. And his
> sons used to go and hold a feast in the house of each one on his
> day, and they would send and invite their three sisters to eat and
> drink with them. And it came about, when the days of feasting
> had completed their cycle, that Job would send and consecrate
> them, rising up early in the morning and offering burnt offer-
> ings according to the number of them all; for Job said, "Perhaps
> my sons have sinned and cursed God in their hearts." Thus Job
> did continually. (Job 1:1-5)

These verses unquestionably reveal what a great man Job was. Talk about having your act together! Job had it all. Spiritual integrity. Loving father. Successful businessman. Sterling reputation. Job was the total package. There's not a one of us who wouldn't have loved to trade sandals with Job. Even God said, "There is no one like him on the earth" (Job 1:8). This man played at the top of the big leagues! His faith, his family, his fortune, his fame, his fathering. He touched all the bases!

His Faith—Strong and Alive!
The most important area of any man's life is his faith—his spiritual life. The Bible says Job was a man of great faith—"blameless, upright, fearing God, and turning away from evil" (Job 1:1). Job had a deeply personal relationship with God. He walked with Him closely. He knew God intimately. He respected Him greatly.

We learn four key aspects about Job's faith from this early passage.

First, Job was "blameless." This does not mean Job was sinless, but blameless. There is a huge difference. Sinless is vertical, blameless is horizontal. Vertically, *everyone* has sinned and fallen short of God's perfect standard (Romans 3:23)—Job included. But horizontally, as Job lived before the watchful eye of his peers, no one could justly charge Job with moral failure. His reputation was impeccable. He walked with integrity. Not with hypocrisy or duplicity. Without moral blemish. And everyone knew it. No charge could be brought against him.

Second, the text says Job was "upright." The word means, literally, "straight," in the sense of walking a straight path. Not deviating from God's standards. Job walked the straight and narrow path that leads to life. He stayed on track, not drifting away into worldliness. His walk matched his talk. He kept his ball in the fairway.

Third, Job "feared God." Fearing God means to be filled with awe, reverence, and respect for Him. It means to take God very seriously. To honor who He is. To obey what He says. To tremble at what He does. This fear is not the cowering of a young boy before the neighborhood bully, for fear of life or limb. Rather, it is an even higher respect and honor than one would feel at being in the Oval Office and meeting the President of the United States. A fear of being in the presence of one far superior.

In much the same way, Job deeply reverenced God in his heart. He had a high view of God. No flippancy toward God. No taking God lightly. Not Job. He soberly recognized he was living on *God's* green earth, breathing *God's* air, always under *God's* constant gaze. Consequently, Job saw God's hand in all aspects of his life.

"The remarkable thing about fearing God," said Oswald Chambers, "is that, when you fear God, you fear nothing else; whereas, if you do not fear God, you fear everything else."

Fourth, Job "turned away from evil." Job rejected all that was contrary to God's holy character. In today's vernacular, Job knew how to "just say no." Job had the strength of conviction to say no to sin, no to worldly temptation, no to evil seduction. He didn't buckle under peer pressure and go with the flow. He resisted temptation and the enticing lure of the world.

Here is Job's spiritual life. He is no ordinary man. He is an *extra*ordinary man. A sincere believer. A devout man. One fully committed to God.

Hardly a candidate for a disaster.

His Family—Full and Blessed!

If one's faith is most important, what is second? A man's family life. So it's not surprising to discover next that Job was the father of a large, close-knit family. He had "seven sons and three daughters" (Job 1:2).

The numbers seven and three signify completeness in Old Testament Hebrew, signs of God's favor. (And you thought your quiver was full.)

Job was like the man at McDonald's feeding eleven hyperactive kids. As busy as a one-armed paperhanger. Passing out drinks. Scraping onions off burgers. Distributing napkins.

A stranger at the next booth, observing the fiasco, inquired, "Are all those your kids?"

The hurried man laughed and said, "Land's sake, no. I could never take care of all these kids. This one here is my neighbor's kid."

The point is, Job enjoyed an ideal family. His children loved each other, and met regularly to enjoy one another's presence. This was no dysfunctional family. No way. This was one greatly blessed by God. God's smile shone brightly upon Job's family.

Candidates for a whole week's worth of "Focus on the Family." James Dobson would have been proud!

Hardly candidates for disaster.

His Fortune—Vast and Great!

Following one's walk with God and one's home life, a person's career would usually be next in order. So we are not surprised to learn that Job was a very successful businessman. "His possessions also were 7,000 sheep, 3,000 camels, 500 yoke of oxen, 500 female donkeys, and very many servants" (Job 1:3).

In ancient days, wealth was measured by one's property—like land, animals, and servants. Job possessed all three in spades. His 7,000 sheep provided him luxurious clothing and ample food; his 3,000 camels provided him transportation (and probably a bustling trucking business); his 500 oxen provided him even more food and "tractors" for plowing; his 500 female donkeys kept him supplied with more offspring; and a whole host of servants. Sounds like a rich businessman—sort of the H. Ross Perot of his day.

Job had every symbol of success. His garage was full of cars. His closet was lined with suits (all-wool, three-button suits, of course). His walk-in refrigerator was stocked with the finest steaks and pork chops. He had a hired crew always working at his house—cutting the hedge, painting the house, washing and folding the clothes, edging the driveway. He was living out most people's dreams.

Job reminds me of the wealthy Texan who was buried, as his will stated, in his gold-plated Cadillac. They dressed him up in a black tux. Then they propped him up behind the wheel of his favorite car, and a massive crane was lowering his car with him at the wheel into the large grave.

One of his envious friends, there to mourn his death, turned to a bystander, and, with a tear in his eye, said, "Man, that's *really* living."

Well . . . from where everyone else stood, Job was really living.

People can be divided into three classes; the Haves, the Have-Nots, and the Have-Not-Paid-For-What-They-Haves (where most of us live!). Let me tell you, Job was a member in good standing of the Haves. He was loaded!

Job was—and this is still a rare combination to find—both godly *and* wealthy. Two qualities rarely found together. Job played in both leagues. He laid up treasure in Heaven *and* on earth.

Hardly a candidate for disaster.

His Fame—Far and Wide!

Next we learn about Job's reputation. Because of his faith and his wealth, we are not surprised that he cast a long shadow across the surrounding landscape. Anyone who is godly and wealthy is sure to stand out. The Bible calls him "the greatest of all the men of the east" (Job 1:3). The greatest!

Job was great in influence. Great in respect. Great in visibility. He was the pillar of the community. The most influential man in town.

Job was held in highest regard by both God and man, well-known in both Heaven *and* on earth. Not bad!

Hardly a candidate for disaster.

His Fathering—Spiritual and Sacrificial!

Finally, to complete our portrait of Job, we need to know that he was a good father, deeply concerned for the spiritual welfare of his children. Unquestionably, he was the spiritual leader of his house.

Many a man is successful in the marketplace, but a failure at home. Many men sacrifice their children on the altar of their career. But not Job. He avoided such a deadly swap, remaining faithful to his family. He kept his priorities straight and on balance.

Honestly, most of us have trouble juggling the elusive balls of a demanding career, and a spiritual walk, and a growing family. But Job balanced these competing demands with great skill and grace.

Job's seven sons would gather together at least seven times a year, once for each of their birthdays (Job 1:4). There existed a close-knit atmosphere among his children, the result of Job's loving concern. Here they were, a tight family who deeply loved each other. No doubt, the integrity of Job's life earned him credibility with his family. His faith in God was real and molded the fabric of his children. When his seven sons met together, they even invited their three sisters to join with them. Their sisters? Good grief, this was a loving family! Job's family looked like a cast reunion of "Happy Days" or "The Cosby Show."

After each family party, Job would sacrifice burnt offerings on behalf of his children (Job 1:5). As the head of his household, Job was deeply concerned for the spiritual welfare of his children. So he offered burnt offerings to God, a symbol of his dedication of each child to God and a recognition of God's rightful ownership of their lives. It seems all Job wanted was God's best for them. Rather than smothering them with a clenched fist, closed to God's will for their lives, Job held them with an open hand, extended upward to Heaven, open to God's plan for each of them. The burden of his heart was that his children be God's . . . completely. To know God's will. To serve God's purposes.

Every family needs such a dad at the helm. A faithful father. A strong believer. A faithful provider. A spiritual leader. Not perfect. Just committed.

Howard Hendricks has said, "If your faith doesn't work at home, don't export it." In other words, faith that is real will always be faith that first works in the home. Well, Job's faith was definitely real, passing the home test with flying colors.

Here then is Job. Have you ever met anyone like him? If these first five verses of his book were all we had to go on, there wouldn't be one of us who would not want to trade places with this successful man.

Hardly a candidate for disaster.

Job walked with God too closely. He led his family too carefully. He loved his children too deeply. All Heaven has broken loose!

I say, hardly a candidate for disaster.

AN INESCAPABLE STORM

But, the fact of the matter is that God's children do suffer, don't they? We are not exempt from trials. Tragedy is a required course, not a chosen elective.

Look at Jesus. He was the *only* perfect Man who ever lived—fully

God, fully Man—and yet He was marked out for sorrow and tragedy. The same was true of Job. Like a lightning rod in the storm draws the fire, so Job was marked out to suffer. The taller you stand, the more fire you draw.

Those who grow tall spiritually, says the Bible, are like tall trees planted by streams of water. The prophet Jeremiah says,

"Blessed is the man who trusts in the LORD
And whose trust is the LORD.
For he will be like a tree planted by the water,
that extends its roots by a stream
And will not fear when the heat comes;
But its leaves will be green,
And it will not be anxious in a year of drought
Nor cease to yield fruit." (Jeremiah 17:7-8)

Here is what God is saying: Those who trust God are like massive trees. Strong. Tall. Towering. Deeply rooted. Growing upward. Fruitful. Productive. And, yes, exposed to life's storms.

In the storm, it is the tallest tree in the forest that is most likely to draw the lightning. Lightning, more times than not, strikes the tallest object. Consequently, we can expect that *those who stand tallest for God will draw the lightning*. Those who are strong in their faith. Those living fruitful lives. Those deeply rooted in Christ. The taller you stand, the more you will draw the fire—hell's fire!

The scene is the 1991 U.S. Open. The place is Hazeltine National Golf Course, just outside of Minneapolis, Minnesota. The day is peaceful, calm, and nice. A gorgeous summer day.

From far out on the horizon, the front wave of a bank of gray clouds rushes swiftly overhead within minutes. Turbulent skies blacken and boil. Swirling banks of electricity collect overhead.

Lightning is spotted. A golfer's worst nightmare.

Storm sirens soon blast as a fierce thunderstorm blows in, threatening the safety of one of the largest single-day crowds in the history of professional golf.

Forty thousand spectators scramble for any makeshift covering. Anything will work. A refreshment stand. An umbrella. A tree. Anything.

A group of spectators seek shelter under a thirty-foot willow tree near the eleventh tee to keep from being drenched. Wisely, an official asks them to find another spot elsewhere. It is just too dangerous to be under a tall tree with lightning spotted. A few people disperse. A few stay.

The storm heightens and lightning strikes a tree behind the tenth green, splitting its trunk in half, stripping back the bark like a peeled banana. A visible reminder of the storm's fury and power is recorded for all to see.

Then a minute later—BOOM!—another lightning bolt strikes. This time it is the tall willow tree. A dozen bodies topple like bowling pins. The noise is outrageous, likened to a series of M-80 firecrackers exploding.

"All I heard was a boom, boom, like gunshots," said spectator Don Lindley. "Then, all those people fell like bowling pins."

Six men got up. Six remained dazed on the ground. One died. With his hands still in his pockets.

One of the survivors recalled, "Somebody said it would be just our luck if lightning hit this one. We laughed. A few seconds later, we were hit."

Suddenly. Unexpectedly. Cataclysmically. The tallest tree drew the fire. All hell broke loose.

The spiritual lesson here screams out to us. The more we grow spiritually, the taller we stand, like massive trees, the more likely we are to draw the lightning in life's storms. The taller we stand, the more likely we are to absorb hell's fire. Hell just doesn't seem to like God's growing trees.

It is critically important that we understand this lesson. If we don't, so much of our suffering makes no sense. When tragedy strikes, we may automatically and inaccurately assume that God is punishing us. And nothing could be further from the truth. Just the opposite, it may well be that God is pleased with us and considers us worthy to suffer.

We will often suffer simply because we are the tallest tree in the area when the lightning strikes. In our neighborhood. In our office. In our family. Wherever.

This eternal perspective is so important. So affirming. So helpful. Instead of falling victims to discouragement, this critical insight enables us actually to be *encouraged*. It is our spiritual growth that causes us, on one hand, to suffer for God. The other hand is dealt by the presence of evil.

How about you? Maybe you—like Job—are a tall tree planted by streams of water, deeply rooted in your faith in God. You are growing fruitful.

As a result, you can expect to draw the lightning that would pass over other low areas.

Have you been struck by life's storms? Have you absorbed hell's fire? Be encouraged. Instead of crying out, "God, what's wrong with me?" it may be that your faith is the very reason why all hell has broken loose.

Has your life been torched? Has your faith been scorched? Has your heart been singed and seared? Do you bear the scars of hell's fire?

Then the message of this book is for you. An all-wise God who knows what is best for your life loves you very much. He remains completely in control, ruling in unrivaled sovereignty. He is Lord of your storms, able to calm the angry waves and hush the fierce winds. He is Lord over Satan. He is Lord over adversity. He loves you deeply and seeks your best.

There comes a time in every life when all hell breaks loose. Suddenly. Unexpectedly. Cataclysmically. All hell breaks loose.

Just when you think you can't take any more, when all hell is breaking loose around you, remember . . . you may be doing something right.

CHAPTER 2

THE INVISIBLE WAR

▼

A t this very hour, our planet is deeply entrenched in a world war. Not a military campaign for territorial rights. Not a political battle between opposing parties. Not an economic struggle for market superiority. But a warfare far more strategic—a spiritual warfare for the souls of human beings. This age-long conflict is an invisible war between God and Satan. An unseen struggle between elect angels and fallen demons. A cosmic conflict between Heaven and hell. A global battle between the forces of good and evil. The battlefield is the souls of men and women. At stake is the future of the planet and the eternal destinies of humankind.

Each of us is engaged in this invisible war. Everyone is enlisted in active duty. None of us has exempt status. There are no draft-dodgers. No conscientious objectors. No one can sit this one out. We are all foot soldiers, either in God's army or in Satan's.

Unfortunately, most people do not recognize they are at war. Even many well-meaning Christians live as if peacetime conditions exist while a bloody war is being fought all around them. Casualties are strewn across the landscape. None of us can afford to be uninformed about this invisible war. We cannot be ignorant of our great adversary

Satan. This evil emperor is working behind the scenes—covertly, invisibly, stealthily—unleashing his diabolical power with great fury and hatred, intent on destroying our faith in God.

Surprisingly, many today deny the existence of the Evil One. They laugh at him. They think he is a figment of men's minds. A holdover from the Dark Ages. A religious myth. An imaginary imp. A make-believe personality. A team mascot. A cartoon character. A Halloween icon.

But the facts are different. Satan rules planet earth, and he does so with an iron grip. He is the supernatural force behind all evil. The sinister architect of all suffering in the world, he is bent on destroying your life, dividing your marriage, and damning your soul. Jesus Himself said so.

His names are many. Each name reveals a different aspect of his wicked character and evil activities. Consider this roll call: Satan (adversary), the Devil (slanderer), Lucifer (bright shining one), Beelzebub (lord of filth), the Evil One (intrinsically wicked), the tempter (enticing to evil), the prince of this world (ruler of worldly influence), the father of all lies (great deceiver), the god of this age (controlling the world system), the prince of the power of the air (ruler over fallen angels), the accuser of the brethren (opposing believers), the old serpent (crafty deceiver), the great dragon (destructive beast), and a roaring lion (the great destroyer).

Long before Job's birth, Satan was active in the world. Genesis 3 introduces us to this crafty deceiver as a serpent who tempted Adam and Eve to disobey God. The world has not been the same since. Everything changed in the Garden of Eden after the first couple succumbed to the filthy one's influence. Theologians call it "the Fall." Some psychologists call it a "proclivity for evil" in the human race. Sociologists recognize it as the cause of social disorder and civic dysfunction. God calls it sin.

We all must recognize it as very real. Original sin. It was the first penetration of evil into human lives. It has incredible implications. It means that all humans now suffer from indwelling sin. Adam chose to believe the Evil One rather than the Creator. The result? We now live in a fallen world.

If we are to make sense of the fallen world around us, we must see the invisible war being fought between God and Satan for the souls of humanity.

The book of Job takes us behind the scenes into Heaven. It allows us to witness a remarkable exchange between God and Satan. Here is a rare trip to Heaven; a rare glimpse of transcendent reality as the veil to Heaven is temporarily pulled back. Here is the opportunity to see firsthand the invisible war between God and Satan. In Job 1, we will discover seven basic truths about Satan. Each one unmasks a bit more of his true identity.

SATAN IS A FALLEN ANGEL

The curtain is drawn and we are permitted to observe God, the angels, and the Devil conducting their business in Heaven: "Now there was a day when the sons of God came to present themselves before the LORD, and Satan also came among them" (Job 1:6).

As the scene shifts from earth to Heaven, we observe the angelic host—"the sons of God"—appearing before the Father. Before we go any further, we need to consider what angels are, how they operate, and why they were created. What *is* an angel? Let's start with the basics. Here's a mini-course in "Angels 101."

Angels 101

An angel—the name means "messenger"—is a heavenly being created to serve God and His people. These supernatural beings, though lower than God, are superior to humans in their strength and intelligence.

The number of angels is "myriads of myriads, and thousands and thousands," according to the New Testament (Revelation 5:11). This indicates an exceedingly large number meaning "ten thousand times ten thousand." Their number is one hundred million with millions left over! Probably billions. (Perhaps one angel for every McDonald's hamburger sold! That's a lot!) According to Scripture, angels neither die nor procreate (see Matthew 22:30, Luke 20:36).

The "host of heaven" are strategically organized into an arranged hierarchy of positions with various levels of authority. Michael is the archangel (Jude 9) and is surrounded by other "chief princes" (Daniel 10:13). They oversee thrones, dominions, rulers, and authorities in the heavenlies (Colossians 1:16). There's evidence that Michael isn't the first archangel, but we'll get to that in a minute.

Around the throne of God, evidently, we find a very high order of angels who serve as guardians of His holiness—the cherubim. These superior angels possess extraordinary courage, high-level intelligence, supernatural strength, and penetrating insight (see Ezekiel 1,

Revelation 4:6-7).

Similarly, the seraphim are also attendants at the throne of God, worshiping Him day and night. Their name means "the burning ones," revealing the burning intensity of their passionate praise. Both seraphim and cherubim are described in the Bible as six-winged humanlike creatures. That's why we see so many angels with wings in classical high-Renaissance paintings.

The Scriptures tell us that these angels cover their faces with two wings, denoting their reverence for God. With another pair of wings, they cover their feet, indicating a deep humility. With the remaining pair, they appear ready to fly at the Father's prerogative, attesting to their readiness to carry out the will of God. The Old Testament prophet Ezekiel described these angels as having full eyes in front and behind, symbolizing their sharp alertness, advanced knowledge, and comprehensive vision (Ezekiel 10:12).

Angels are given extraordinary ministry assignments of momentous importance. They watch over nations and world rulers (Daniel 4:17). They guard Israel (Daniel 12:1). They directly influence human leaders (Daniel 10:21–11:10). They will administer God's awful judgments upon the nations at the end of this age (Revelation 6–18).

In many ways of which we are unaware, angels are involved in serving us (Hebrews 1:14). At God's bidding they answer our prayers (Acts 12:7). They provide encouragement (Acts 27:23-24). And they care for us at death (Luke 16:22, Jude 9).

What a high and lofty ministry these elect angels are called to perform! Oh, if only elect angels were in the universe! Unfortunately there are more! Let's return to Job to see the others.

The Satanic Presence
Among this holy contingent appears another angel. He is identified simply by name. He is Satan.

Who is Satan? Where did he come from? What was his beginning? Why is he in Heaven? To answer these questions, we must hear from two ancient prophets—Ezekiel and Isaiah.

In the Old Testament, it's recorded that God addressed a godless king, the king of Tyre, by the prophet Ezekiel. However, God also directed His message to another person. He addressed none other than Satan himself—the evil power behind the throne, the one who controlled the human king:

Again the word of the LORD came to me saying, "Son of man, take up a lamentation over the king of Tyre, and say to him,

'Thus says the Lord GOD,
"You had the seal of perfection,
Full of wisdom and perfect in beauty.
You were in Eden, the garden of God;
Every precious stone was your covering:
The ruby, the topaz, and the diamond;
The beryl, the onyx, and the jasper;
The lapis lazuli, the turquoise, and the emerald;
And the gold, the workmanship of your settings and
     sockets,
Was in you.
On the day that you were created
They were prepared.
You were the anointed cherub who covers,
And I placed you there.
You were on the holy mountain of God;
You walked in the midst of the stones of fire." ' "
     (Ezekiel 28:11-14)

While we picture Satan as a dark, ugly, and evil creature, he did not start out that way. He was created by God as the most wise and beautiful being ever made. He was the highest of all the angels. There was none greater in the heaven except God Himself.

Satan was God's most important angel, the anointed cherub—the highest ranking position God could offer. He guarded all access to God's throne as His prime minister over all of creation.

So what went wrong?

Pride. Satan chose to rebel against the very God who had created him. The prophet Ezekiel tells us why.

"You were blameless in your ways
From the day you were created,
Until unrighteousness was found in you.
By the abundance of your trade
You were internally filled with violence,
And you sinned." (Ezekiel 28:15-16)

Satan no longer wanted to submit to God's authority. He became full of pride and rebelled against his Sovereign. He wanted to be worshiped himself; he rejected worshiping Another. In due time Satan attempted to overthrow the government of Heaven and seize control of God's throne. This started a great war against the Rightful Ruler. A treacherous takeover attempt of God's Kingdom occurred. A heavenly mutiny. Satan wanted Heaven as his own.

Satan wanted to replace God and rule the angels on his own. He wanted all the other angels to worship him and join in his rebellion against God. He wanted to sit on God's throne and rule over the universe.

Another Old Testament prophet, Isaiah, describes Lucifer's sin when he reveals God's address to the king of Babylon. Like Ezekiel, Isaiah was speaking not only to the earthly king but also to Satan, the power behind the throne. Isaiah records Satan's rebellion against God in the heavens:

> "But you said in your heart,
> 'I will ascend to heaven;
> I will raise my throne above the stars of God,
> And I will sit on the mount of assembly
> In the recesses of the north.
> I will ascend above the heights of the clouds;
> I will make myself like the Most High.'" (Isaiah 14:13-14)

Five times Satan defiantly asserts his arrogant will above God's. "I will . . . I will . . . I will . . . I will . . . I will." He wanted to be like God so that he would not have to answer to anyone. Such incredible pride is the core of all sin. It is pushing God out of His rightful place and choosing my way over His.

Betrayal filled the heavens that day.

Because of Satan's sinful rebellion, God severely judged him. The Lord condemned him, relieving him of his privileged responsibility over the angels, and sentencing him to the earth, where he became the ruler of this world. The prophet Ezekiel describes this fall from Heaven:

> "Therefore I have cast you as profane
> From the mountain of God.
> And I have destroyed you, O covering cherub,

From the midst of the stones of fire.
Your heart was lifted up because of your beauty;
You corrupted your wisdom by reason of your splendor.
I cast you to the ground;
I put you before kings,
That they may see you.
By the multitude of your iniquities,
In the unrighteousness of your trade,
You profaned your sanctuaries.
Therefore I have brought fire from the midst of you;
It has consumed you,
And I have turned you to ashes on the earth
In the eyes of all who see you." (Ezekiel 28:16-18)

God stripped Satan of his authority as the anointed cherub, protector of God's throne, and He expelled the evil from Heaven. Lucifer and the army of angels enlisted in his cause were forcibly removed and thrown down to the earth by a holy and angry God.

That's how Satan came to be Satan.

Back to Job. Here is Satan, standing before God's throne. Appearing right alongside the other angels, those who had remained faithful. Once the highest of all angels. Now a fallen creature. At war with God.

SATAN HAS DIRECT ACCESS TO GOD

Strange as it sounds, Satan still has access to God's throne. Although cast out of Heaven, he is still permitted by God to appear back in Heaven. Let's read this verse again: "There was a day when the sons of God came to present themselves before the LORD, and Satan also came among them" (Job 1:6).

Talk about being out of place! Here is the filthy, fallen Devil in the presence of the holy, pure God of Heaven. Face to face. Eyeball to eyeball.

Ray Stedman writes, "You can see him sauntering about among the angels, hands in his pocket, picking his teeth, disdain for all the angels, looking for an opportunity to accuse."

Accuse. That's precisely why Satan is here. He appears before God to accuse His people of their sins (Revelation 12:10). Filled with unholy hatred, the Devil seeks to accuse those whom God loves—you and me—of sin. While Satan is powerless to defeat God, he can hurt

God by destroying those whom God loves.

It's the same today. Satan is accusing us of our sins before God. Day after day, he is like a grave-digger, stirring up dirt against us. He says, "Look there, God. Steve Lawson is the biggest hypocrite on earth. He says he loves You, but look at the way he's living his life. He is disobedient. He is selfish. God, You've got to judge him."

I don't fully understand why God allows Satan this opportunity to accuse us. But He does. In fact, his very name—Satan—means adversary. His other name—the Devil—means slanderer. That's precisely what he's doing! Opposing and slandering us.

We desperately need someone to defend us before God. We need an Advocate to represent us in Heaven's courtroom. Well, I have good news. We have the best Defense Attorney ever—Jesus Christ. He's never lost a case. Never. The Bible says, "If anyone sins, we have an Advocate with the Father, Jesus Christ the righteous" (1 John 2:1), and He is at the right hand of God. Every time Satan accuses us, Jesus is there, pleading His blood, releasing us of every charge. He lives forever to intercede for us with God (Hebrews 7:25).

SATAN SEARCHES THE EARTH FOR PREY

Like a hungry lion, Satan stalks the earth looking for unsuspecting prey to devour. He is restless and relentless in tracking down innocent victims to destroy. Listen now to the opposing summit leaders. "And the LORD said to Satan, 'From where do you come?' Then Satan answered the LORD and said, 'From roaming about on the earth and walking around on it'" (Job 1:7).

Do you see who initiates this battle? God takes the offensive, not Satan. God elects to take the opening kickoff and go on the offensive first. Not Satan.

With the formality of courtroom procedure, God asks a question to raise an issue. "Devil, from where do you come?" In other words, "What have you been doing?" God already knows the answer. The question is judgmental in nature, causing Satan to accuse himself with his own words.

"I've been roaming about on the earth," Satan snarls. In truth, he has been roaming the earth, like a roaring lion, looking for someone to eat for lunch.

Be forewarned! Satan is prowling after you and me, too. The Apostle Peter writes, "Be of sober spirit, be on the alert. Your adversary, the devil, prowls about like a roaring lion, seeking someone to devour" (1 Peter 5:8). He's hot on our trail! He has our scent. He's hungry to devour our lives, our marriages, and our souls. Look out!

Specifically, what does Satan do down here on earth? He's no caged animal. He's on the loose!

Satan *blinds our minds* (2 Corinthians 4:4). He *seduces our hearts* (2 Corinthians 11:3). He *hinders our ministries* (1 Thessalonians 2:18). He *inflicts our bodies* with physical diseases and even death (Matthew 12:22, Revelation 9:14-19). He *divides our relationships* (Matthew 13:40). He *tempts our flesh* (1 Corinthians 7:5). He *attacks our faith* (Genesis 3:1). He *deceives our minds* (1 Timothy 4:1). He *controls our politicians* (Revelation 16:14). He *causes our persecution* (Revelation 2:10).

Do you see Satan's work? The devil stalking the earth for you? There are those who say Satan is in hell already. If so, he must be on a mighty long leash. He rules planet earth with relish.

SATAN IS LIMITED BY GOD'S SOVEREIGNTY

Despite Satan's great power, he is limited by God's sovereignty. He has great power, but he's not all-powerful. He has great power over his domain, but remains under God's power. The ensuing dialogue reveals who is sovereign in this invisible war.

> The LORD said to Satan, "Have you considered My servant Job? For there is no one like him on the earth, a blameless and upright man, fearing God and turning away from evil." . . . The LORD said to Satan, "Behold, all that he has is in your power, only do not put forth your hand on him." (Job 1:8,12)

It is God who tosses Job's name into the ring. Not Satan. It is God who defines the limits of the Devil's access into Job's life. He says, "Devil, you can do this and this and this to Job. But you can go no further. You cannot cross the line and do this." Despite Satan's ferocious power, God remains fully in control. Later, God will choose to remove the boundaries and allow Satan greater access into Job's life. But only to the extent that God allows. Spiritual warfare is not an eternal tug of war between two equal powers. It is the triumph of a greater power over a lesser one.

We must guard against two dangers in our view of Satan. One is to think too highly of him. The other is to think too little of him. With one extreme, we see a demon behind every bush. With the other, we fail to see his presence at all. We must maintain a balanced, biblical view of the invisible war. Satan is powerful, but limited by the boundaries established by a sovereign God.

This is a great comfort! In the middle of combat, we must never forget we're fighting a winnable war. We wrestle with a mighty foe, but he can be defeated in God's power. Our Commander in Chief will not allow the Devil entrance into our lives beyond what we can withstand.

SATAN IS SHREWD AND CUNNING

As Satan continues his great debate with God, he subtly tries to turn God against Job. The Apostle Paul warned against the shrewd schemes of the Devil (Ephesians 6:12). Don't get the idea that he is a bumbling idiot. With stunning brilliance, he attempts to pit God against us and vice versa. Watch how Satan tries to outsmart God. While God always sees through this diabolical strategy, we often do not.

> Then Satan answered the LORD, "Does Job fear God for noth-
> ing? Hast Thou not made a hedge about him and his house and
> all that he has on every side? Thou hast blessed the work of his
> hands, and his possessions have increased in the land. Put forth
> Thy hand now and touch all that he has; he will surely curse
> Thee to Thy face." (Job 1:9-11)

What a bold frontal attack! Satan mounts his evil campaign of hostility, accusing Job of serving the Lord for selfish reasons and charging God with buying worshipers. He challenges God to take away all Job's temporal blessings, hoping that will prove the hypocrisy in Job's heart.

Satan is saying this: "God, it's obvious why Job fears You. No wonder! You've *bought* him! You've spoiled him! You keep blessing him. That's the only reason he serves You. If You withheld Your blessing, he wouldn't give a rip about You. He would never worship You for who You are. Do You think Job would look upon You and be attracted by Your beauty? Take away his blessings and Job won't just quit worshiping You. He'll curse You to Your face."

Never forget that the Devil's tactic is to pit God against you and you against God. He tries to play both ends against the middle. Without even lifting a finger! Do you see how shrewd he is? He learned much from his early rebellion when he pitted a third of the angels against God. He is enraged that he was cast out of Heaven. He knows he must win this war for long-term survival, and he's become a master at mind-to-mind combat in his quest for victory.

We learn how the Devil works by studying the three places in the Bible where his words are recorded. We've just seen the second occurrence here in Job. Let's note the other two.

The first time we read Satan's words is in Genesis 3. God put Adam and Eve in paradise and gave them everything they could ever want. They had it all. The only prohibition was that they could not eat from the tree of the knowledge of good and evil. But even that restriction was good.

Satan appeared to Eve and said, "God's just holding out on you. God's not a good God. He said you can't eat fruit from this tree. You think He is a good God? He's not. God's holding out on you." Essentially, he whispered in her ear, "God's not good to you."

The second time Satan speaks is recorded here in Job 1. To God he says just the opposite of his claim to Adam and Eve: "God, you're too good for them." Evil tactics. Lies. Deceit.

The final time we hear Satan's words is in Christ's temptation (Matthew 4:3,6,9). He says to Jesus, "I'll be better to you than God. Follow me and I will give you the whole world."

This is the Devil's diabolical strategy: cause division, create hostility, destroy trust, then conquer. First, he's slithering in the garden, whispering to man, "God's not good to you." Then he's in Heaven, saying to God, "You're too good to man." Then he's tempting the God-man saying, "I'll be better to you than God." How cunning!

Satan says the same to God about you: "The only reason she serves You is because You've bought her." If God were to remove your blessings, would you still serve Him?

The Devil has become an accomplished field general in the theater of war known as the human soul. Can he be defeated? How can mere foot soldiers like you and me cross spiritual swords with such a skillful foe? How do you face the enemy's leader?

SATAN HAS GREAT POWER OVER CIRCUMSTANCES

While Satan is not all-powerful, he has been given greater power than any other creature. Notice how the Devil wields this power in Job's life with destructive force: "Then the LORD said to Satan, 'Behold, all that he has is in your power, only do not put forth your hand on him.' So Satan departed from the presence of the LORD" (Job 1:12).

Armed with divine permission, the Evil One departs from God's throne and descends to earth. Hovering over the globe, he spies the land of Uz and makes for Job like a "smart bomb" seeking an Iraqi military command center. He can't wait! God's laser shield of protection has now been turned off. Job is defenseless!

> Now it happened on the day when his [Job's] sons and his daughters were eating and drinking wine in their oldest broth-er's house, that a messenger came to Job and said, "The oxen were plowing and the donkeys feeding beside them, and the Sabeans attacked and took them. They also slew the servants with the edge of the sword, and I alone have escaped to tell you." (Job 1:13-15)

While Job's ten children are together celebrating at one of the sibling's houses—a picture of love, closeness, and unity—suddenly, a messenger bursts into Job's house with a frantic look on his face. With a dramatic voice, he reports that a great disaster has struck Job's business. The Sabeans have attacked Job's animals, stealing five hundred oxen and five hundred donkeys, and killing all but one of his servants. This is a crushing blow!

In reality, Satan was behind the scenes, influencing and manipulating the Sabeans like pawns on a chessboard. The prince of this world inflamed their passions and incited their hearts to kill Job's servants and steal his animals. Yes, Satan has great power over people. He can fill people's hearts with rage to kill, steal, and inflict great harm. The great dragon is the evil power behind the rioting and looting that we see in major cities today.

But, wait. More disaster follows!

> While he [the first messenger] was still speaking, another [mes-senger] also came and said, "The fire of God fell from heaven and burned up the sheep and the servants and consumed them, and I alone have escaped to tell you." (Job 1:16)

While the words are still pouring from the first messenger's mouth, a second messenger bolts into Job's house. He, too, has a panicked look on his face. He blurts out that fire fell from Heaven—perhaps a lightning bolt—and burned up Job's seven thousand sheep and all of his servants except one. This one servant has escaped the catastrophe to report to Job.

We can only conclude that Satan swings great power over the weather. Not all power over all weather. But some power over some weather. To the extent that God allows, the Devil has supernatural power at his disposal to direct the elements to accomplish his evil purposes.

But, there's more.

> While he [the second messenger] was still speaking, another
> [messenger] also came and said, "The Chaldeans formed
> three bands and made a raid on the camels and took them and
> slew the servants with the edge of the sword; and I alone have
> escaped to tell you." (Job 1:17)

Another traumatized messenger breaks in to announce yet another disaster. Gasping for air, he informs Job that attacking raiders captured all three thousand of his camels and massacred all but one servant in the process.

Think about it! Satan can fill the hearts of men with an unquenchable hatred, provoking them to murder and steal. Jesus said that the Devil "was a murderer from the beginning" (John 8:44). Jesus charged Satan with the first-degree murder of Abel. The Bible says that Cain "was of the evil one, and slew his brother" (1 John 3:12).

At this very hour, Satan fills the hearts of men with murder, greed, and hatred. "The whole world lies in the power of the evil one" (1 John 5:19). Unbelievers are "held captive by him to do his will" (2 Timothy 2:26). After all, for an evil enemy to succeed he must brainwash the people who follow. To seduce anyone into believing a lie you must control the flow of information. You need a solid propaganda machine. Today, Satan holds in his iron grip many unbelievers in the media, politics, Hollywood, and the music industries. He even controls many preachers in pulpits. Some of us would probably be surprised at who hell's mouthpieces are, unknowing puppets carrying out Satan's agenda for this world.

Another disaster hits Job!

> While he [the third messenger] was still speaking, another [mes-
> senger] also came and said, "Your sons and your daughters were
> eating and drinking wine in their oldest brother's house, and

behold, a great wind came from across the wilderness and struck the four corners of the house, and it fell on the young people and they died; and I alone have escaped to tell you." (Job 1:18)

Escalating his attack, Satan concludes with what he believes will be his knockout punch. Here is the blow to break Job's faith. While Job's ten children were celebrating together, a great wind—perhaps a whirlwind or a twister—struck the house. It immediately collapsed the structure and crushed his children to death.

A fourth messenger with a face as white as a ghost's breaks into the room to tell Job the sad news. Like a dagger thrust deeply into his heart, Job receives the report of his children's death.

All that he has worked for has been stripped and removed from his life. All that he loves has been cruelly taken. If we live to be a thousand years old, few of us will ever grasp the depths of Job's grief at this moment.

Satan has great power. If permitted by God, he has the power to invade your life as well. Martin Luther once wrote,

For still our ancient foe
Doth seek to work us woe—
His craft and power are great,
And, armed with cruel hate,
On earth is not his equal.[1]

SATAN IS DEFEATED BY OUR FAITH!

We see Job standing over ten fresh graves on a barren hillside. His world has come to a screeching halt. Think of his shock. His disbelief. He feels grief too deep for words.

Would Job's faith crumble? Would he curse God?

No. Job did not respond the way Satan had hoped he would. Rather than blaspheme God, he blessed Him. Job bowed his head to God in humble prayer and worship. This remarkable man chose to accept God's sovereign will without knowing why he was suffering. The following verses record one of the most remarkable acts of faith ever.

Then Job arose and tore his robe and shaved his head, and he fell to the ground and worshiped. And he said, "Naked I came from my mother's womb,

And naked I shall return there.
The LORD gave and the LORD has taken away.
Blessed be the name of the LORD."
Through all this Job did not sin nor did he blame God.
  (Job 1:20-22)

Here is faith in action! We learn from Job's response five key lessons to overcoming personal disaster.

Allow the Grief Process to Occur

First, Job tore his robe and shaved his head. These were expressions of deep sorrow in his ancient culture. Reeling under the impact of these great losses, Job was too crushed in heart to put up any false front of cheerful courage. He wept openly with boundless grief.

Emotionally, he was allowing the natural grief process to occur. Some people think that to be spiritual, they cannot cry or let anyone else see their crushed heart. Some believe it unspiritual to let their broken spirit show.

Not so. It is unhealthy not to allow the grief process to occur. If all that emotion remains pent up on the inside, we become like a teakettle on a stove—ready to explode! It is emotionally healthy and therapeutic for our souls to cry. Didn't Jesus weep over the death of Lazarus?

Chuck Swindoll writes to this very point: "I am disappointed that someone, somewhere, many years ago, introduced the ridiculous idea that if you know the Lord, you don't grieve. That even if you lose something or someone significant, you shouldn't weep. With my whole heart, I disagree! Granted, we don't grieve 'as those who have no hope.' But, no tears? No grief? I find that unthinkable. Since when does becoming a Christian make a person less than human . . . or more than human?"[2]

Choose to Worship God

Second, Job worshiped God with humble reverence. I can't imagine the deep struggle within Job. He wasn't Superman. But, as an act of his will, he chose to worship God. He did not shake an angry fist toward Heaven. Rather than curse God the Father—as Satan said he would—Job chose to worship Him.

Job was able to worship because God never changes. Circumstances change. But God never changes. He is immutable. Rock-solid. Pristine. Unaltered. Therefore, in any and every circumstance, we can praise God. He is always worthy to be praised.

How about you? Are you going through deep water? When the Sabeans attack, when the fire falls, when the Chaldeans raid, when the roof caves in, how will you respond? Don't blame God. Worship Him. Give Him the glory. If you're worthy to suffer, He's worthy to praise.

Maintain an Eternal Perspective

Third, Job maintained an eternal perspective. "Naked I came from my mother's womb, and naked I shall return there." Job realized he came into this world without anything. He also knew he would leave without anything. "I came into this world empty-handed," Job said, "and I'm going to leave empty-handed." Only such an eternal perspective can produce this sort of contentment!

It's been well said, you'll never see a U-Haul behind a hearse. Why? Because you can't take it with you. Someone asked how much money a rich man who recently died had left behind. "That's easy," his friend replied, "He left it *all* behind."

What about you? Do you have an eternal perspective? All that you worry about will one day be left behind. True riches are what money can't buy and death can't take away.

Trust in God's Sovereignty

Fourth, when troubles break loose, we must always remember that God is sovereign. Always. Job said, "The Lord gave and the Lord has taken away." It is God's divine prerogative to give His blessings, and it is His decision to receive them back.

Job viewed his possessions as gifts from God. Temporarily on loan. Undeserved. Unearned. Consequently, God had every right to take them back at His pleasure.

Personally, I don't know how anyone can go through a trial without believing in the sovereignty of God. Some Christians have a limited view of God. They see the Devil, or circumstances, or their own mistakes in control. But God alone is sovereign. He controls everything that comes into our lives. Whether He *sent* the ordeal or whether He *allowed* it, it is there, nevertheless, by divine appointment. Without overlooking our pain, and without sounding glib, we must remember: "God causes all things to work together for good to those who love God" (Romans 8:28).

As Charles Spurgeon once said, "When you go through a trial, the sovereignty of God is the pillow upon which you lay your head."

Refuse to Allow Bitterness to Fester

Finally, Job refused to allow bitterness to fester in his heart. He said, "Blessed be the name of the Lord." Through all this, Job did not sin nor did he blame God.

Rather than blame God, Job chose to magnify Him. He didn't play the "blame game" with God. He refused to allow a root of bitterness to grow, choosing instead to bless the name of God.

Trusting God is a matter of the will and is not dependent upon my feelings. I choose to trust God and my feelings will eventually follow. Too often, we live our lives by feelings rather than by faith.

I do not mean that the choice is as easy as choosing whether or not I'll go to the grocery store. We must choose to look to God or we will be ruled by our feelings of despair. Faith must ultimately dictate our feelings.

Trusting God does not mean we do not experience pain. It does mean we believe that God is at work through our adversity for our ultimate good.

Despite the attack, Job has stood strong in his faith. After one inning, the score is Job 1, Satan 0. No runs, no hits, no errors.

Perhaps disaster has struck your life. Maybe your world is crumbling around you. Perhaps your worst fears have become a living nightmare.

Have faith in God that He will give you the victory. Satan is a destructive force intent on destroying our lives. But his defeat is assured. You can count on God's winning the invisible war!

Have faith in God.

NOTES

1. Martin Luther, "A Mighty Fortress Is Our God."
2. Charles Swindoll, *Growing Wise in Family Life* (Portland, OR: Multnomah, 1988), page 220.

CHAPTER 3

LIVING HELL

▼

S ometimes our lives become microcosms of hell. Just ask Michael
Benson, Chris Duddy, and Craig Hosking.

On location in Hawaii, this Hollywood crew was filming
for the upcoming thriller "Sliver." They found themselves flying in a
helicopter inside the Pu'u'O'o crater of Kilauea, filming the world's
most active volcano, which has been erupting for the past ten years.

As the helicopter descended into the bowl of fire, hovering just
ten feet above the floor of the fiery inferno, steam and foul-smelling
gases rose upward from bubbling pools of red-hot lava, obscuring their
vision.

Suddenly, the pilot shouted, "We've got a problem." They looked
up just in time to see the wall of the volcano directly in front of them.

"We're dead," yelled Duddy.

The two rotor blades hit the volcano's wall and were instantly
sheared off, plunging the chopper down into the fiery pit. Unexpectedly,
they were living a thriller far more real than the one they had been
filming.

Baptized into harsh fumes, Duddy and Benson tried climbing
straight up the nearest wall, only to keep slipping back in the loose

45

cinder. Eventually, Benson managed to climb to a narrow ledge about seventy-five feet below the outer rim, while Duddy climbed thirty feet higher.

In the meantime, Hosking got the chopper's radio working and frantically called for help. But with fog and clouds closing in, their hopes of escaping disappeared. When Benson and Duddy heard the sound of a helicopter hovering overhead, they shouted to Hosking, who was not in sight. When he didn't reply, they assumed he had fallen or been overcome by the fumes. In fact, Hosking had been spotted by the helicopter and been lifted to safety. The problem for Benson and Duddy was that they were in an inaccessible spot in the volcano.

With darkness falling, Duddy and Benson realized they were going to have to spend the night clinging to ledges inside the seething volcano.

Throughout the night, a ranger up on the rim blew a whistle to keep the men's spirits up. Below them, the lava lake glowed fiery red, lighting the canyon walls. It looked like hell itself.

Duddy started losing hope. He looked up at the cliff walls and concluded, "I can die trying to get out of here, or I can die waiting, curled up in a fetal position." There seemed to be no way out.

So he said a prayer, took a deep breath, and started climbing up. Against all odds, he made it to the top of the cinder wall and propelled himself over the top to safety.

Only Benson remained inside the volcanic crater. The whole ordeal seemed as incredible as any action movie he had filmed, only scarier. "I was waiting for the director to say, 'Cut!'" he said. "But reality set in. This is not a movie. This is real, and I'm actually sitting here, dying."

That night sleep evaded him. He lay awake with terrifying hallucinations. At one point, he saw Madam Pele, the supposed fire-goddess of this volcano. "All these faces of everyone I had known came by me," he said. "I heard maybe two thousand voices and every one of them said, 'You have everything to live for. You're a fighter. You're too young to die.'"

Salvation came the next morning.

Risking his own life, Maui pilot Tom Hauptman lowered his chopper down into the smoldering crater and held it rock-steady. He dangled a seventy-foot cable with a chair-sized basket on the end in Benson's vicinity. On the fourth cast, Benson grabbed hold and climbed aboard.

"They lifted me out of there and gave me the ride of my life."

Yes, sometimes life gets hotter than hell. Sometimes we find our-selves in a living hell. Just ask Benson, Duddy, and Hosking.

Just ask Job.

Disaster overtook Job and he found himself in a living hell. Literally. He was in a fiery pit with no relief in sight. With hell's flames below him, impossible walls around him, and seemingly, no help from above, his fiery trial seemed to be without any escape in sight.

It is the same with you and me. Sometimes we find ourselves in a living hell. Just when it seems like life can't get worse, that's precisely what happens. Life goes from bad to worse. Sometimes the light at the end of the tunnel is an oncoming train.

Let's return to the story of Job and discover that lightning is about to strike twice. His already charred life is about to go from bad to worse. The heat is going to be turned up and Job is going to crash and be dropped into the middle of a living hell.

SATAN'S PERSISTENCE BEFORE GOD

Satan was not through with Job. Not yet.

The Devil is relentless in his accusation and attack. This is no solo skirmish, nor isolated battle, in which Job is embroiled. This is a long, protracted military campaign. An endless series of battles. It's a *war!* Consequently, we are not surprised to see Satan coming again before God's throne. He's back! "Again there was a day when the sons of God came to present themselves before the LORD, and Satan also came among them to present himself before the LORD" (Job 2:1).

Please don't overlook the first word of this chapter. *Again!* Again, Satan comes to accuse Job and do greater damage to his life.

Again and again and again, the Devil comes after us. Resist the Devil today and he'll be back tomorrow. We talk about the patience of Job. What about the perseverance of the Devil!

I heard about a lady who never spoke ill of anyone. A friend told her, "I believe you would say something good even about the Devil."

"Well," she said, "You certainly do have to admire his persistence."

Beware of his persistence, yes. Admire, no.

Satan never gives up. After Satan tempted Christ in the wilderness, "he departed from Him until an opportune time" (Luke 4:13). So, here we see Satan back before God's throne to accuse Job. Again. "And the

LORD said to Satan, 'Where have you come from?' Then Satan answered the LORD and said, 'From roaming about on the earth, and walking around on it' " (Job 2:2).

There has to be some sarcasm here in God's question. "Devil, where have you been? Down on the earth, haven't you? Who have you been attacking? Job? You can't get to him, can you? You said he would curse Me to My face if I allowed you to take away his possessions. Well, what did you discover? Job still loves Me, doesn't he?" We can see God's face light up with delight over Job's faith.

Satan answered the Lord the same as before. But this time there is a curious omission. The Devil makes no mention of Job. Why bring up the name of your last opponent if you lost? I wouldn't.

> The LORD said to Satan, "Have you considered My servant
> Job? For there is no one like him on the earth, a blameless and
> upright man fearing God and turning away from evil. And he
> still holds fast his integrity, although you incited Me against
> him, to ruin him without cause." (Job 2:3)

The dig goes deeper now. God puts the fork into the Devil's pride and turns the handle. "Say, have you considered My servant Job? You remember Job, don't you? He's the one who just threw a shot out at you."

Consider him? Satan has just been to the earth and attacked Job to the fullest extent that God would allow. Satan has thrown everything at him but the kitchen sink. He has unloaded all the artillery of hell and blasted Job with both barrels. All to no avail. Not even a dent.

Consider him? Satan has been considering *no other but* Job. That's like asking a college freshman, "Have you considered girls?" Job is on Satan's mind morning, noon, and night.

God repeats that Job is in a league by himself. Blameless. Upright. God-fearing. Turning away from evil. No one is in his class. Remember, Job didn't get into this mess because there was some sin in his life. He's here because there's everything *right* about his life.

God gladly acknowledges that, despite the Devil's hellish assault, Job still holds fast his integrity. He has not wavered in his faith. Not one iota. Job still stands strong in his trust in God.

SATAN'S PERSUASION WITH GOD

Satan then seeks permission to step up his attack.

Satan answered the LORD and said, "Skin for skin! Yes, all that
a man has he will give for his life. However, put forth Thy hand,
now, and touch his bone and his flesh; he will curse Thee to
Thy face." (Job 2:4-5)

Satan suggested to God a new test for Job. Physical suffering. Pain
can weaken our resistance and make everything look and feel worse
than it really is. More than one person has withstood tragedy only to
fall apart under the onslaught of pain.

Here is the first Skins Game.

In Job's ancient culture, "skin for skin" was a bartering term meaning to trade one skin for another. The Devil is accusing Job of being
willing to risk the skin of his children and livestock in order to protect
his own skin. This is self-protection run amok. Satan's saying: "All this
righteousness is only to save Job's own hide."

Satan argues that it was a selfish tradeoff. "Job willingly gave up
the lives of his own family to keep his own life—that's all. Their skin
for his skin."

Satan now goes for the jugular. He asks God for permission to
inflict disease upon Job's skin. If he can, the Devil boasts that Job will
crumble like a proverbial house of cards.

Do you see the subtle scheme here? While the Devil is falsely
accusing Job of bartering with God, Satan himself is bartering with
God to get at Job. He is doing the very thing that he accuses Job
of doing.

SATAN'S PERMISSION FROM GOD

The narrative continues, "So the LORD said to Satan, 'Behold, he is in
your power, only spare his life'" (Job 2:6).

The Devil is given a green light to torment Job. But notice, it's still
within the divinely ordained limits permitted by God's sovereignty.
Again, Satan has had to receive permission from God before he can
move further into Job's life and afflict him.

Job is now turned over to Satan's power for further testing. Satan
can do anything to him except take his life. This time, the Devil is
permitted to touch Job's body.

You would think this man had endured enough. Surely Job has
experienced more than his quota of suffering. Surely God will now
choose to spare Job any further pain. Surely God will announce that

the test is over and restore Job's future now.

Wrong.

The agony will become worse. It's not enough that Job loses his farm and his family and his fortune. Now he must lose his health. Put that into your theological pipe and smoke it!

If you are suffering a deep tragedy, remember it first had to pass through God's permissive will. Nothing—not even our worst nightmare—can occur without His permission.

SATAN'S PERSECUTION OF JOB

We read on: "Then Satan went out from the presence of the LORD, and smote Job with sore boils from the sole of his foot to the crown of his head" (Job 2:7).

Satan hotfooted it (no pun intended) out of Heaven again and descended to earth on another sinister mission of destruction. His mission is to afflict Job physically—yet leave Job short of death—so that he will curse God.

With Heaven's permission and all of hell's power, Satan smites Job's body with gruesome sores. From the crown of his head to the bottom of his feet, Job is nothing but boils, boils, and more boils. This poor guy is now *covered* with boils!

The skin covering his entire body is afflicted. He may have had elephantiasis, or a cancer of the skin. His gruesome condition was characterized by ulcerous sores (2:7), itching (2:8), degenerative changes in facial skin (2:7,12), loss of appetite (3:24), depression (3:24-26), worms in the boils (7:5), hardened skin and running sores (7:5), difficulty in breathing (9:18), dark eyelids (16:16), foul breath (19:17), weight loss (19:20), continual pain (30:17), blackened skin (30:30), and fever (30:30). All this for months on end (7:3; 29:2).

Job knew nothing about Satan's challenges to God. He was completely unaware of the scenes being played out before God and Satan. He had no idea that the Enemy was using him as a reason for slandering the Lord. Not a clue. He had no idea that God was holding him up to be a lightning rod. Even later, when the Lord will answer Job from a whirlwind, he will not be informed of the reason for his suffering.

God's people are soldiers on the battlefield, but there are times when they *are* the battlefield. Such is Job's pain.

Not only did this smite Job, but it also smites today's "health and wealth gospel." The "name it and claim it" teachers don't quite know what to do with this. Their gospel teaches that God's sovereign will is for every one of God's people always to be healthy and wealthy. Sure, and I've got some swampland in Florida to sell you. Don't buy it!

Here, the will of God included sickness and poverty for the choicest of all men. It certainly included tragedy for Christ Himself as He lived without earthly riches and died a tragic death on the cross—all within the predetermined plan of God (Acts 2:23).

This "prosperity gospel" is a cruel message. It isn't "good news" at all. It tells people they are suffering the loss of personal health or wealth because of a lack of faith. Go tell that to a faithful mother who has suffered a miscarriage. Tell it to an elderly saint who has walked with Christ for sixty-plus years and now contracts cancer. Or a missionary couple overseas serving Christ when their financial support back home begins to suffer. The "prosperity gospel" is, in actuality, a bankrupt gospel. Here we see that this lie has been around since the earliest stages of recorded history. Job is its first victim.

Satan, cruel monarch that he is, used the fullest extent of his power allowed by God toward Job. Nothing was held back. God said that Satan could go so far, and Satan pushed it to the limit. He held back none of his diabolical fury. Not one bit.

Satan will do the same in our lives as well. Don't think for one minute that the "good ol' Devil" will cut you any slack. If you take a stand for Christ, he will come after you to the fullest extent that God will allow. He will push the envelope every time.

TAKE MY WIFE . . . PLEASE!

In Job's hour of greatest need, surely his wife will be there for him. To comfort his heart. To console his hurts. Right?

Wrong again. We pick up the story: "Then his wife said to him, 'Do you still hold fast your integrity? Curse God and die!'" (Job 2:9).

Talk about the spiritual gift of discouragement!

Mrs. Job melts like an angelfood cake in water. She can't bear to see her husband suffer like this. Her heart, already crushed by the loss of her ten children, is now without hope. She is saying, "Curse God and He'll strike you dead, too. Then you can escape this pain. Death would be better than this."

Job's wife was certainly outspoken. She reminds me of the wife of a man who was asked, "Was your wife outspoken?"

"Not by anyone I know of," he replied.

What keeps Job going? His faith in God. He holds all his life in an open hand before God. His wealth, his health, his family. He trusts God to do right. Period. Paragraph.

When you cut to the bottom line, Job's faith is deeply rooted in the sovereignty of God. He is unshaken in his belief that God alone possesses the right to give blessing. And He alone possesses the right to take back blessing. It is God's to give and take; ours to accept. He is the Creator; we are His creation.

How about your faith? Only a belief that God is absolutely in control of our circumstances—both good times and bad times—can carry us through our trials. He alone is the solid rock upon which our faith stands. Job's words bear out his faith: "But he said to her, 'You speak as one of the foolish women speaks. Shall we indeed accept good from God and not accept adversity?' In all this Job did not sin with his lips" (Job 2:10).

Job has won again!

The score is now Job 2, Satan 0. After two innings, the Devil is shut out. No runs, no hits, no errors.

Satan's tactical assault has failed again. Job has won another battle. But the war continues on a different front. The deadliest front.

JOB'S THREE "FRIENDS"

Satan now pulls out his heaviest artillery. Job has suffered financial ruin, family loss, physical pain, marital tension. Yet Job has endured strong in his faith. So where does the Devil point this heaviest artillery? Where else? At Job's relationships! Having failed to make enough progress in breaking up his marriage, the Old Schemer now seeks solace in that staple evil of television soap-opera—friends!

Three friends enter the ring. These three will manage to do what all of Job's affliction was unable to accomplish. Like bobbing and weaving heavyweight fighters, they will wear him down round after round, until they leave this champion hanging on the ropes.

Now when Job's three friends heard of all this adversity that had come upon him, they came each one from his own place, Eliphaz the Temanite, Bildad the Shuhite, and Zophar the Naamathite; and they made an appointment together to come to sympathize with him and comfort him. (Job 2:11)

Of course these three men came. Job was the most respected man in the community. His bankruptcy sent shock waves throughout the entire land. Everyone knew about it. This was front-page stuff!

Sincere. Concerned. Wanting to help. That's how these three friends came. But with best of intentions, they became instruments of Satan to yield the final blow to Job's faith.

Strange, but those who love us the most can hurt us the deepest. They came to sympathize, but stayed to antagonize Job. They came to comfort, but stayed to confound.

> And when they lifted up their eyes at a distance, and did not recognize him, they raised their voices and wept. And each of them tore his robe, and they threw dust over their heads toward the sky. (Job 2:12)

Job was so disfigured from the disease that they did not recognize him when they saw him. Could this really be their beloved friend, Job? They expressed their grief for him in four ways. They wailed in emotional shock. They wept in sorrow. They tore their robes in brokenheartedness. They threw dust into the sky in deep grief. You really didn't express yourself this way in Job's day unless you truly loved someone. These guys really loved Job. Sort of. "Then they sat down on the ground with him for seven days and seven nights with no one speaking a word to him, for they saw that his pain was very great" (Job 2:13).

They all sat on the ground, the friends observing Job in silence for seven days. They were so horrified at his pain that words of sympathy escaped them.

Following the custom of the day, they remained quiet allowing the grieving person to speak first. Little did they know the invisible war that was being fought in their very midst.

HOW TO ESCAPE THE PIT

Do you remember the story I told you at the beginning of this chapter? Like Job and that film crew, we, too, will find ourselves in fiery trials. How do we escape the pit?

First, *accept the gift of eternal hope*. By now you have probably noticed that Job has not yet cracked under Satan's barrage. Even though the heavy artillery has arrived and Job is clearly discouraged, he has not yet succumbed to total despair or complete depression. The last time we heard from him he had just affirmed his faith despite his wife's urging to "Curse God and die!" How did he do it? He had eternal hope. At least for now Job recognizes that problems don't last forever. Perhaps he rests in the fact that God is a perfect God. Perhaps he trusts that God's judgment is perfect and that His children are in His good hands.

Second, *remember God's goodness*. Job has spent a lifetime serving God and recognizing his earthly rewards. He doesn't have a short memory. He realizes that although things look bleak now, God has always proved faithful. Job remembers that faithfulness just as you and I can.

Why forget about all the blessings we've received from God when a trial confronts our path? Shall we engage in some sort of purposeful cosmic amnesia? No! If we're sincere about God, we must remember that we're sincere because He first loved us and sent His only Son to redeem us. And that in spite of our rebellion! Surely our memories aren't so short that we cannot recall the day of our salvation. That encouragement can keep us out of the pit.

Third, *never forget that others have been where you are . . . and have survived*. Job survived! Benson, Duddy, and Hosking—the film crew in the volcano—all survived. If we know God, we will survive, even if we become a casualty on earth! God's plan is to populate Heaven with overcomers (Revelation 2–3). True survival depends on trusting and loving God. In any war there are casualties. Just ask the mother of the little Somalian girl who trusted Christ, only to die of malnutrition a few weeks later.

As God's foot soldiers on the front lines we're going to stand tall and be hit with the Enemy's fiery darts. That means injury. It means pain; sometimes excruciatingly so. It may mean suffering or even death. But if we're worthy of such pain, we may be assured that our heavenly General is not asking us to undergo such terror for no reason. Our survival is in His worthy hands.

Finally, *know it's only temporary!* It encourages me to know that I've survived some very difficult times. At first it didn't seem as if my storms would ever pass, but in due time, they did.

In the early stages of writing this book (I should have known this would happen), I experienced a torturous conflict with some people very close to me. The dispute was mostly over some of my failures, along with typical miscommunication. There were several men involved in the situation, some of them my closest friends. All were believers. What's interesting is how quickly the thing got resolved once we all sat down and worked through our grievances. Frankly, things in this group are better now than they ever were before.

JOB'S DILEMMA AND OUR SITUATION

Before we leave Job 2, we need to be realistic about where he is. Certainly, he's still hopeful about his relationship with God. And his friends, so far, are treating him with respect. But he's dangerously close to depression. It is only his eternal perspective and his view of God that keep him going.

What about you?

Remember, if lightning strikes twice, even if you find yourself in a living hell, that Job survived.

When you're in a living hell, you can count on a living hope.

CHAPTER 4

I JUST WANT
TO LIE DOWN AND DIE

▼

ave you ever had a time in your life when you wished that you
could die? I mean, just lie down and die? I sure have.

For me, one of those times occurred when I graduated from
college. I was twenty-two years old and had just moved back home for
the summer. While away at college, I had become used to coming in
late at night. There would be many nights—now, I never got in any
trouble, mind you—that I would just drive around late with my buddies.
We would go to a drive-through, order food, cruise around town, and
listen to music.

So when I moved back home, it was a difficult adjustment to live
under the same roof with Mom and Dad again. Very likely an adjustment for them, as well!

I remember one night. I was out on a date. Not just any date. A
very special date. This girl was just a knockout. (Can I say that in a
Christian book?) She had been our homecoming queen in high school
and our head cheerleader. I had waited five or six years to have a date
with this girl, just waiting for the competition to kill itself off. Finally,
the opportunity was there to go out with her and, needless to say, I was
walking on clouds. So it was late at night—well past midnight—and we

went to her parents' house. We were just talking, listening to music, and sitting on the sofa in her den with the lights down low. (Honest, we were just talking!)

As we were sitting on the sofa together, I heard a rustling in the bushes outside. Hmmmm. It stopped, so I didn't think anything about it. Probably just the wind blowing. We kept talking, but, in a little bit, I heard some more rustling in the bushes. I thought, *I think there's something in the bushes.*

In a few seconds, I heard a knock on the pane-glass window. "Tap, tap, tap." Like someone knocking on it. "Tap, tap, tap." There it was again. "Hey," I said. "Somebody is knocking on your window."

So I turned around, pulled back the curtains, and looked through the large, plate-glass window over the sofa. There, to my total astonishment, was the head of a man peering through the hedges and looking right at me. It was . . . my father! And he was pointing to his watch.

Here it is after midnight and this grown man—a professor in medical school mind you—looking like a camouflaged "tree man" with his head peering out of the hedge. He is motioning in the direction of our house, "informing" me of the lateness of the hour and that I needed to head home!

I can't tell you how embarrassed I was. Humiliated! (For some reason, it's funnier now than it was then.) I could have just died. If I could have been raptured to Heaven at that moment, I would have gladly gone. "Beam me up, Scottie!"

I remember turning back around to my date, shrugging my shoulders and saying, "I've never seen that man before in my life!"

Well, I think that is something of how Job is now feeling. He just wants to die. Not out of embarrassment. But out of deep pain and acute suffering. In a far greater way than my embarrassment—in a way that's really *not* funny—Job felt as if he wanted to die.

For Job, his life has gone up in smoke. Satan has burned him. Well-done and crisp. The Devil has inflicted him with adversity that few of us can fully fathom. In one fell swoop, his family has been stripped away, his possessions reduced to rubble, and his fortune decimated. Then—as if that were not enough—Satan, with permission from God, has ravaged his skin from the top of his head to the bottom of his feet. The man is devastated financially, physically, and emotionally.

When the first onslaught occurred, Job responded with faith. "The Lord gives and the Lord takes away, blessed be the name of the Lord."

But, with blast after blast, his strength has been eroded and his soul eaten away. All his suffering has not been without profound impact. Job is down; he is discouraged; he is ready to throw in the towel.

Have you ever felt this way? Have you ever hurt so bad that you simply wished you could go to Heaven? I have.

Every person has a breaking point. A point at which he or she can become deeply discouraged. Even depressed. Such despair can cause a person to want to give up on life. Either we want Jesus to come back right now and take us home, or we want to give up on life and die. Either way, we just want to graduate to glory to escape life's pain.

Maybe this is where you are. Maybe you are tired of the constant pain and suffering. Maybe you are worn down by the heaviness of trials. It just won't go away.

That is precisely where Job is. He is longing for relief. Any kind of relief. He just wants to get out of this life and into the next. Job doesn't want to take his own life. Instead, he wants God to take his life.

Job has no life left in him. Except pain, torment, suffering, and misery. No reason to live.

He is looking for immediate relief.

I WISH I WAS NEVER BORN!

In Job 3 we now see what it's like for a person who loves God to go through the dark night of his soul. The downward spiral begins when Job says, "I wish I had never been born."

It has been a period of time since we last saw Job. Perhaps weeks. Maybe months. But sufficient time for his faith to begin to erode. Remember, his three friends have been sitting there with him, silently observing, waiting for Job to break his silence:

> Afterward Job opened his mouth and cursed the day of his birth.
> And Job said,
> "Let the day perish on which I was to be born,
> And the night which said,
> 'A boy is conceived.'"(Job 3:1-3)

Job is undergoing the darkest of miseries in his innermost heart. He literally thinks, *I wish I had never been born so I wouldn't have to experience all the suffering that I am going through.* He wants to give up on life. For him, the day he was conceived should never have existed.

Job wishes to eradicate his very conception. Erase his beginning. If God would take that date off the calendar, it would be all right with him. For Job, that day should be annihilated. Obliterated. If only that day had never existed, all this misery would go away.

Then Job's mood takes a step deeper into the abyss of despair. Notice the rejoicing in hell. The evil prince and his hideous hordes think they have him.

> "May that day be darkness;
> Let not God above care for it,
> Nor light shine on it.
> Let darkness and black gloom claim it;
> Let a cloud settle on it;
> Let the blackness of the day terrify it.
> As for that night, let darkness seize it;
> Let it not rejoice among the days of the year;
> Let it not come into the number of the months."
>   (Job 3:4-6)

Five times in this brief comment Job speaks of darkness, black gloom, or blackness. That precisely reflects his feelings on the inside. Who can blame him?To have never been born would have been fine with Job. God should have just skipped that day and gone on to the next. Ripped it out of the eternal calendar:

> "Behold, let that night be barren;
> Let no joyful shout enter it.
> Let those curse it who curse the day,
> Who are prepared to rouse Leviathan." (Job 3:7-8)

Job summons the ancient soothsayers to curse his birthday. I don't believe Job personally believed in their mystical power, nor was he committing himself to them. Rather, he is simply communicating vividly: "I wish I could call upon those who make their living pronouncing curses to put a curse on the day I was born. I wish they would rouse Leviathan [a monster that devoured great objects in the sea]. I want a sorcerer to conjure up a sea monster that would gobble up that day from the past so that I could have never been born."

Have you ever been this low? So low that you are ready for any way out, desperately grabbing for any relief?

"Let the stars of its twilight be darkened;
Let it wait for light but have none,
Neither let it see the breaking dawn." (Job 3:9)

Job wishes that the day on which he was born had just waited and waited and waited. He wishes that the sun had never come up. That the light of day had never broken.
Why?

"Because it did not shut the opening of my mother's womb,
Or hide trouble from my eyes." (Job 3:10)

Job's reaction is not uncommon. Pain, tragedy, and suffering can cause us to lose perspective on life. We make exaggerated comments we don't really mean, but we *feel*: "Nobody loves me. This isn't worth it. Nobody cares about me. If I died, nobody would come to my funeral."
Job's emotional state has now come to acute depression.

I WISH I HAD DIED AT BIRTH!
Job now goes a step further.
First, he says, "I wish I had never been born." Now, he says, "All right, I was conceived. Since I had to be born, that day is on God's calendar. But I wish I had died at birth. If I *had* to be born, then I wish I had died at birth."

"Why did I not die at birth,
Come forth from the womb and expire?" (Job 3:11).

Job now shifts gears and asks God why. Have you ever asked God why? Job did.
It's not wrong to ask the Lord why. It's only wrong to demand that God answer you. God may choose to reveal His reason. Or He may not. But He doesn't owe you an answer.
Jesus Himself asked God why. When He died on the cross, He asked the Father why. "My God, My God, why hast Thou forsaken Me?" (Matthew 27:46).

Why is a very natural question to ask the Lord—especially in a time of heartache. But it is a question that must be asked humbly, without a demanding spirit toward God. It's a request for hope. Not a demand for relief.

The amazing thing throughout Job's entire experience is that God never does give him an explanation. All God does is reveal Himself. He shows Job who, not why. Knowing God is what we need to endure the crunch. Not why.

Let me illustrate. When you break a leg and they rush you into the emergency room of the hospital, they take an x-ray of your broken limb. There you are, lying in one of those cubicles, in deep pain. The doctor brings the x-ray and puts it up on the screen. He flicks on the light and shows you why the break occurred. Does knowing why really take away the pain? No, not really. But so often, we think if we just knew why, our heart would be healed. But really, we need to know *who* and not *why*.

As Warren Wiersbe says, "We don't live our Christian lives on explanations; we live them on the promises."

Job continues,

"Why did the knees receive me,
And why the breasts, that I should suck?" (Job 3:12)

It was common practice during Job's time to take a little child, just from the womb, and put him upon the father's knee. "Why did that ever happen to me?" Job asks. "Why did my mother continue to give me nourishment and life only for this to happen to me? I've been set up for a fall."

Job gives us his multifaceted view of death. A profound thinker, Job views death as a rest (verse 13), a reunion (verse 14-15), a relief (verses 17-19), and a reward (verse 21). You know what? Job is right. Death is each of these realities.

First, Job begins by picturing death as a *rest*.

"For now I would have lain down and been quiet;
I would have slept then, I would have been at rest." (Job 3:13)

He is saying, "If I could have just died when I was born, I could have lain down and gone to sleep and found rest. But instead of rest,

I get only misery, affliction, and torment. Death would have been an afternoon nap."

Second, he pictures death as a *reunion*. With whom?

"With kings and with counselors of the earth,
Who rebuilt ruins for themselves;
Or with princes who had gold,
Who were filling their houses with silver." (Job 3:14-15)

Job reasons, "If I could have just died at birth, I would have graduated to glory. I would have been promoted onto the same level with kings and princes in the next world. There would have been a reunion in Heaven with all the mighty kings, counselors, and princes."

Third, Job views death as a *relief.*

"Or like a miscarriage which is discarded, I would not be,
As infants that never saw light.
There the wicked cease from raging,
And there the weary are at rest.
The prisoners are at ease together;
They do not hear the voice of the taskmaster.
The small and the great are there,
And the slave is free from his master." (Job 3:16-19)

Job wishes he had been stillborn at birth. He says death would have brought him relief from the pain and the torment of this life. The wicked cease from raging in death. In death man ceases from sinning. That's true. In Heaven, our sin nature will be eradicated. And we will be like our true image in Christ.

In death, Job says there will be relief from punishment because then "the prisoners are at ease together." In other words, death is like a jailbreak from the imprisonment of suffering. Right now, we are imprisoned in our bodies. Subject to affliction and torment. We are imprisoned in our circumstances. Only death will free us from this prison house. Only in death will we have relief.

Death blots out the voice of the slave driver. We hear pain's voice no longer. In death, we prisoners no longer hear the voice of our cruel taskmaster. Only in death do we have relief from pain. We will be no longer enslaved to life's torment. Both the small and the great will have the relief of death one day. We will be free from the affliction of this life. If we can just escape life, we will have relief from life's pain.

But Job has not yet hit the bottom. First he says, "I wish I had never been born." Next, he says, "I wish that I had died at birth." Since neither of those has happened, he wishes for today—"I wish I could die right now."

I WISH I COULD DIE NOW!

I don't believe Job is saying, "I want to commit suicide." Not at all. He doesn't want to take his own life. He wants God to take his life. There is a vast difference.

Have you ever felt such despair? Have you ever thought, *I just wish Jesus would come back today and rapture me out of this dilemma?* I have. You may have thought that this morning. I think that's where Job is. He's not contemplating suicide. He just wants to check out of this life. This world is full of misery, suffering, and heartache. The longer we live, the more pain we suffer. That is what Job is saying. That's what most of us feel at one time or another.

Maybe you heard about the man who went to his doctor for a checkup. He came back the next day to get the results from the tests.

"Doc, how do I look?"

The doctor said, "I have good news and bad news. Which do you want first?"

The man said, "Let me hear the good news first."

The doctor said, "Well, the good news is, you have twenty-four hours to live."

"Good grief! That's the good news?" the man gasped. "I've got twenty-four hours to live? Then, what's the bad news?"

The doctor replied, "The bad news is I was supposed to tell you yesterday."

That's where Job is. This bad news would be good news to Job. Why? Because Job wants to die today. He has sunk so low as to say,

"Why is light given to him who suffers,
And life to the bitter of soul?
Who long for death, but there is none,
And dig for it more than for hidden treasures;
Who rejoice greatly,
They exult when they find the grave?" (Job 3:20-22)

Again, Job asks God why. "Why does God continue to give light to the one who suffers?" To give extended life to one who suffers seems cruel and pointless.

Job is a candidate for Dr. Doom's Death Machine. Death would be a welcome release. If it could be found, it would be better than discovering a valuable treasure chest in the ground. That's why Job is aggressively pursuing death. If he could just find it, there would be the riches of relief for him.

A casket in the ground would be like a treasure chest buried beneath the surface. Death is that treasure chest—that welcomed reward.

> "Why is light given to a man whose way is hidden,
> And whom God has hedged in?" (Job 3:23)

Why does God continue to give life to a man who can't even see his way to navigate through his affliction? He's trapped in an intricate maze with no way out. Whichever way he turns, he runs into a wall. No way out. Why does God hedge him in? To Job, it seems that God is cruel to keep him alive in this inescapable maze.

Before Job's catastrophes, Satan said, "God, no wonder Job serves You. You've built a hedge, a wall of protection, around him. I can't get to him." God said, "All right, I'll remove that hedge. You can come at him. You can do anything except take his life."

As Satan invaded Job's life and brought great harm, God had built *another* hedge around Job's life. But this hedge is to keep Job from escaping his trials. He is now locked in. Instead of a wall of protection to keep Satan out, now there is a wall of affliction that keeps Job in.

Have you ever wanted your problems just to go away? Surely you have. So did Job. But God had hedged Job into his problems and he couldn't get out.

> "For my groaning comes at the sight of my food,
> And my cries pour out like water." (Job 3:24)

Job's stomach is in such a knot, he can't even eat. He has lost his appetite and food is repulsive. He can't eat, he is so eaten up with despair. He "cries" like a lion (Job 4:10). He sounds like a roaring lion in the jungle as he groans in the night and pours out his anguished heart to God. The anguish pours out.

"For what I fear comes upon me,
And what I dread befalls me." (Job 3:25)

Job fears that there is "no escape" from his misery. "I wake up in the morning hoping that this was just a nightmare, and I wake up to the grim reality that, yes, my children were taken. Yes, my fortune was taken. Yes, my health has been taken. Yes, I am hurting very deeply. And there is no end in sight and no way out of my problem. My worst fears have become reality."

"I am not at ease, nor am I quiet,
And I am not at rest, but turmoil comes." (Job 3:26)

In the aching of his heart, Job says, "I have no peace and I have no rest. All I have are problems and heartaches and despair."

Have you ever been there?

Maybe that's where you are right now. Or, perhaps somebody you know. Take heart, all is not lost. I want to give you some steps to overcome such despair. I don't want to leave you here.

OVERCOMING DESPAIR: GOD'S WAY

Despair is very real. I've been there and so have you. How can we overcome deep discouragement? Let me give you some steps.

First, *realize that even the strongest believer can become discouraged.* Not one of us is Superman. Nor the Bionic Woman. None of us is exempt from such discouragement.

Remember, Job was the most righteous man on the earth when God said to Satan, "Have you considered Job? There is no one like him." I think He was saying, "Listen, Job is My Mount Everest. He stands taller than anyone else on the earth in his love and devotion for Me."

Job has sunk into a dark, black pit of depression. Despite being strong in his faith, he bears all the marks of someone who is depressed: gloom, anger, anxiety, bitterness, confusion, fatigue, cynicism, fear, hopelessness, insomnia, dejection, sadness, pessimism.

Can a believer in Christ be depressed? Yes. Most of us have been or will be depressed.

The Apostle Paul experienced it. In 2 Corinthians 1, he says, "We were burdened excessively, beyond our strength, so that we despaired even of life; indeed, we had the sentence of death within [us]" (verses

8-9). King David of Israel enjoyed the heights of worship. But he also hit the valleys of despair.

Warren Wiersbe, who has written some great biographical books on walking and talking with the giants of our faith, points to a clear theme woven through the lives of many devout servants of God. At times they all were overcome with oppression and discouragement and even depression in their ministry and service for God.

Even such a stalwart of the Christian faith as Martin Luther experienced such deep depression. He wrote of his grief: "For more than a week I was close to the gates of death and hell. I trembled in all my members. Christ was wholly lost. I was shaken by desperation and blasphemy of God."[1]

Second, *we can suffer deeply on many levels at one time.* I see Job suffering on four different levels simultaneously. He's suffering *physically*. We know that from the end of the previous chapter. Added to that, Job says, "I can't eat and I'm crying. I'm knotted up, physically, on the inside."

He is suffering *intellectually* as his mind is flooded with "Why? Why? Why, God?" He is confused and bewildered.

He is suffering *emotionally*. He says in verse 26, "I am not at ease, I am not at rest, I am not quiet in my heart, I am full of turmoil."

Job is suffering *spiritually* as well. He is realizing that God has hedged him in, and he wishes God had never even allowed him to be born.

There are times in our lives when we will go through a dark night of adversity in which we suffer physically, intellectually, emotionally, and spiritually all at the same time—and this will touch the deepest recesses of our souls.

Third, *discouragement can cause us to lose perspective.* That's what is happening to Job here. He is losing his perspective of God. He is overreacting and making exaggerated statements. He is jumping to wrong conclusions and he has lost sound judgment.

Depression affects your whole view of life. It gives a twisted perception of reality. It produces a distorted view of God and self, often yielding an inaccurate and unhealthy negative self-image.

When you and I become discouraged over an extended period of time, we can lose perspective on life and we, too, can begin to draw wrong conclusions, to make exaggerated statements, and to see life in an irrational perspective that is not right.

Often when people are discouraged they say, "I'm going to quit and go to another church" or "I'm going to divorce my wife" or "We're just going to up and leave town." In the midst of your discouragement when you have lost perspective, you'll make your worst decisions.

Fourth, *don't keep your deep pain to yourself.* Share your hurt with someone else.

One of the things that crushed Job's spirit as he and his friends sat in the garbage dump was his own silence. All they have done so far is simply to stare at one another. All the while, Job could have been pouring out his heart and sharing his burdens with them. But he kept it on the inside. And Job became like a teakettle on a stove and the pressure built up and up and up so that when finally released, it came spewing out. Eruption. Gusher. Explosion. Job could have prevented this by exposing his heart all along. We need our friends to help us bear our heavy loads.

Galatians says, "Bear one another's burdens." Romans says, "Weep with those who weep."

Job should have freely shared what he was going through. So should you.

Fifth, *remember that God always has a purpose behind suffering.*

As long as you are alive, God has a purpose for your being here on the earth. And until the moment we die, we are still in the process of fulfilling that purpose. Therefore, we need to stay here upon the earth until God determines our time is over. God will not take us home until we have fulfilled our purpose.

Jesus said, "We must work the works of Him who sent Me, as long as it is day; night is coming, when no man can work" (John 9:4). While we have life and while we have opportunity, we need to do what God has called us to do.

Sixth, when discouraged, *take proper steps to avoid depression.* May I give you several things that I share with counselees who are deeply afflicted and discouraged and even depressed? These are practical steps on how to overcome deep discouragement.

Memorize and meditate upon Scripture. The Word of God can be a soothing balm to a breaking heart.

Listen to Christian music. God inhabits the praises of His people (so try some praise music). And God has designed us so that praise should lift our hearts to God. One of the greatest things you can do is listen to Christian music that elevates God and Christ with celebration.

David played his harp for Saul. It softened, if only for a time, Saul's bitter soul. I'd wager David also played his harp for himself. And it was a soothing comfort.

Stay plugged in to Christian fellowship. You need the strength that others provide. Don't isolate yourselves from others. You need to allow others to affirm you and to communicate value to you. We all need to be around others as they laugh and enjoy life. Charles Swindoll has said that the Christian life should include some outrageous joy. Look for that kind of contagious fellowship.

Find someone else to encourage. One way to work through problems is to take your focus off yourself and put it onto others. Begin to serve others who are in need, and it will help heal your own heart.

Have a prayer partner. Find someone you can pour your heart out to and share your needs with. Someone who will pray for you and with you. Someone who is truly trustworthy. There is something powerful about hearing another person's voice pray for you and offer your requests up to God, perhaps at a time when you are so weak you can barely even bring your heart before God's throne. To hear someone else pray on your behalf can lift your battered spirit.

Remember that God is sovereign. He is in control. As we see in Job's life, God was in control of Satan and He had a master plan. He allows our suffering for a greater purpose to help weave that marvelous tapestry that He will one day reveal and that will bring glory to Himself. Remember that nothing will come into your life except that which is either allowed or sent by a sovereign God.

Maintain physical exercise. You need to walk, you need to jog, you need to ride a bike, you need to plant a garden, you need to go walk the golf course (then again, that may be why you're depressed—that back nine). Physical exercise is critical.

HELP IS ON THE WAY

Long ago, in the days of sailing ships, a terrible storm arose and a ship was lost in a very deserted area. Only one crewman survived, washed up on a small, uninhabited island. In his desperation, the castaway daily prayed to God for help and deliverance from his lonely existence.

Each day, he looked for a passing ship and saw nothing. Eventually, he managed to build a very crude hut in which he stored the few things he had recovered from the wreck, and those things he was able to make to help him.

One day, as the sailor was returning from his daily search for food, he saw a column of smoke. As he ran to it, he saw that it was arising from his hut, which was in flames.

All was lost.

Now, not only was he alone, but he had nothing to help him in his struggle for survival. He was stunned and overcome with grief and despair. He fell into a deep depression and spent many a sleepless night wondering what was to become of him and questioning whether life itself was even worth the effort.

Then one morning, he arose early and went down to the sea. There to his amazement, he saw a ship lying offshore, and a small rowboat coming toward him.

When this once-marooned man met the ship's captain, he asked him, "How did you know to send help? How did you know I was here?"

The captain replied, "Why, we saw your smoke signal last week. But, by the time we could turn our ship around and sail against the wind, it had taken us several days to get to you. But here we are."

Calamity may strike, but we must remember that God *can use* that calamity as a means to bring greater blessing to our lives.

Right now, you may feel as if your life has gone up in smoke. You may feel as if your heart is going through fiery trials. I want you to know that your trial may be used by God as the very instrument that will bring you closer to Him and bring blessing from His hand.

That reality would eventually become true in Job's life. God drew Job closer to Himself than ever before.

God will use our times of testing and trials to bring us even closer to Himself.

NOTE
1. Roland Bainton, *Here I Stand* (Nashville: Abingdon, 1950), page 36.

CHAPTER 5

WITH FRIENDS LIKE THESE . . .

▼

W e've all had one. That well-intentioned friend who means well but is grossly misguided. You know, the one who constantly throws cold water on the flickering flame of our hope. It could be an overprotective parent. A ubiquitous friend. A nosy sibling. A demanding boss. We've all had one.

They mean well. Their intentions are honorable. But their effect is devastating. Demotivating. Deflating. Just plain discouraging.

No doubt about it. They are experts on every subject. Their advice is meant to help. But it never does. If these folks have a spiritual gift, it must be that of discouragement.

Intending to be the voice of God to help, they often unwittingly become the mouthpieces of Satan to hurt. Their words cut so deeply that there's no blood. Only pain, injury, and despair. Discouragement has to be one of the Devil's very chief tools.

THE DEVIL'S GARAGE SALE

The story is told that the Devil decided to have a garage sale. Taking out all his finest tools of deception and death, he priced and placed each one on the driveway. They were each marked according to their value.

There was hatred, envy, and jealousy all marked for sale. There was deceit, lust, lying, and pride with their appropriate price tags.

But, set over by itself, totally removed from the other instruments, was an unassuming plain-looking tool. It was quite worn. In fact, it was the most worn of all the tools, and yet it carried the highest price. A customer sauntered up and began browsing through the tools. He picked it up, looked it over, and casually asked the Devil, "Say, what's the name of this tool?"

With a shrewd sneer, the Devil boldly replied, "Ahh, my favorite tool. I know it well. That's the tool called discouragement."

"Is that high price negotiable?" the customer asked.

"No, absolutely not. That tool is more powerful than any other tool I have. When I use the tool of discouragement on a person's heart, I can pry open that person's heart and then use all of my other tools. It is the key tool—my most strategic tool—and therefore comes at a very high price."

There is much truth in that little parable. When Satan discourages us and gets us down and defeated, we become easy prey for his hellish host, who then use the Devil's cheaper instruments of destruction.

What is discouragement? Discouragement is the state of being deprived of confidence and hope. It is being dejected, disheartened, and deflated. It is being despondent, despairing, and dismayed. (I can't find any more *d*'s, but that's what it is to be discouraged.)

This is exactly where Job is. Discouraged. Despairing. Dismayed. Job's friends have picked up the Devil's tool of discouragement and are prying open Job's heart. He is now easy prey for the Devil.

Can you relate to this?

Do you know what it is to be discouraged? Easy pickin's for the Devil? I sure do. I've been there and so have you.

We've all had trouble down at work. The ministry is no exception. Let me tell you about a doozy that happened to me.

I was still wet behind the ears, fresh out of seminary, when I pastored my first church. (That means I knew enough theology to be dangerous.) The first two years were one big honeymoon. Everybody loved me. I loved everybody.

Until it happened. I invited a speaker into our church—a close, personal friend who had performed the wedding for my wife, Anne, and me—to hold a conference on prayer. Somehow, the messages got off track and deviated into some highly explosive subject matter.

What he said was controversial. Jolting. Shocking. He was partly right, but partly wrong. And our little church was torn asunder.

After my friend left town, I was left to deal with the fallout. And, believe me, the fallout was epidemic. Hurt feelings. Broken trust. Severed relationships. Emotional barriers. Deep wounds. Personal attacks. Counterattacks. Tense meetings. Hidden agendas. Power plays. Lines drawn. Sides taken. Let me tell you, I was at the center of it all with no way out. My honeymoon was now officially a nightmare. A lot was my fault. A lot wasn't.

Just coming to the office was a chore. My calendar was cluttered with people wanting an explanation. I spent a month in the office every day. My evenings were occupied with endless boards wanting to debate what happened. My nights were filled with lengthy phone conversations with church members all wanting to discuss it. Every time it was rehashed, it seemed I sank into deeper depression. I couldn't sleep. I stopped eating and lost weight. I honestly didn't laugh for over a year. I withdrew into isolation. At night, I would walk the streets in lonely solitude. I would pace back and forth under our streetlight.

But God used this experience for good in my life. I see that now. He used it to break me in order to remake me. Before I entered the ministry, I could be very abrasive and harsh, especially with my humor. I was often explosive and out of control in making fun of people. I could put someone down and make others laugh at someone in a heartbeat. It was insensitive. Selfish. Self-serving. Unfortunately, this carried over to other areas of my life.

I needed to be brought down off my high horse. That's precisely what God did through this excruciating experience. The pillars of my life were removed and the whole temple came crashing down upon me. God tore down the old building in order to rebuild a new one. That's what He is still in the process of doing. But it all began with this crashing blow.

Even though it was deeply painful, God used it to remold me into a fit vessel. Because I was so hurt, I developed a higher sensitivity to others in pain. Only when I was humbled could God begin to use me.

Someone has said, "Before God uses a man or woman greatly, He must first break them deeply." He did it with me.

My personal pain lasted a year. A whole year. But I believed that God would see me through it. Somehow. Some way. Some day.

God will do the same in your life. He will use a time of personal tragedy and heartbreak to remake you into His image.

Everyone is going to make mistakes that lead to suffering. I did and still do. Sometimes the consequences are devastating. What is most important is the realization that God sovereignly uses these defeats to make us victorious.

What about you? How has God used your personal tragedies to get your attention and make you like Himself?

Let's now meet three instruments of humility in Job's life. His friends: Eliphaz, Bildad, and Zophar. I call them Eliphaz the Exterminator, Bildad the Brutal, and Zophar the Zealot. They will speak to Job with good intentions, but become major stumbling blocks for him. Their speeches will contain elements of truth, but never the whole truth. The problem will not be so much what they say, but what they don't say. Half a truth when it becomes the whole truth, is no truth at all.

MEET ELIPHAZ THE EXTERMINATOR

The first friend to speak was Eliphaz. He was probably the oldest of the three and appealed to experience for authority. He was also the most sympathetic of Job's three friends. Eliphaz came from Teman, a town noted for wisdom.

Eliphaz begins in a courteous tone. He appears to be genuinely concerned for Job's well-being. The problem is he really doesn't know how to help.

> Then Eliphaz the Temanite answered,
> "If one ventures a word with you, will you become
>   impatient?
> But who can refrain from speaking?
> Behold you have admonished many,
> And you have strengthened weak hands.
> Your words have helped the tottering to stand,
> And you have strengthened feeble knees.
> But now it has come to you and you are impatient;
> It touches you, and you are dismayed.
> Is not your fear of God your confidence,
> And the integrity of your ways your hope?" (Job 4:1-6)

He is saying, "Job, I've got something I want to share with you. I need for you to be patient and listen. Job, God has used you in a great way to teach and encourage others. You've been a great teacher, but . . . *you* need to be taught now. Sit down, take a dose of your own medicine, and you'll be well again."

Eliphaz now states the basic principle he thinks will cure Job's ills:

"Remember now, who ever perished being innocent?
Or where were the upright destroyed?
According to what I have seen, those who plow iniquity
And those who sow trouble harvest it.
By the breath of God they perish,
And by the blast of His anger they come to an end.
The roaring of the lion and the voice of the fierce lion,
And the teeth of the young lions are broken.
The lion perishes for lack of prey,
And the whelps of the lioness are scattered." (Job 4:7-11)

We can hear Eliphaz's voice become intense. His eyes glare. His finger begins to motion and point at Job. Eliphaz says, "Job, if you're going through a tough time, it has to be because you have done something wrong. You're not right with God. Just confess your sin and everything will turn around in your life."

His argument is that the righteous are never afflicted. Only the unrighteous suffer.

The implication is clear. Job's problem is that he must be hiding some sin in his life. "Job, if you will only admit it, you'll be all right."

Eliphaz draws an illustration from the jungle. When a hunter captures a lion, his young cubs are destroyed because the king of beasts didn't do a good job of protecting them. The point is obvious. "Job, if you were doing a good job of protecting your family, your children would have never been taken away." Now, that's cruel! Eliphaz is systematically destroying Job's hope.

Eliphaz says he learned this truth in a vision that is hair-raising. His interpretation of the dream is harebrained.

"Now a word was brought to me stealthily,
And my ear received a whisper of it.
Amid disquieting thoughts from the visions of the night,
When deep sleep falls on men,
Dread came upon me, and trembling,

And made all my bones shake.
Then a spirit passed by my face;
The hair of my flesh bristled up.
It stood still, but I could not discern its appearance;
A form was before my eyes;
There was silence, then I heard a voice:
'Can mankind be just before God?
Can a man be pure before his Maker?
He puts no trust even in His servants;
And against His angels He charges error.
How much more those who dwell in houses of clay,
Whose foundation is in the dust,
Who are crushed before the moth!
Between morning and evening they are broken in pieces;
Unobserved, they perish forever.
Is not their tent-cord plucked up within them?
They die, yet without wisdom.'" (Job 4:12-21)

In this dream, a spirit appeared to Eliphaz and gave him supernatural revelation. But this spirit was no holy messenger, it was a demon spirit from hell sent to delude Eliphaz and discourage Job.

The revelation given was unbalanced theology. Heavy on God's holiness but devoid of any grace. The spirit said if God charges even the angels with error, there's no way man can be righteous or trusted before God. Yes, man is sinful, but Job can be trusted to serve God without cursing Him.

A clock that doesn't even run is right twice a day. Sure, Eliphaz is right in asserting God's holiness, but he is dead wrong in saying that Job cannot be trusted. In fact, God Himself has said that Job will not curse him. But this doesn't stop the Exterminator!

Eliphaz now taunts Job not to appeal to the angels for help. After all, they will just tell him the same thing.

"Call now, is there anyone who will answer you?
And to which of the holy ones will you turn?
For vexation slays the foolish man,
And anger kills the simple.
I have seen the foolish taking root,
And I cursed his abode immediately.

His sons are far from safety,
They are even oppressed in the gate,
Neither is there a deliverer.
His harvest the hungry devour,
And take it to a place of thorns;
And the schemer is eager for their wealth.
For affliction does not come from the dust,
Neither does trouble sprout from the ground,
For man is born for trouble,
As sparks fly upward." (Job 5:1-7)

Fools start off well but eventually lose their family and fortune to calamity. First there's confusion (vexation), then anger, and more foolish behavior. Eliphaz is so disgusted by such foolishness, he curses their homes. Again, the implication is painfully obvious: "Job, you've lost your children because of some moral failure in your life. You're foolish, therefore you're cursed. Your trouble comes from within yourself. It comes from sin, like a crackling campfire sure to send sparks heavenward."

Eliphaz urges Job to plead his case with God. If Job would repent, God would restore all his blessings. But he's not through.

"But as for me, I would seek God,
And I would place my cause before God;
Who does great and unsearchable things,
Wonders without number.
He gives rain on the earth,
And sends water on the fields,
So that He sets on high those who are lowly,
And those who mourn are lifted to safety.
He frustrates the plotting of the shrewd,
So that their hands cannot attain success.
He captures the wise by their own shrewdness
And the advice of the cunning is quickly thwarted.
By day they meet with darkness,
And grope at noon as in the night.
But He saves from the sword of their mouth,
And the poor from the hand of the mighty.
So the helpless has hope,
And unrighteousness must shut its mouth." (Job 5:8-16)

Even though Eliphaz doesn't address Job directly here, the inference is clear: If Job would just repent, God would shower down blessings upon him and restore his hope. "Job, just fear God, confess your sin, and things will be all right. Until that confession comes, Job, you'll just be groping in the dark."

A FAULTY VIEW OF HUMAN NATURE

Notice how loftily Eliphaz places himself. He judges the fool. He even curses the fool's house. He judges the shrewd, explaining that God frustrates the unrighteous but cunning individual. Here the "shrewd" and the "cunning" are those who don't love God. And in the same breath Eliphaz raises up the "lowly," "those who mourn," and "the poor."

Eliphaz now confuses the issues surrounding Job's afflictions even more—at once claiming his suffering is disciplinary and that God's deliverance is near. But we know his suffering is not disciplinary—remember chapter 1. Again Eliphaz contends, if Job would acknowledge his sin, God would bless him; he would be delivered from affliction. In the meantime, Eliphaz continues:

"Behold, how happy is the man whom God reproves,
So do not despise the discipline of the Almighty.
For He inflicts pain, and gives relief;
He wounds, and His hands also heal.
From six troubles He will deliver you,
Even in seven evil will not touch you.
In famine He will redeem you from death,
And in war from the power of the sword.
You will be hidden from the scourge of the tongue,
Neither will you be afraid of violence when it comes.
You will laugh at violence and famine,
Neither will you be afraid of wild beasts.
For you will be in league with the stones of the field;
And the beasts of the field will be at peace with you.
And you will know that your tent is secure,
For you will visit your abode and fear no loss.
You will know also that your descendants will be many,
And your offspring as the grass of the earth.
You will come to the grave in full vigor,
Like the stacking of grain in its season.

Behold this, we have investigated it, thus it is;
Hear it, and know for yourself." (Job 5:17-27)

What a sensitive thing to say. "Hey, cheer up, Job! God's disciplin-
ing you. Smile! The harder the discipline, the better off you'll be."

Eliphaz has no compassion for Job. No tenderness. No love. Only
harsh discipline and judgment. Because he has such a rigid, harsh view
of God, he has no room for God's mercy.

Eliphaz explains to Job what would happen if he would repent and
ask for God's forgiveness. His confession would bring relief from pain,
healing of his sores, deliverance from death, no more slander, no more
famine, and more children.

Smug, cold, and callous is Eliphaz. There's no desire to help Job.
No desire to come alongside and encourage him. No attempt to breathe
hope back into him. No attempt to bear his burden. Instead, Eliphaz is
just standing at a distance, looking down a long, self-righteous nose at
Job, the man he had earlier claimed to love.

GET OFF MY BACK!

Job now responds, but it's not exactly to Eliphaz. He is a broken man.
He feels alienated by God and isolated from his friends. His speech
seems to ignore Eliphaz's "words of encouragement" completely, since,
in Job's mind, those words didn't get at his problem.

Then Job answered,
"Oh that my vexation were actually weighed,
And laid in the balances together with my iniquity!
For then it would be heavier than the sand of the seas,
Therefore my words have been rash.
For the arrows of the Almighty are within me;
Their poison my spirit drinks;
The terrors of God are arrayed against me.
Does the wild donkey bray over his grass,
Or does the ox low over his fodder?
Can something tasteless be eaten without salt,
Or is there any taste in the white of an egg?
My soul refuses to touch them;
They are like loathsome food to me."
(Job 6:1-7)

Job is claiming that if his anger and misery (vexation) were placed on one side of the scales of justice, and the indignities he has suffered as a result of God's attack on the other, we would plainly see that his anger and misery are no match for the indignities. They would weigh as much as the sand in the sea! Who could weigh that? Job appeals for sympathy in light of the fact that God was directly attacking him. He claims the right to complain since he has been wounded so deeply. He basically picks up where he left off in chapter 3. He cries for understanding for his harsh words: "Guys, don't you understand, God Himself has wounded me! It's terrifying! You'd use rash language too if you were in my shoes. It feels as if I've become the enemy of God!" It's this last realization that has Job distressed more than any other.

Job is incredulous. "Why me?" is his cry. The donkey doesn't complain (bray) if he gets the grass he usually eats. The same with an ox. Why is Job then receiving the opposite of what he, a righteous man, deserves? By the same token, just as any sane person would reject taste-less food, Job refuses to swallow the bitter pill God has prescribed.

Job begins sinking back into the pit of despair. He wants to end his pain. He has a death wish.

> "Oh that my request might come to pass,
> And that God would grant my longing!
> Would that God were willing to crush me;
> That He would loose His hand and cut me off!
> But it is still my consolation,
> And I rejoice in unsparing pain,
> That I have not denied the words of the Holy One.
> What is my strength, that I should wait?
> And what is my end, that I should endure?
> Is my strength the strength of stones,
> Or is my flesh bronze?
> Is it that my help is not within me,
> And that deliverance is driven from me?" (Job 6:8-13)

If Job could just die now, he believes he would be happy. That way, he could die knowing he had remained true to God. He has no strength. No help. No hope. He is no longer "rock-solid, market-wise." No longer does he feel the impenetrable, uninjurable immortality of youth—he knows his flesh isn't as strong as a bronze shield. He longs to die because that would relieve him of his suffering.

Job appeals to his friends to show him kindness. He recognizes he cannot succeed on his own. His message to them is: "I need you on my team, not on my back."

> "For the despairing man there should be kindness from his
>   friend;
> Lest he forsake the fear of the Almighty.
> My brothers have acted deceitfully like a wadi,
> Like the torrents of wadis which vanish,
> Which are turbid because of ice,
> And into which the snow melts.
> When they become waterless, they are silent,
> When it is hot, they vanish from their place.
> The paths of their course wind along,
> They go up into nothing and perish.
> The caravans of Tema looked,
> The travelers of Sheba hoped for them.
> They were disappointed for they had trusted,
> They came there and were confounded.
> Indeed, you have now become such,
> You see a terror and are afraid.
> Have I said, 'Give me something,'
> Or, 'Offer a bribe for me from your wealth,'
> Or, 'Deliver me from the hand of the adversary,'
> Or, 'Redeem me from the hand of the tyrants'?"
>   (Job 6:14-23)

Job wasn't getting that kind of sympathy, was he? He paints a vivid picture that needs some explanation. He describes his friends as like a wadi. Now, what's a wadi? It's the Hebrew word for riverbed. His friends are like a riverbed full of rocks. In the wintertime, the river is full of water, snow, and ice. But that's not when water from the riverbed is needed. It's in the summertime that water is needed. But the problem with the wadi is that when the summer comes, all of the cool, cold, refreshing water has evaporated. When it is needed the most is when it is not there.

Job says, "Eliphaz, that's exactly the way you are. When I need help and encouragement, you're not there for me. When I need someone to come put his arm around me and care for me, your kindness has evaporated. There is no encouragement or comfort from you when I need it the most."

Can't you just see this dry riverbed winding along through the wilderness, into the desert, and across the terrain? Picture a caravan out in the middle of the desert, desperately needing water. They see this dry riverbed and decide to follow it in hopes of finding water. But as they follow it, it just peters out into nothing.

Job is saying, "Eliphaz, that's exactly the way you are in my life. The longer I listen to you, the more you lead me out into the desert without any help."

Job asks, "Have I even asked you to get involved in my life? Have I even invited you to be doing this?" The answer is no.

Job next pleads with his friends to teach him where he went wrong. Watch out, Job, you're asking for it! He asks, "How can I confess a sin of which I'm unaware?"

> "Teach me, and I will be silent;
> And show me how I have erred.
> How painful are honest words!
> But what does your argument prove?
> Do you intend to reprove my words,
> When the words of one in despair belong to the wind?
> You would even cast lots for the orphans,
> And barter over your friend.
> And now please look at me,
> And see if I lie to your face.
> Desist now, let there be no injustice;
> Even desist, my righteousness is yet in it.
> Is there injustice on my tongue?
> Cannot my palate discern calamities?"
>   (Job 6:24-30)

He turns to Eliphaz and says, "You say I'm suffering because of sin, but you've never pointed anything out specifically. Teach me and tell me what my sin is. But until you do, there's no proof of your argument."

Job felt as if he were being sold like an orphan. He's quite perceptive about their lack of true concern for him, discerning accurately that each is only trying to win a theological debate.

Having responded to Eliphaz, Job now expresses bitter complaints to God.

"Is not man forced to labor on earth,
And are not his days like the days of a hired man?
As a slave who pants for the shade,
And as a hired man who eagerly waits for his wages,
So am I allotted months of vanity,
And nights of trouble are appointed me.
When I lie down I say,
'When shall I arise?'
But the night continues,
And I am continually tossing until dawn.
My flesh is clothed with worms and a crust of dirt;
My skin hardens and runs.
My days are swifter than a weaver's shuttle,
And come to an end without hope." (Job 7:1-6)

Job complains that he's like a slave working under the hot sun. He is like a man toiling under forced labor, longing for shade, waiting to be paid. His life is continual toil and misery.

He wants to sleep and he can't even sleep!

Job is saying, "If God is going to help me, He had better hurry up and do it now because my life is escaping fast."

"Therefore, I will not restrain my mouth;
I will speak in the anguish of my spirit,
I will complain in the bitterness of my soul.
Am I the sea, or the sea monster,
That Thou dost set a guard over me?
If I say, 'My bed will comfort me,
My couch will ease my complaint,'
Then Thou dost frighten me with dreams
And terrify me by visions;
So that my soul would choose suffocation,
Death rather than my pains.
I waste away; I will not live forever.
Leave me alone for my days are but a breath.
What is man that Thou dost magnify him,

And that Thou art concerned about him,
That Thou dost examine him every morning,
And try him every moment?
Wilt Thou never turn Thy gaze away from me,
Nor let me alone until I swallow my spittle?
Have I sinned? What have I done to Thee,
O watcher of men?
Why hast Thou set me as Thy target,
So that I am a burden to myself?
Why then dost Thou not pardon my transgression
And take away my iniquity?
For now I will lie down in the dust;
And Thou wilt seek me, but I will not be." (Job 7:11-21)

Job now sees his life as short as a breath. When he dies, he will go down to Sheol and never return. Anything but this! Job then spoke out again in bitter complaint against God, who he felt, was harassing and frightening him.

Job just wanted God to leave him alone.

"God, why have you set me up to be a target just to shoot at? Why?"

MEET BILDAD THE BRUTAL

Enter "friend" number two—Bildad the Brutal. He's highly intelligent, a cold, calculating thinker, and skilled debater. He has essentially the same view that Eliphaz has, which is: If there's something going wrong in your life, it's because you're not right with God. If you were right with the Lord, you wouldn't be going through this trouble. Whatever suffering a human experiences, it was "begotten" by him (compare Job 4:8). All you need to do is confess your sin, get right with the Lord, and all of these problems will go away. You can see how Bildad unknowingly plays right into the Devil's hands. He becomes an evil mouthpiece.

Then Bildad the Shuhite answered,
"How long will you say these things,
And the words of your mouth be a mighty wind?
Does God pervert justice
Or does the Almighty pervert what is right?
If your sons sinned against Him,
Then He delivered them into the power of their transgression.

If you would seek God
And implore the compassion of the Almighty,
If you are pure and upright,
Surely now He would rouse Himself for you
And restore your righteous estate.
Though your beginning was insignificant,
Yet your end will increase greatly." (Job 8:1-7)

Bildad's style is to ask questions. He tries to approach Job's problems with a precise logical framework.

His first question is, "Can God do wrong?"

That's a great question and, of course, the answer is no. How can anyone argue with such a lofty premise?

When Job's children were killed, the only conclusion Bildad cares to draw is that *they* did something wrong. After all, *God* cannot do wrong. Because God punishes all sin, any tragedy must be the result of some hidden sin. Calculating logic. Incomplete premises. Bildad is ignoring the obvious. But he's not through with his tirade.

"Please inquire of past generations,
And consider the things searched out by their fathers.
For we are only of yesterday and know nothing,
Because our days on earth are as a shadow.
Will they not teach you and tell you,
And bring forth words from their minds?" (Job 8:8-10)

Bildad says that because life is so short, we really don't have enough time to gather up enough wisdom to live it. That's why we need to look at tradition and the people who have lived before us. We need to gather up their collective insight, and that will give us the wisdom we need to live.

Warren Wiersbe writes some very helpful words here, "To be sure, we can today learn from the past, but the past must be a rudder to guide us into the future and not an anchor to hold us back. The fact that something was said years ago is no guarantee that it is right. The past contains as much folly as wisdom."

To Bildad, the past was a parking lot. A safe place to sit out life. But God wants the past to be a launching pad into the future. There is nothing wrong with learning from the past—providing it does not paralyze the present into a dusty old museum that only displays bygone days. Neither the present nor the future needs to become a cemetery for the possibilities of today. Yet Bildad persists in his faulty argument.

Finally, Bildad appeals to the realm of science to establish his point with Job.

> "Can the papyrus grow up without marsh?
> Can the rushes grow without water?
> While it is still green and not cut down,
> Yet it withers before any other plant." (Job 8:11-12)

Bildad's logic is, "If you don't water a plant, it will wither and die." So, if someone's life is withering, the problem must be that this person is a hypocrite. Our culprit simply cannot be deeply rooted in the Lord.

Likewise, those who fail to trust God are as flimsy as a spider web.

> "So are the paths of all who forget God,
> And the hope of the godless will perish,
> Whose confidence is fragile,
> And whose trust a spider's web.
> He trusts in his house, but it does not stand;
> He holds fast to it, but it does not endure." (Job 8:13-15)

Also, the one who does not trust God is like a green plant that may initially thrive under the sun, but be easily uprooted and die.

> "He thrives before the sun,
> And his shoots spread out over his garden.
> His roots wrap around a rock pile,
> He grasps a house of stones.
> If he is removed from his place,
> Then it will deny him, saying, 'I never saw you.'" (Job 8:16-18)

The implication is clear. "Job, that's the way your life is. From outward appearances, you had it all. Fame. Fortune. Family. But now look at you. It's all gone. It's a sure sign that your faith was shallow and superficial."

Was that true? Well, let's think back. God said that Job was the most righteous man on earth. He was a man who feared the Lord and put his whole trust in God. Job's calamity does not seem to be the result of a faulty root system. Didn't God choose to allow the Devil to totally uproot Job's life and turn his whole world upside down? And did God say that this was through any fault of Job's? Well, Bildad? Wasn't that a part of the sovereign plan of God to use the Devil to bring greater glory to Himself?

God will also do that in our lives. There will come times when God will allow the Devil to attack our lives and cause our world to be turned upside down and uprooted. Not because anything is wrong with our lives. It may just be because everything is *right* with our lives.

A FRIEND TO THE HURTING
How can we be a friend to people in distress, like Job?

Be There for Them
Eliphaz was there physically, but emotionally his heart remained miles away. He was there more to make theological points for himself than to comfort Job.

We can be like that, can't we? We can hardly wait to say "I told you so," to make us look good, rather than to comfort the hurting party.In order to be a friend to someone who is hurting, we must come alongside that person in his or her sorrow. That's what the word *encourage* means. It means to come alongside someone in need—to help, to encourage, to comfort, to guide. Proverbs 18:24 states,

> A man of many friends comes to ruin,
> But there is a friend who sticks closer than a brother.

Eliphaz never really did that. Sure, he was standing before Job. But I don't think he was standing *with* Job. Job needed a friend to come put a gentle arm around him rather than shake an accusing finger in his face.

Feel Their Pain and Hurt
Eliphaz never did sympathize with Job and enter into his pain. It was all so intellectual. So theological. So analytical. So bottom-line–oriented.

Aren't we supposed to *bear* one another's burdens (Galatians 6:2)? That means to get under a brother's burden with him and help carry the weight of his hurt. Not just sit across the room and explain where he went wrong. It takes no size to criticize.

Be on Their Team

Eliphaz took an adversarial role. He lost sight of the original goal, which was to actually *comfort* Job. He spent his time trying to pin Job down rather than lift him up. He tried to criticize Job and condemn him, and to document that Job was in sin. There was no comfort at all from Eliphaz. No help, only harassment.

A few years back, Pepper Rogers, head football coach at UCLA, was going through a terrible season. He was so upset about it, and he didn't think his wife was encouraging him enough. He said, "My dog is my best friend. I told my wife that a man needs at least two friends. She told me to go buy another dog."

That's what Eliphaz is saying to Job.

Proverbs 17:17 states,

A friend loves at all times
And a brother is born for adversity.

Listen More Than You Talk

Part of Eliphaz's problem is diarrhea of the mouth. He just wants to talk, talk, talk. The guy goes on like a broken record. He goes on and on . . . as if he has an Energizer battery inside him.

God gave us two ears and one mouth. We need to use them accordingly. Be quick to hear and slow to speak.

Job didn't need a lecture, he needed love. He didn't need a sermon, he needed sympathy. He didn't need criticism, he needed comfort. He didn't need a treatise, he needed tenderness.

Don't Try to Explain Everything

Quite frankly, Eliphaz really did not know what he was talking about. He thought he had all the divine mysteries figured out. He just knew he was wise to why everything was going wrong in Job's life. But really, he didn't have a clue.

When I hear somebody try to explain something in somebody else's life, or in my life, I sometimes think, *When did you go to Heaven and come back?*

Don't try to explain everything.

Help Instill Hope

The flame of hope had been extinguished within Job's heart. He needed to have that flame rekindled. He needed to be told, "Job, there is a bright tomorrow out there. God's going to work through this. We're going to work through this together. God's going to work through this for *good*."

But Eliphaz was so focused on the negative, he had nothing positive to say. No wonder Job had no hope.

Someone has said, "Real friends are those who, when you make a fool of yourself, don't think you've done a permanent job."

Look Beyond Your Friend's Faults to His or Her Needs
Eliphaz could only see Job's faults—or what he *thought* were his faults. That's all he could see. He attacked Job's shortcomings, but he never did see his need. Never.

To be a friend to someone who's hurting, you and I must look beyond that person's faults to his or her needs. Isn't that what God has done for us?

Emphasize God's Love and Compassion
Do you know what's missing from all that Eliphaz has to say? God's love. His tenderness. His compassion. All he sees is a God of strict justice, harsh judgment, swift discipline, and severe condemnation. He has a very rigid view of God that allows for no mercy or grace.

If we are to help someone who is hurting, we need to emphasize God's love, tenderness, and mercy.

Yes, God is a God of judgment, but He is also a God of love. One without the other is not God. Again, half the truth, when it becomes the whole truth, becomes no truth at all.

There are people all around us—perhaps now more than ever—who are going through some very difficult times. They need a friend just like you to help them through these days.

What a shame it would be to be like Eliphaz and only add to their sorrow. God can use you in the lives of others. As we follow the steps just prescribed, we will learn what it is to minister to one another, comfort one another, and encourage one another. Something Job never had.

Most of all, we have a friend in the Lord Jesus Christ. If you have been without such a friend, may I point you to Him. What a friend we have in Jesus!

He will never, never disappoint you. He will never, never leave you. And His love and mercy shall never, never cease flowing from His heart to yours.

CHAPTER 6

THE FOUR SPIRITUAL FLAWS
▼

I heard about a father who was watching his small son draw a picture. Intensely focused, the young lad was totally engrossed in his work of art. Crayons were scattered everywhere. Unfinished sketches were wadded and cast aside.

Without wanting to break the boy's concentration, the dad gently inquired, "Say, son, what are you drawing?"

Never looking up, the small boy replied, "God."

Somewhat taken back, his father said, "Well, no one knows what God looks like."

Confidently gazing at his masterpiece, the boy retorted, "They will when I get through."

We all have a picture of God in our minds. And our picture of God is critically important to who we are. In fact, our picture of God is the most important thing about us.

A. W. Tozer once said, "The most important thing about you is what comes into your mind when you think of God." If so—and I believe he is correct—then a spiritual flaw regarding our mental picture of God can have a devastating effect on our faith. We *must* have a right view of God, or else it will be distorted and out of focus.

91

Too often, we allow circumstances to shape our picture of God. If our circumstances are good, it's easy to believe that God must be good. But if our circumstances are bad, then sometimes we draw some false conclusions about God. In a time of personal adversity and deep struggle, our picture of God can become flawed.

Yes, I said flawed. In the midst of trials, our picture of God can become influenced by tragic circumstances. We begin to see God through our circumstances rather than seeing our circumstances through God.

If our circumstances are good, we tend to see God as good. But when tragedy strikes and bad things happen, the divine picture can become greatly distorted. Out of focus. A misrepresentation of who He is. Unfortunately, when the picture becomes flawed, so does our faith. Our faith can only be as strong as our right picture of God.

More times than not, a distorted picture of God occurs in the midst of severe trials and personal troubles. When we become discouraged, we can soon become greatly disillusioned about who God is.

The colors of Job's palette have become blurred by his circumstances. Discouragement has marred his picture of the Almighty. He has lost sight of the true God. Such malady could be diagnosed as the "Four Spiritual Flaws." They are flaws in Job's perception of God.

Notice I said flaws, not laws. I'm sure you are familiar with *The Four Spiritual Laws*, a widely distributed and greatly used booklet that distills the essentials of the gospel into four spiritual laws that govern God's spiritual Kingdom.

Well, I'm talking about *flaws*. You know what a flaw is. An imperfection. A distortion. In this case, anything that hinders a right view of God.

Job is not the only one who suffers from these flaws. Anyone can suffer from a wrong picture of God. Especially when life isn't going our way. We, too, can succumb to the Four Spiritual Flaws.

As a pastor, I hear these flaws again and again from people who are going through difficult times. And as a believer, I myself have fallen victim to their untruths. We all want to be aware of them and then avoid them like the plague.

Back to Job. In this epic encounter with Job's friends, the Devil uses a new approach. After attacking Job's family, fortune, and health, Satan vandalizes Job's picture of God. In essence, the Devil draws a mustache on the Mona Lisa. He spray-paints graffiti on Job's image of

God. Using Job's friends to do the deadly work, Satan is gaining access to the canvas of Job's mind.

Satan will do the same with our image of God. If he can't get us to curse the true God, he'll get us to believe in a wrong picture of God. There is nothing—I repeat, nothing—more devastating to your life than a wrong view of God. It colors all that you are and do.

God.

Is your picture of Him flawed? Job's was. Let's examine these four flaws one at a time. Here is spiritual flaw number one:

GOD WON'T LISTEN TO ME!

As the intensity of his suffering mounts, Job cries out to God for relief. But there is no immediate answer. No miraculous deliverance. No dramatic change. No nothing. So what is Job's conclusion? "God won't listen to me."

Here's the scene. Bildad has just spoken discouraging words to Job, and now Job responds to his friend's misguided advice.

> Then Job answered,
> "In truth I know that this is so,
> But how can a man be in the right before God?
> If one wished to dispute with Him,
> He could not answer Him once in a thousand times."
> (Job 9:1-3)

Ouch! No, Job. Don't agree with your buddy! Bildad's wrong! He hasn't told you the truth. Bildad's got Job believing his half-truths about God.

Job's flaw is in thinking God is too big, too powerful, too sovereign to listen to him. God is too awesome to pay attention to Job. "Why would God listen to me?" he reasons.

Job pictures God as a severe Judge. Unapproachable. Unmerciful. So he approaches God accordingly. Job appeals to God to appear in court so that he can present his case that he hasn't done anything to deserve this kind of treatment. He's confident the divine Judge will change His decision and reverse His judgment once He discovers Job's innocence.

However, Job fears that were God to cross-examine him and ask just one question, he couldn't answer. Not one question. He reasons,

"God is so intimidating, how could I talk to God? How could I have communication with God? If He asked me one question, I'd dissolve."

Why does Job feel so insignificant? Because his picture of God is so powerful that he doesn't feel God would give him the time of day. Listen to his description of God.

> "Wise in heart and mighty in strength,
> Who has defied Him without harm?
> It is God who removes the mountains, they know not how,
> When He overturns them in His anger;
> Who shakes the earth out of its place,
> And its pillars tremble;
> Who commands the sun not to shine,
> And sets a seal upon the stars;
> Who alone stretches out the heavens,
> And tramples down the waves of the sea;
> Who makes the Bear, Orion, and the Pleiades,
> And the chambers of the south." (Job 9:4-9)

God is the subject, the actor, in all these phrases. God the all-wise. God the shaker of the earth. God the creator of the heavens. God the suspender of the planets. How can Job answer the Almighty?

> "Who does great things, unfathomable,
> And wondrous works without number.
> Were He to pass by me, I would not see Him;
> Were He to move past me, I would not perceive Him;
> Were He to snatch away, who could restrain Him?
> Who could say to Him, 'What art Thou doing?'"
>   (Job 9:10-12)

Job rightly sees God as incomprehensible, but wrongly pictures Him as unapproachable. Yes, God is sovereign, but He is not so distant and far removed that we cannot know Him and have a close, personal relationship with Him. But Job is at a disadvantage compared to you and me. We have the luxury of the New Testament revelation. All of the Old. The history of the Church before us. Yet with all these advantages, broader perceptions, fuller revelation, we still find ourselves in Job's shoes all too often, don't we? Forgetting that God is merciful, full of grace, truth, love.

What a contrast to Job's next perception. Here, Job says God is a monster.

> "God will not turn back his anger;
> Beneath Him crouch the helpers of Rahab.
> How then can I answer Him,
> And choose my words before Him?
> For though I were right, I could not answer;
> I would have to implore the mercy of my judge.
> If I called and He answered me,
> I could not believe that He was listening to my voice."
>   (Job 9:13-16)

Rahab was a mythological sea monster ready to devour its helpless victims. Job sees God as Rahab. A monster ready to pounce on innocent victims like Job.

Job insinuates he would have to throw himself on the mercy of the court before he could get God to hear him. Job says, "If I pray, I can't believe that God is even listening to me." Why is that? Because Job's circumstances aren't changing. *If God were listening*, he thinks, *my circumstances would change.* "I call out day and night but God's not listening. My prayers aren't going any higher than the ceiling. No matter how much I pour my heart out to God, I know that God is not listening to me." That's how low he has sunk. Job is so low he could play handball against the curb.

Have you ever felt like that in prayer? You pray fervently for a family member to be saved, but nothing happens. Or, you pray faithfully for a loved one to get well, but nothing happens. The only conclusion you may come to is, "God, you're not listening to me. I'm praying, but nothing is happening. You can't be listening."

But just because nothing is happening does not mean God is not listening. Perhaps you have heard it said that when we pray, God answers with "Yes," "No," or "Wait." Right now, Job is having to wait on God. But he is misreading "wait" as "God's not listening." Because he's having to wait, he's falsely assuming that God's not hearing his prayer.

But is that the case? Is that true? Does God not hear our prayers? Of course God hears our prayers: "Call to Me, and I will answer you

and I will tell you great and mighty things which you do not know"
(Jeremiah 33:3); "The righteous cry and the LORD hears. . . . The LORD
is near to the brokenhearted" (Psalm 34:17-18); "The LORD is near to
all who call upon Him" (Psalm 145:18).

Job has bought the Devil's lie. He is now believing a flawed view
of God. Job falsely assumes that God is so big, so busy, and so preoc-
cupied that He's not listening to his cries for help. But God did hear.
God simply chose to wait before He answered.

A lawyer was at home one pleasant Sunday afternoon. He retired
into his study, closed the door shut behind him, and began to busily
prepare for a case that he was to try the next morning.

As the lawyer was working hard, all of a sudden the door burst
open and a basketball came bouncing into the study. It bounced up on
his desk and hit his inkwell, spilling it across his papers.

His young son, Jimmy, came running in looking for his ball.

His dad looked at him and said, "Jimmy, I've told you not to be
playing ball in the house. I've told you to knock before you come in.
Daddy's busy. Now, what do you want?"

"Aw, Dad," Jimmy said, "I just wanted to see if you would play
ball with me. Would you come outside and play ball with me?"

With that, the heart of his father melted. He put down his pen and
said, "Why, sure, son. Let's go out and shoot some baskets."

Aren't you glad that God is not so busy hanging out Orion, setting
Pleiades in place, and suspending the planets that He doesn't have time
for you or me? Aren't you glad that God hears our call? Every time we
call out to Him, He hears us. He listens. Just remember, He isn't always
going to give you a quick answer. And sometimes His answer may be
quite different from the one you wanted. But He does listen. He created
you. He'll do the very best for you, even though you may not be able to
see what that is right away.

Here's spiritual flaw number two:

GOD ISN'T FAIR!
When we get down emotionally, we often question God's justice. We
say, "God, this isn't fair." By that we mean, "God, I don't deserve this."
Job is at that point:

> "For He bruises me with a tempest,
> And multiplies my wounds without cause.

He will not allow me to get my breath,
But saturates me with bitterness.
If it is a matter of power, behold, He is the strong one!
And if it is a matter of justice, who can summon Him?
Though I am righteous, my mouth will condemn me;
Though I am guiltless, He will declare me guilty."
     (Job 9:17-20)

Job's reasoning here makes some sense, doesn't it? The punishment should fit the crime. If a man parks his car in a no-parking zone, should he get the death penalty? No, because the punishment doesn't fit the crime. Job is bruised and wounded, but innocent. "What have I done to deserve this?" he asks.

Job wants to appear before God in court and present his case. He knows he is right. But if he goes into the courtroom with God, he feels his own mouth will condemn him. He would become so confused and so intimidated, he would end up condemning himself. Indirectly, Job is declaring God to be unfair.

When Job says he is guiltless, he is not claiming to be sinless. He's not espousing moral perfection. Just relative innocence. He doesn't believe he's done anything to deserve this kind of treatment. And, as we think back on Job 1, he hasn't.

Job's mood has taken a sudden swing. Now filled with hopeless despair, Job feels even if he confessed his sins, God would still declare him guilty. His bitterness has taken a sudden turn inward; instead of merely questioning God's scrutiny, his anxiety turns to soulful despair. Is Job beginning to believe God is the author of the evil that has befallen him? Has his faith completely deserted him? The image swirling about in his mind now turns to a soulful mourning wherein he sees time as irrelevant, attempts at productivity vain, his inevitable condemnation already determined by an unjust Sovereign:

"I am guiltless;
I do not take notice of myself;
I despise my life.
It is all one; therefore I say,
'He destroys the guiltless and the wicked.'
If the scourge kills suddenly,
He mocks the despair of the innocent.

The earth is given into the hand of the wicked;
He covers the faces of its judges.
If it is not He, then who is it?" (Job 9:21-24)

Job moans; there is no justice with God. If both the guilty and the guiltless suffer in life, what justice is that? Bottom line, if one man keeps God's Word and another doesn't and, yet, both suffer, what justice is that? Is that fair? The argument is now at a fever heat.

Job takes it a dangerous step further. He risks everything. He is actually saying that God punishes the good and rewards the evil. Talk about injustice! Talk about boldly blaspheming where no man has gone before! Two facts about Job are clear: he is blameless, yet he was blasted! Job's conclusion? This means God is unjust, even cruel. Another thing that seems to be on his mind here—perhaps it's his main complaint—is that God is aloof: "He covers the faces of the earth's judges." Not only is God unjust, he's cruel and aloof. Ouch!

But wait! Haven't *you* ever thought such?

I thought that very thing recently when I was standing with seven thousand pro-life demonstrators in our town. There were only fifty pro-death demonstrators. But guess who got on the front page? Guess who got the interview? I thought, *God, this isn't fair. Seven thousand of us and only fifty of them. We're right. They're wrong. And, yet, they're in the spotlight.* I thought, *God, that's not right! It's not fair! Why don't You do something?!*

There's a young girl who keeps herself sexually pure, yet the guys aren't asking her out. Here is another girl who is promiscuous and morally unfaithful, and the guys are chasing after her. The pure girl's heart aches, "God, that's not fair! Why does the one who does right seem to be punished, while the one who does wrong is rewarded? God, that's not fair!"

How about at the office? A businessman remains honest and turns in his sales report honestly, yet he gets passed over for a promotion. Somebody else pads his records and gets the raise. The honest man cries out, "God, that's not fair! Why does this happen?"

Someone else says, "I pray and go to church. I serve the Lord and yet it was my spouse who came down with cancer. Why was it *my* spouse? It just doesn't seem fair."

Have you ever wrestled with such discouragement?

Listen, that's flawed thinking. God *is* just and fair. We must remember that God doesn't settle His accounts until the end of time. One day, God is going to make everything right. But, presently, this world is upside down. Life *isn't* fair. But don't think God isn't fair. Just because God hasn't made a matter right yet doesn't mean He won't one day. "Shall not the Judge of all the earth deal justly?" (Genesis 18:25).

Picture it this way. God deals with the righteous on a cash basis, and the unrighteous on a credit basis. When the righteous sins, he pays for it as he goes. God disciplines us *now* when we sin. But for the unrighteous, it's all on credit. He doesn't necessarily pay for his sin right now. God doesn't presently discipline those who are not His children. But that doesn't mean that He won't one day deal with their sin. At the end of time, God will settle His accounts with the unrighteous. There's a payday someday. God *is* fair. It's just a matter of time.

As for God's aloofness and cruelty, Job was at a disadvantage. Let's not forget the spiritual warfare that's going on behind the scenes. Satan wants Job discouraged.

"God's not fair." That's the second spiritual flaw. Don't believe it! That's the Devil's lie. God will do you right.

Here's spiritual flaw number three:

GOD WON'T FORGIVE ME!

Have you ever thought, "God won't forgive me?" That's an easy conclusion to come to if you feel you are suffering for past sins even after you have confessed them. Listen to what Job says:

"Now my days are swifter than a runner;
They flee away, they see no good.
They slip by like reed boats.
Like an eagle that swoops on its prey." (Job 9:25-26)

Job feels that his days are passing by quickly without any relief from God. He fears God is not going to do anything to make it right. The image of the reed boats passing by—light, very fast, easily maneuverable skiffs made of braided reeds and commonly used on rivers in the ancient Near East—reinforces Job's perception of a life that is now quickly fading in significance. As Job sees these vessels fading in the distance, a new thought occurs—why do anything?

Do you remember in the old movies where, with the passing of time, a calendar would be shown on the screen? A fan would be blowing the pages of the calendar off the screen. Leaves would come blowing by, signifying the coming of winter. Then snow would fall behind the calendar, picturing the coming winter. Then grass would grow, representing the arrival of spring. All showed the passing of time.

That's the picture Job has. His life is passing by quickly, but God's not doing anything to get him out of this trial.

> "Though I say, 'I will forget my complaint,
> I will leave off my sad countenance and be cheerful,'
> I am afraid of all my pains,
> I know that Thou wilt not acquit me.
> I am accounted wicked,
> Why then should I toil in vain?
> If I should wash myself with snow
> And cleanse my hands with lye,
> Yet Thou wouldst plunge me into the pit,
> And my own clothes would abhor me." (Job 9:27-31)

Job sinks even lower. He believes God is never going to forgive him. He feels he is going to go to his grave paying for his sin. Even if he cleans up his life, and washes himself with snow and cleanses his hands with lye—a picture of a purification ritual—God won't forgive him. "If I confess my sin, repent, and turn to the Lord, still God will throw me back into a mud hole. I'll clean myself up and God will make me dirty again, just as if I never cleaned myself up to begin with." Job is losing all hope that God will forgive him.

A haunting sense of guilt is echoing and vibrating in Job's conscience. He doesn't know what sin he's done. He just feels guilty, and unclean.

Do you know the difference between the correction of the Holy Spirit and the accusation of Satan? The Holy Spirit will point out specific sins in our lives. He puts His finger on sin that has *not* been confessed. However, the Devil, when he accuses us of sin, will either be so vague as to not specifically point out the sin, or will accuse us of sin that we have *already* confessed to the Lord. Although we are already forgiven, Satan doesn't want us to feel that way.

Just as Job's despair takes him dangerously close to the very pit of hell, right where Satan would like him to remain, a small light illumines a bit of hope.

"For He is not a man as I am that I may answer Him,
That we may go to court together.
There is no umpire between us,
Who may lay his hand upon us both." (Job 9:32-33)

Of course, Job is right. God is not a man. Man is not on an equal footing with God. God is too far beyond Job for him to hope to reach the Creator by standard human methods. God is too "other," too transcendent, too unfathomable. Job is longing for somebody to represent him before God. Someone who can plead his case.

Job wants a mediator. An advocate. Unknown to Job, his statement looks forward to the coming of Jesus Christ, who will be that mediator, that umpire, equal to both sides. From the cross, Jesus will be able to lay His hand upon God and His hand upon man and bring the two parties together who have had the biggest dispute in the history of creation. Job's heart cry ultimately looks to Christ.

"Let Him remove His rod from me,
And let not dread of Him terrify me.
Then I would speak and not fear Him;
But I am not like that in myself." (Job 9:34-35)

In the absence of a mediator, Job pleads with God to remove the rod of discipline from him. If God would ease up, Job could go into court and plead his own case with God and be shown right for suffering unjustly.

Is God really unforgiving? Must God be coerced to pardon our iniquity? Is He begrudging to wash away our sins? Not at all. God is in the business of forgiving our sins. All our sins. If we will confess our sins, He delights to forgive them all. God's Word says, "If we confess our sins, He is faithful and righteous to forgive us our sins and to cleanse us from *all* unrighteousness" (1 John 1:9, emphasis added).

You or I will never commit a sin that the blood of Jesus Christ is not powerful enough to wash away. As far as the east is from the west, so far will He remove our transgressions from us (Psalm 103:12). God will place our sins behind His back where He can't see them anymore. God will bury our sins in the sea of His forgetfulness, where they will be of no effect anymore.

He invites us,

> "Come now, let us reason together. . . .
> Though your sins be as scarlet,
> They will be as white as snow;
> Though they are red like crimson,
> They will be like wool." (Isaiah 1:18)

If God can forgive David of adultery and murder, if God can forgive Noah of drunkenness, if God can forgive Abraham of lying, if God can forgive Saul of persecuting the Church, if God can forgive Peter of denying the Lord, if God can forgive the thief on the cross for stealing, if God can forgive Zaccheus for cheating, then He can forgive you and me of sins. All of them, fully. Completely. Immediately. Unconditionally.

Here's spiritual flaw number four:

GOD DOESN'T LOVE ME!

Job doesn't believe that God cares for him. He doesn't believe God loves him and has a wonderful plan for his life. If this is how God treats his children, I'd hate to be an enemy.

Why does Job believe this lie? Because Job is looking at his circumstances. His view of God is colored by his circumstances. Job sees only bad circumstances and concludes God doesn't love him. Listen to Job:

> "I loathe my own life;
> I will give full vent to my complaint;
> I will speak in the bitterness of my soul.
> I will say to God, 'Do not condemn me;
> Let me know why Thou dost contend with me.
> Is it right for Thee indeed to oppress,
> To reject the labor of Thy hands,
> And to look favorably on the schemes of the wicked?
> Hast Thou eyes of flesh?
> Or dost Thou see as a man sees?

Are Thy days as the days of a mortal,
Or Thy years as man's years?
That Thou shouldst seek for my guilt,
And search after my sin?
According to Thy knowledge I am indeed not guilty;
Yet there is no deliverance from Thy hand.'" (Job 10:1-7)

Job is saying, "God, I'm not guilty! I know it and You know it. Yet You won't stop. What's worse, God, You won't tell me what I've done wrong to deserve this. I'd confess my sin and I'd make it right, but, God, You won't even tell me what my sin is."

You know what? There is no sin for Job to confess to under this trial. There is basically nothing to forgive. "God, why are You oppressing me—the object of Your love? I think You've got me mixed up with somebody else. You must need some bifocals. God, You see like a man sees. Surely You're not seeing my life, are You?" Job feels that God is getting older, and He's not seeing like He once did.

To Job, God is just looking and looking for some dirt to hold against Job. It's like an eternal entrapment. Job perceives God, like some sort of intergalactic IRS agent, as sifting through his files for anything to hold against him. Job continues his lament to God:

"Thy hands fashioned and made me altogether,
And wouldst Thou destroy me?
Remember now, that Thou hast made me as clay;
And wouldst Thou turn me into dust again?
Didst Thou not pour me out like milk,
And curdle me like cheese;
Clothe me with skin and flesh,
And knit me together with bones and sinews?
Thou hast granted me life and lovingkindness;
And Thy care has preserved my spirit.
Yet these things Thou hast concealed in Thy heart;
I know that this is within Thee." (Job 10:13)

As Job sees it, God has made him just to destroy him. God had set him up just to knock him down. He created him just to crush him.

Job looks back on life in the womb. Symbolically, Job says it was like pouring milk into a glass that, after a while, begins to settle, compress, and become cheese. So was he wonderfully fashioned by God in the womb.

What puzzles Job the most though is that God has known all along that He was going to do this harm to him. "Why did You keep it from me?" he asks with a confused heart. "You've been keeping this from me all along." So why doesn't God tell him? Why does He keep the plan concealed? Worse, why does the intensity of the attack constantly increase?

> "If I sin, then Thou wouldst take note of me,
> And wouldst not acquit me of my guilt.
> If I am wicked, woe to me!
> And if I am righteous, I dare not lift up my head.
> I am sated with disgrace and conscious of my misery.
> And should my head be lifted up,
> Thou wouldst hunt me like a lion;
> And again Thou wouldst show Thy power against me.
> Thou dost renew Thy witnesses against me,
> And increase Thine anger toward me,
> Hardship after hardship is with me." (Job 10:14-17)

Job feels that God has made him wonderfully with great design, only to have a pretty target at which to shoot. "God, You don't care about me. God, what have You got against me?" cries Job. "Whether I am innocent or guilty, my life is destroyed all the same."

> "Why then hast Thou brought me out of the womb?
> Would that I had died and no eye had seen me!
> I should have been as though I had not been,
> Carried from womb to tomb."
> Would He not let my few days alone?
> Withdraw from me that I may have a little cheer
> Before I go—and I shall not return—
> To the land of darkness and deep shadow;
> The land of utter gloom as darkness itself,
> Of deep shadow without order,
> And which shines as the darkness." (Job 10:18-22)

This passage shows the depths of Job's despair. He laments that he was ever born. He pleads with God to leave him alone and let him have a few days of peace, perhaps even some joy, before death. But even here Job's existential desperation is compounded, for Job does not see death as a restful solace.

"God, I wish I could have bypassed life completely. I wish You could have transported me from the womb to the tomb and spared me all of this pain."

Job wishes that, before he dies, God would cut him some slack and allow him a few moments of peace. "God, if You would just leave me alone for a few days, I could catch my breath and be happy. God, if You'd just let me take a vacation from You, everything would be great in my life. God, You don't care about me! This plan for my life that You've got—You've planned all along just to crush me."

Is that a right view of God? It sounds pretty convincing, at times, to read these verses through the grid of circumstances.

God had a good plan for Jeremiah's life: "'For I know the plans that I have for you,' declares the LORD, 'plans for welfare and not for calamity to give you a future and a hope'" (Jeremiah 29:11).

And God is not finished with Job yet, either.

God told Joshua, "This book of the law shall not depart from your mouth, but you shall meditate on it day and night, so that you may be careful to do according to all that is written in it; for then you will make your way prosperous, and then you will have success" (Joshua 1:8).

That was God's plan.

The Apostle Paul wrote, "The will of God is . . . good and acceptable and perfect" (Romans 12:2). That is true. It's just that within God's will, there are times that He has ordained trials to come into our lives. But God has a purpose and God has a reason. God's will is never without a higher purpose. God's will is ultimately for His glory and our good.

The psalmist tells us,

The LORD God is a sun and shield;
The LORD gives grace and glory;
No good thing does He withhold from those who walk uprightly.
  (Psalm 84:11)

God is a good God.

If we look at our losses and our trials and our circumstances, so many times we would come to the same conclusion—that God doesn't love us.

But we must be careful to see God not through our circumstances, but through His Word.

God is a good God who has provided so very much for us.

OUR RESPONSE TO BILDAD

As I look back at Job's response to Bildad, I think two messages clearly stand out.

First, this is a *message of warning*. Job was the most righteous man on the earth. He feared God and walked with God. Yet Job descended to the low point of believing these lies about God. If it can happen to Job, it can happen to you and me. In an argument from the greater to the lesser, we are just as vulnerable, if not more so. So we must refuse to buy into Satan's lies.

If we look at God through the prism of our circumstances, our view of God will become distorted. We must see God clearly through His Word and then see our circumstances accordingly.

Yes, this cry of Job's is a message of warning to you and me. Many times, we believe what we *feel* about God rather than what we *know* to be true.

Second, this is a *message of hope*. Hope, you say? I really don't see a whole lot of hope here. Well, it's there.

Through all of Job's collapse, God was still there for him. Listening. Forgiving. Caring. God never, never left Job's side.

Yes, this is a message of hope. God will never give up on you and me, even when we go through the valley. When we are faithless, God remains faithful. Let me say that again. When our faith falters, God remains faithful. Solid as a rock.

David found this to be true.

The steps of a man are established by the LORD;
And He delights in his way.
When he falls, he shall not be hurled headlong;
Because the LORD is the One who holds his hand.
    (Psalm 37:23-24)

God promises: "I will never desert you, nor will I ever forsake you" (Hebrews 13:5).

Paul believed it while sitting in a Roman jail. "I am confident of this very thing, that He who began a good work in you will perfect it until the day of Christ Jesus" (Philippians 1:6).

When it seemed that God was the farthest away, God was still a part of Job's life. That is a message of encouragement.

If you are presently going through a dark valley, know that God is right there with you. If it seems as if God is far away, know that God is right there with you. Even if the circumstances are not yet changing. We can trust Him.

MAYBERRY REVISITED

Let me illustrate. This past summer, our family was vacationing in Florida. While we were there, it was time for haircuts.

On this sleepy little island off the coast, there was only one barbershop and one beauty salon. My wife, Anne, forbade me to take the boys to the beauty salon. So I took all three of them—my twins, age nine, and John, one—to the barbershop. You know, where all the guys go.

I drove over there with Andrew, James, and John, while Anne and Grace Anne headed to the beauty salon. The boys and I walked into the barbershop. It was like stepping back in time. It was Mayberry all over again. I kept thinking Andy Griffith would show up. I didn't know there was still a place like that around. The whole place seemed frozen in time.

As I walked in, I entered a long, narrow corridor of worn-down linoleum to which were fixed four huge, metal barber chairs. The air was thick with talc. Ancient sinks lined the wall. Corroded softball team trophies sat on the shelves.

The first barber wore Coke-bottle lenses. He was a short guy missing some teeth. As I walked in, he was smiling from ear to ear, revealing what looked like a white picket fence with some slats missing. He greeted us with a high-pitched voice that only dogs could hear.

A quick glance around the room assured me I was in the local "good ol' boys club." Five or six men sat clustered in front of the first barber's chair, holding court, discussing politics, fixing the economy, and solving the world's problems.

Then I noticed a second barber at the end of the shop, which got darker and darker as you moved away from the door. All the chairs in front of him were empty. No one was waiting. Later I would find out why.

To get the job done as quickly as possible, we continued down the dark corridor. I could faintly see the second barber. He was about seventy-five years old. Maybe eighty. He had his hair greased straight back. One of those "around the world" hairdos. This was like going to a dentist with brown teeth.

The ancient name tag above the mirror told me his name. Preacher.

Sweeping up the striped barber's apron, he dusted out the chair and mumbled, "Hop up, son." I didn't know what to do, so I took John, my one-year-old, and put him in the chair first. I thought, *John, you're not old enough to know the difference. Before I sit in that chair, I want to see what happens to you.* I felt kind of like Abraham offering up Isaac on the altar.

As I sat down, Andrew and James were both looking at me like, "Dad, you can't be doing this to us."

Preacher started cutting John's hair. And cutting. And cutting. I had told him, "I want it really short, okay? I want a summer beach haircut."

Well, Preacher went around the sides. I saw a lot of hair falling to the floor. After a few minutes I thought, *I need to get up and do a closer check on John. It's so dark I can't really see.*

As I stood next to John, he was just deadpan. Showing no emotion. Scared to death. I looked at him closely and about fainted. Huge massive divots had been cut out of the side of his hair. It looked like he had the mange or scurvy. It was just unbelievable. I thought, *Well, it will grow out by the time he graduates from college.*

Preacher looked at me and asked, "How does it look?"

I said, "Well, it looks . . . it looks . . . it's there."

As he began to cut on John's crown, I said, "Preacher, that's fine. Why don't I just take John down?" So I rescued John and sat him in another chair and turned to Andrew. "Andrew, your turn, buddy. Hop up there."

Andrew wanted a buzz. I thought, *Well, there's no way to mess up a buzz.* So I thought.

"Preacher," I said, "go ahead and cut both Andrew's and James' hair. I'll pay you when I get back. I'm going to take John around the block." As I walked John out of the shop, everybody said, "Oh, he can stay, he can stay."

"He gets a little restless," I said. "I'm going to drive him around the block."

So I put John in the car and drove straight to the beauty salon. I walked in and negotiated with the owner: "Listen, I'll pay you half a haircut if you'll just try to shape up the top of my son's head."

She looked at his head, shook hers, and said, "Looks like you've been to see Preacher."

Embarrassed, I admitted, "Yes, ma'am, I sure have. Please do something to help me."

She tried to shape up John's hair. She did the best she could, but said, "Really, it's just going to take a couple of months for this to grow back out."

I took John back to the barbershop, where Andrew and James were standing out front totally bald, dying to hide in the car.

What's my point? Simply this: Sometimes we think if we turn our lives over to the Lord and trust Him, it's going to be like getting into Preacher's barber chair. God's going to make a mess of our lives. We're just going to get whacked. Scalped. Clipped. Carved up. Humiliated. Embarrassed.

That is the Devil's lie. He's trying to flaw our image of God. The Lord is not like Preacher. He's not blind. God can still cut it straight in our lives. We can trust Him.

What God wants us to do is simply trust Him. He calls us to have faith in Him. He invites us to turn our lives over to Him. He bids us to allow Him to have full sway in our lives.

He listens. He cares. He is fair. He forgives.

You *can* trust Him.

CHAPTER 7

I NEED YOU ON MY TEAM, NOT ON MY BACK

▼

L et me ask you a question. How well do you handle criticism? Recently, I asked my congregation this question, and I was amazed at the nervous laughter that broke out. Obviously, I had hit a live nerve. It confirmed what I had suspected. For all of us, handling criticism can be difficult.

Let's face it, none of us really likes to be told we are wrong. We love to be praised, not put down. We like to be stroked, not stabbed.

By nature, we all react negatively to criticism. Even constructive criticism is hard to swallow. But it's even tougher when the criticism is unjust. That's when it is really difficult to choke down.

The story is told of an old man whose grandson rode a donkey while they were traveling from one city to another. The old man heard some people mumbling, "Would you look at that old man walking, suffering on his feet, while that strong young boy is totally capable of walking?"

The criticism cut deeply, so he changed positions. The old man started riding the donkey while the boy walked.

Sure enough, others started grumbling, "Would you look at that—a healthy man riding the donkey and making that poor little

111

boy suffer! Can you believe that?"

To avoid further criticism, the old man changed again. This time, he and the boy both hopped up on the donkey. They *both* started riding.

You guessed it, people still criticized him. He could hear people saying, "Would you look at those heavy brutes making that poor donkey suffer."

So he and his grandson jumped down and they both started walking. He thought, *No one will criticize us for this.* But people are fickle. He soon heard some people say, "Would you look at that waste—a perfectly good donkey not being used."

The old man was at his wits' end. What could he do to avoid the criticism altogether? Then it dawned on him. To avoid all criticism, the old man decided to carry both the donkey and boy.

The moral of the story is this: No matter what we do, someone will always criticize us. The key is how well we respond to the criticism.

Like the old man in this story, when we listen to our critics without discernment, we end up carrying a heavy load unnecessarily. That's where Job is. He's got his critics on his back. No matter what he does, these friends continue to ride him hard. It's difficult to know how to respond to criticism. Sometimes, no matter what we do, it's never going to be good enough.

Can you relate to that?

Who's on your back?

Do you have overbearing parents with unrealistically high standards for your life? No matter what you do, it just doesn't seem to be enough? Do you have a perfectionist boss who, regardless of your good work, seems to always find something to criticize you for? Maybe you have a doting father-in-law, and you're just not good enough for his daughter, no matter what you do.

We can all suffer from unjust criticism, whether at home, at work, at school, or at church. When wrongly communicated, or improperly directed, criticism can become very demotivating in our lives. It can paralyze us and strip away the will to excel. We need to learn how to respond to criticism well.

Job finds himself in the hot seat, drawing the heat of unjust criticism. He is a lightning rod in the storm, drawing the Devil's fire. He's lost his fortune, his health, his family, and his wife's support. Now, he's a target for his friends' criticism.

IN THE CRITICS' DEN

Let's meet Job's third "friend"—Zophar the Zealot. You may want to name one of your children Zophar. Nice name, don't you think?

Zophar is probably the youngest of the three friends because he speaks last. He speaks with the angriest tone of all. He speaks with animosity. He gives a scorching rebuke. He is rude. Blunt. Insensitive. Impatient. If you thought Eliphaz and Bildad were bad news, wait until you hear from Zophar. It just gets worse!

Zophar gives Job a piece of his mind. Unfortunately, it seems that those who want to give you a piece of their mind are the ones who have the least to share. Here now are three ways *not* to offer *constructive* criticism.

Begin Negatively

Constructive criticism, if possible, first builds up and affirms before it points out the negative. But the criticism that tears down first goes for the person's jugular. It is immediately negative.

That's how Zophar begins. Negatively. Abrasively. Obnoxiously. Offensively.

> Then Zophar the Naamathite answered,
> "Shall a multitude of words go unanswered,
> And a talkative man be acquitted?
> Shall your boasts silence men?
> And shall you scoff and none rebuke?
> For you have said, 'My teaching is pure,
> And I am innocent in your eyes.'
> But would that God might speak,
> And open His lips against you,
> And show you the secrets of wisdom!
> For sound wisdom has two sides.
> Know then that God forgets a part of your iniquity."
>   (Job 11:1-6)

Zophar is saying, "Job, I'm listening to you babble at the mouth, and somebody has got to answer you. We just can't let you get away with declaring yourself innocent. We're going to rebuke you for that, Job. You think you're innocent? No way that's possible. You need to have God open your eyes and convict you, Job. That's the problem!

God needs to show you His wisdom!"

That's the encouragement Zophar offered to Job. Maybe God wouldn't fully punish him for his sin. Maybe God would just grade him on the curve. Maybe God would let him off light.

Use Intimidation

If you want to tear down another person, follow up your negative beginning with intimidation as soon as possible. Intimidation tries to bully someone into a course of action.

Steve Aschburner wrote about a certain coach's power to intimidate refs: "If the IRS auditors wore whistles around their necks, Bobby Knight would pay exactly $3.41 in income taxes each year." That's Zophar's tactic. Like one preacher wrote in the margin of his Bible, "Weak point. Yell here."

> "Can you discover the depths of God?
> Can you discover the limits of the Almighty?
> They are high as the heavens, what can you do?
> Deeper than Sheol, what can you know?
> Its measure is longer than the earth,
> And broader than the sea.
> If He passes by or shuts up,
> Or calls an assembly, who can restrain Him?"
> (Job 11:7-10)

The most deadly intimidation you can hold over someone's head is, strangely enough, God. The Pharisees were experts at this game. Use God like a club and put everyone to shame.

Zophar asks Job, "Can you discover the depths of God?" No, but who can? Apparently, Zophar thinks he knows the depths of God's wisdom.

What is so dangerous about Zophar's words is that some of what he is saying is true. God is too deep for Job. But it's only one side of the truth. And half the truth, when it becomes all the truth, is no truth at all. God has also made Himself known to Job. That part of Him, and of His wisdom, that Job could know and understand, He chose to reveal to Job. If only Zophar knew the height and the depth and the breadth and the length of the love of God, as Job does.

But Zophar sees only one side of God:

"For He knows false men,
And He sees iniquity without investigating."
    (Job 11:11)

Zophar builds his case, in essence, saying, "Job, God sees you. He sees everything you have been doing. You might as well go ahead and confess it."

"And an idiot will become intelligent
When the foal of a wild donkey is born a man." (Job 11:12)

Now here's a verse to put on your refrigerator! We may print this one on the bottom of our church stationery.

Zophar's intimidation tactics turn to name-calling. He labels Job an idiot. He's saying, "Job, you are so stupid. You've redefined the word. Look up 'idiot' in the dictionary, Job, and you'll see your own picture." Zophar claims Job will become intelligent when a donkey is born a man. In other words, when hell freezes over.

This reminds me of the guy who went to the doctor and said, "Doc, I need for you to check my brain."

After running a few tests, the doctor said, "I'm sorry to tell you this, but you're an idiot."

The man said, "I need a second opinion."

The doctor said, "All right. You're ugly, too!" That's the sensitivity with which Zophar speaks to Job. You're stupid, but don't worry, you're also ugly.

Assume the Worst
Zophar now assumes the worst and tells Job to get right with God. Only then will everything be okay. He assumes Job is guilty until he's proven innocent.

"If you would direct your heart right,
And spread out your hand to Him;
If iniquity is in your hand, put it far away,
And do not let wickedness dwell in your tents.
Then, indeed, you could lift up your face without moral defect,
And you would be steadfast and not fear.

For you would forget your trouble,
As waters that have passed by, you would remember it.
And your life would be brighter than noonday;
Darkness would be like the morning.
Then you would trust, because there is hope;
And you would look around and rest securely.
You would lie down and none would disturb you,
And many would entreat your favor." (Job 11:13-19)

Zophar is the first "fightin' fundie" saying, "Just confess your sin and repent. Open your heart to the Lord and say, 'God, I've sinned!' Then He will hear your prayers and restore your life."

"But the eyes of the wicked will fail,
And there will be no escape for them;
And their hope is to breathe their last." (Job 11:20)

Zophar says, "But, if you don't repent, you'll never see a bright tomorrow. You'll never get out of your troubles."

This is the kind of person you don't want doing your year-end evaluation. Negative. Intimidating. Faultfinding. Assuming the worst.

This is not how Jesus deals with common, ordinary people. The woman caught in adultery. Tax gatherers. Sinners. He looked beyond people's faults to their needs. Sure, He dealt with sin, but He did so in a corrective way. He certainly played hardball with the Pharisees, but He wouldn't use Zophar's method with hurting people. Isaiah prophesied,

"A bruised reed He will not break,
And a dimly burning wick He will not extinguish." (Isaiah 42:3)

To the contrary, Zophar broke this bruised reed and all but snuffed out Job's dimly burning wick of hope.

HOW TO HANDLE CRITICISM

Someone has said, "It doesn't take much size to criticize." If that's true, then it takes far greater maturity to receive it well.

From Job's life, we will now discover four key principles to coping well with criticism. Here's how to handle criticism well.

Study the Criticism Carefully

First, we must receive criticism with a teachable spirit. Listen with an open heart. Examine what is said. Evaluate it. Consider carefully what has been spoken and then determine whether it is true or not. Sometimes the criticism will be right on target. A bull's-eye. God will use it in your life to correct and mature you. If properly spoken, it can be a means to help us be on target with our lives.

But at other times, the criticism we receive is not true. It misses the mark. It is neither constructive nor correct. In such cases, if followed, it will actually steer us off course and bring us harm. We must study what is said and decide whether or not it is true. We must filter the criticism through the Word of God and our own conscience and determine whether it's right or wrong. Don't buy it just because someone is selling it.

Job has heard his friends' criticism, and he studies it carefully. Consequently, Job comes to the conclusion that it just isn't correct. Listen to his response.

Then Job responded,
"Truly then you are the people,
And with you wisdom will die!
But I have intelligence as well as you;
I am not inferior to you.
And who does not know such things as these?
I am a joke to my friends.
The one who called on God, and He answered him;
The just and blameless man is a joke.
He who is at ease holds calamity in contempt,
As prepared for those whose feet slip.
The tents of the destroyers prosper,
And those who provoke God are secure,
Whom God brings into his power." (Job 12:1-6)

What a sarcastic comment Job makes! His words have some punch to them. He's saying to his friends, "Fellows, you've got all the wisdom in the world. When you die, there won't be any wisdom left in the world. You've got a monopoly on wisdom."

Using sarcasm is not always wrong. When we come to the end of this book, God Himself will voice the most sarcastic statements made anywhere in Scripture. God can be very sarcastic. So can we. But there is a proper and improper use of sarcasm. Job uses it here to put some punch to his words.

Job says, "I've studied your criticism and I reject it. It isn't true. Look at me, for example. I call on God. I am blameless and just. Yet I suffer greatly, making me the laughing stock of this community."

Bewildered, Job looks at the wicked and sees them prospering in their businesses. He sees the unbeliever getting ahead in the world. Job says, "Guys, your criticism isn't correct. You say the wicked suffer and the righteous prosper. I see just the opposite. I see the wicked prosper and the righteous suffer."

On what basis would we evaluate any criticism? Every criticism must square with God Himself. He is the standard. It must square with His Word. His character and His will.

Job is saying, "Zophar, your criticism is wrong because it does not conform with who God is and how He operates. It doesn't square with my understanding of my own motives."

God is sovereign and He does whatever He pleases. In God's sovereignty, many times He will act mysteriously, even unpredictably. He will act in ways that will puzzle and bewilder us. God can't be confined to a tight little formula. Consequently, God will not always physically and financially prosper the righteous, any more than He will *always* chastise the unbeliever in this life.

> "But, now, ask the beasts, and let them teach you;
> And the birds of the heavens, and let them tell you.
> Or speak to the earth, and let it teach you;
> And let the fish of the sea declare to you." (Job 12:7-8)

Job says, "You need to learn some very elementary and basic truths that all of creation knows; even the birds, the fish, the animals, and the earth know this."

Specifically, what is it that his critics need to learn?

> "Who among all these does not know
> That the hand of the LORD has done this,
> In whose hand is the life of every living thing,
> And the breath of all mankind?
> Does not the ear test words,

As the palate tastes its food?
Wisdom is with aged men,
With long life is understanding." (Job 12:9-12)

Job's friends needed to learn that all of our days are in God's hands. God is sovereign. Everything about our lives is in His hands. Even our suffering. Job's comment indicates he realizes he is being tested.

"With Him are wisdom and might;
To Him belong counsel and understanding.
Behold, He tears down, and it cannot be rebuilt;
He imprisons a man, and there can be no release.
Behold, He restrains the waters, and they dry up;
And He sends them out, and they inundate the earth."
    (Job 12:13-15)

The psalmist says, "Our God is in the heavens; He does whatever He pleases" (Psalm 115:3). When God closes a door, no man can open it. When God opens a door, no man can close it. When God sends calamity, no man can avoid it.

God is a sovereign God. As He works in our lives, it is mysterious and unpredictable. His ways are above our ways and His thoughts above our thoughts (Isaiah 55:8-9). It is beyond our comprehension, but nevertheless true (Romans 11:33-34).

Specifically, God is in control over individuals, even the wisest and most powerful people on the earth. Even Job and friends.

There are times when God will send trials into our lives. It's all His doing.

"With Him are strength and sound wisdom,
The misled and the misleader belong to Him.
He makes counselors walk barefoot,
And makes fools of judges.
He loosens the bond of kings,
And binds their loins with a girdle.
He makes priests walk barefoot,
And overthrows the secure ones.
He deprives the trusted ones of speech,

And takes away the discernment of the elders.
He pours contempt on nobles,
And loosens the belt of the strong."
        (Job 12:16-21)

A counselor walking barefoot is the image of a wise man being led into captivity and defeat. Even his own wisdom can't save him from an invading army if God sends the trial. When an invading army would come and capture a city, they would take the people, tie them up with ropes, lead them captive out of the city, and take them back to serve them. They would take off their shoes, sometimes even their clothes, and force them to walk back barefoot to become their servants.

What is Job's point? There are times when God will send trials into our lives for purposes and reasons known only to Himself. It's God who makes counselors walk barefoot. Even their own ingenuity and intelligence cannot deliver them out of their trials. God does the same with judges. He loosens the bond of kings; that is, He removes their power. One day, the king is upon his throne; the next, God removes him and elevates another king. It's all the sovereignty of God. Job is arguing, rightly, that even those who seem secure in life face trials that are beyond their ability to escape. It's all God's doing.

"He reveals mysteries from the darkness,
And brings the deep darkness into light.
He makes the nations great, then destroys them;
He enlarges the nations, then leads them away.
He deprives of intelligence the chiefs of the earth's people,
And makes them wander in a pathless waste.
They grope in darkness with no light,
And He makes them stagger like a drunken man."
        (Job 12:22-25)

What is true of individuals is true of nations. God is sovereign over even the nations. He sets them up and then takes them down. History is His story. God will destroy a nation by depriving its leaders of the intelligence to make right choices. Bad decisions thus lead them into a wasteland from which there is no return, only wandering.

Job is saying, "Guys, what you have been telling me—that God will always reward the righteous and they won't have any problems in life, and God will always punish the wicked and they'll never get ahead in this world—it just ain't so! The criticism that you have of me—that I must be in sin because all of this calamity is happening in my life—that is a false criticism. It's not so. Do you know why? It doesn't square with who God is and how God operates. Because God is a sovereign God and He intervenes in our lives in ways that are unpredictable and mysterious. There are times when He will bring us into a storm and lead us through a dark valley. It's all a part of His plan for our lives."

What must we do when we are criticized as Job was? First, study the criticism carefully and see if it squares with who God is and how God operates.

You're going to be facing criticism. Always square it with God Himself.

Speak to Your Critics Openly
Sometimes criticism triggers a wrong response in our heart. If we keep that response on the inside, it will smolder into a building resentment. It will brew and brew until it erodes our emotional strength. Instead, we need to be transparent, honest, and open with our critics.

One thing we can say for Job. He certainly communicated with his critics. Certainly some of what he said crossed the line, but I think we have a tendency to go to the other extreme and never respond to our critics. How healthy it is for us to speak to our critics honestly and openly. That's what Job does now. He tells them how he feels and why he disagrees.

> "Behold, my eye has seen all of this,
> My ear has heard and understood it.
> What you know I also know.
> I am not inferior to you." (Job 13:1-2)

Job says, "Quit looking down your long nose at me as though I don't know a thing in the world. I know as much as you do." Sometimes people will walk all over you and take advantage of you. There comes a point when we should say to our critics, "Enough is enough!"

> "But I would speak to the Almighty,
> And I desire to argue with God.
> But you smear with lies;

You are all worthless physicians.
O that you would be completely silent,
And that it would become your wisdom!
Please hear my argument,
And listen to the contentions of my lips." (Job 13:3-6)

Notice what Job says to these guys. Getting very confrontive, Job says, "Read my lips!" Job opens his emotional kimono and shares his innermost thoughts with these hypocrites.

Job calls them worthless physicians who can't make a right diagnosis. How could they possibly prescribe the proper cure? Because their diagnosis is wrong, their prescription is deadly. So, Job tells them just to be quiet.

"Will you speak what is unjust for God,
And speak what is deceitful for Him?
Will you show partiality for Him?
Will you contend for God?
Will it be well when He examines you?
Or will you deceive Him as one deceives a man?
He will surely reprove you,
If you secretly show partiality.
Will not His majesty terrify you,
And the dread of Him fall on you?" (Job 13:7-11)

Emphatically, Job tells them, "You are improperly representing God to me. You speak as though you have the mind of God, but you don't. If you were to take your own medicine, you would die. If you were to take your own exam, you would fail."

"Your memorable sayings are proverbs of ashes,
Our defenses are defenses of clay." (Job 13:12)

Job speaks honestly with his critics, calling their cynical counsel charred ashes and crumbling clay. There comes a time when we are receiving unjust criticism that we need no longer to be a punching bag and absorb the criticism. In such cases, we should speak to our critics openly when their words err.

How we answer our critics is very important. Speak with a loving attitude. Speak with kind words. Speak with a reconciling heart. But when the criticism is unjust and does not square with God Himself, then we should speak with honesty, transparency, and openness.

Seek to Please God Ultimately

When criticized, our natural tendency is often to please our critics simply to get them off our backs. But when we try to please our critics, we become people pleasers rather than God pleasers. Such a direction is devastating. Ultimately, we must seek to please God, not man.

> "Be silent before me so that I may speak;
> Then let come on me what may.
> Why should I take my flesh in my teeth,
> And put my life in my hands?
> Though He slay me,
> I will hope in Him.
> Nevertheless I will argue my ways before Him.
> This also will be my salvation,
> For a godless man may not come before His presence.
> Listen carefully to my speech,
> And let my declaration fill your ears.
> Behold now, I have prepared my case;
> I know that I will be vindicated.
> Who will contend with me?
> For then I would be silent and die." (Job 13:13-19)

Job is careful to seek to please God. Zophar, Bildad, and Eliphaz are not the holy Trinity. God is. Consequently, Job desires to argue his ways before God, not man. He seeks to be vindicated by his Creator, not his critics.

Job says, "Though He slay me, I will hope in Him." What a statement of faith in God! What a declaration of confidence and trust in God. "No matter what befalls me, I will put my hope and trust in the Lord. Not in my critics."

Rather than arguing with his friends, Job desires to be vindicated by God alone. Why? If you please God, it doesn't matter whom you displease. And if you displease God, it doesn't matter whom you please.

George Whitefield repeatedly said, upon receiving criticism, "The judgment seat of Christ will bear me out." In other words, he didn't want to get into the business of having to defend himself. That's God's business. "No, I'll wait until the judgment seat," he would say, "and let Christ vindicate me."

Job is saying the same. "Despite your criticism, I ultimately seek to be vindicated by God in Heaven. That is far more important than to be approved by men."

There's a story told of a young violinist who was a child prodigy. He could play the violin with great skill. This young maestro was scheduled to play for the first time in Carnegie Hall.

The hall was packed for this teenage prodigy. With every number that he played, the crowd rose to its feet and cheered and applauded.

When the performance was over, he left the stage to a standing ovation. A star was born! They begged him to come back out. The young sensation came back out to the delight of the audience. "Bravo! Bravo!" the audience shouted as they applauded even louder. He left the stage again and they begged him to come back again.

He came back and played again. This scene was repeated several times until the final encore when he left the stage with a very downcast look.

As he walked behind the curtain, his startled manager said, "Why are you so downcast? This was the night of our life. We've looked forward to this for the last six years. You were wonderful. The people loved you."

The young violinist pulled the curtain back to peer out into the large meeting hall. The audience was still cheering. But there was one man in the audience who was not cheering. The violinist pointed to that man.

He said, "Do you see that man?"

The manager said, "Yes."

The violinist said, "He's not cheering."

The manager said, "Well, so what? There are 2,300 other people who are cheering you and loved everything that you've played tonight. You're downcast about only one man who's not cheering?"

The violinist replied, "You don't understand. That man seated on the front row is a master violinist. He is my teacher. He taught me to play the violin. If he is not pleased, then I am not pleased."

That must be our attitude. We must please God, not the crowd. Even if the world is cheering us, please God. Even if others are criticizing us, please God.

Search Your Heart Honestly

Fourth, we must look within our own hearts and see if what our critics say truly applies to us. Is what they say applicable to me? We must search our hearts, asking, "God, is there really sin in my life? Show me if I am wrong."

> "Only two things do not do to me,
> Then I will not hide from Thy face:
> Remove Thy hand from me,
> And let not the dread of Thee terrify me.
> Then call, and I will answer;
> Or let me speak, then reply to me.
> How many are my iniquities and sins?
> Make known to me my rebellion and my sin." (Job 13:20-23)

Job is a wise man. He says to God, "Lord, show me if there is sin in my life. Show me what needs to change about me."

Why do we need to ask God to reveal our sin? Because the Bible states,

> "The heart is more deceitful than all else
> And is desperately sick;
> Who can understand it?" (Jeremiah 17:9)

It is hard to know our own hearts. Only the Spirit of God can truly convict our hearts and reveal our sin. Job is saying here, "God, if what Zophar is saying is true—if I am suffering because of sin in my life—then, God, show me what that sin is."

That is a humble man. Job is a teachable man with a ready heart, wanting to learn what his sin is so that he may deal with it.

The psalmist cried,

> "Search me, O God, and know my heart;
> Try me and know my anxious thoughts;
> And see if there be any hurtful way in me,
> And lead me in the everlasting way." (Psalm 139:23-24)

Our tendency can be to resist what our critics say. But, like Job, we must open up our hearts to the Lord and say, "God, is it true in my life?"

"Why dost Thou hide Thy face,
And consider me Thine enemy?
Wilt Thou cause a driven leaf to tremble?
Or wilt Thou pursue the dry chaff?
For Thou dost write bitter things against me,
And dost make me to inherit the iniquities of my youth.
Thou dost put my feet in the stocks,
And dost watch all my paths;
Thou dost set a limit for the soles of my feet,
While I am decaying like a rotten thing,
Like a garment that is moth-eaten." (Job 13:24-28)

Job asks God, "Is there something I did when I was a teenager that I'm still paying for today? God, is the cause of all of this some hidden sin in my early years?"

If we are going through a difficult trial, this is a question we must ask ourselves. Does the criticism apply to my life? Is it on target? If so, confess your sin and change. If not, then pass over it.

But we must have the integrity to honestly consider it. Job honestly searched his heart. In reality, he was suffering, not because there was anything outwardly wrong in his life, but because his life was so right that he was singled out for Satan's heat. Even though he doesn't realize it at this point.

When we receive criticism, we need to search our own hearts honestly and ask God, "Is this true?"

WHERE THE CRITICS WENT WRONG

What was it about Job's three friends' counsel that was so bad? I mean beyond their curtness, self-righteousness, and unwillingness to listen to Job's explanation that he wasn't aware of any outward sin?

Their words drip with self-righteousness. Accusations. Pharisaical judgments. Heck, they make the Pharisees look humble.

By charging Job with outward sin, they seem to be unaware of their own. They seem to be saying, "We're not having these problems, Job, because we're not 'in sin'! You know, like you are!"

They've failed to understand indwelling sin. Every member of the human race is plagued by this indwelling sin problem.

Every person is a descendant of the first man, Adam. When Adam sinned, the Bible teaches, we all sinned (Romans 5:12). His original sin was imputed to our accounts, and his sin nature was imparted to the human race endemically. None of us can get out of it (Psalm 51:5). Consequently, when we're born, we're born in sin, depraved (Romans 3:10-18). Every part of our humanity—mind, emotions, will—is tainted by deadly sin. Every human.

At conversion, the believer becomes "a new creature" (2 Corinthians 5:17). Legally, justification by faith in Christ imputes His righteousness to our account (Romans 4:11). Practically, as we grow (the process called sanctification), Christ's righteousness is imparted to our inner man (Romans 6:1-7). The power of sin is defeated and reversed.

Still, we experience a lifelong conflict with indwelling sin. It constantly assaults us and will until the day we die. The more we grow and mature spiritually, the more aware we become of sin's presence in our lives. The closer we're drawn into the light, the more we become aware of our imperfections and blemishes.

The Apostle Paul continued to wrestle with indwelling sin, even after being a Christian for more than twenty years (see Romans 7:14-17). Why do we struggle? Paul says it's because we're confined to a body of sinful flesh.

The "flesh" is the place where our sinful selfishness dwells, even after salvation. It is the locale of indwelling sin, which remains in us and drags us repeatedly into sin—even the very sins we hate. As believers, our flesh is still active and powerful, subject to sin's deceit, and attracted by sin's allurements.

Although we desire to rid ourselves of indwelling sin, we cannot. It is still present in our flesh. We will not be rid of our residual sinfulness until we die and are glorified.

Neither Eliphaz, nor Bildad, nor Zophar is aware of this theological truth. Certainly, they were without benefit of the New Testament. But tragically, they wrongly assumed that Job was suffering because of some specific outward sin in his life. The fact of the matter is, though, everyone has sin in their lives. Even Eliphaz. Even Bildad. Even Zophar.

I'M WORN OUT

Job's response to all this criticism? He goes into an emotional tailspin. He downshifts to a melancholy lament. He suffers a tremendous mood change. As Job asks God to reveal his sin, he considers how frail and full of turmoil his life is. His heart begins to sink. Listen to the words of a man in despair.

"Man, who is born of woman,
Is short-lived and full of turmoil.
Like a flower he comes forth and withers.
He also flees like a shadow and does not remain.
Thou also dost open thine eyes on him,
And bring him into judgment with Thyself.
Who can make the clean out of the unclean?
No one!
Since his days are determined,
The number of his months is with Thee,
And his limits Thou hast set so that he cannot pass.
Turn Thy gaze from him that he may rest,
Until he fulfills his day like a hired man.
For there is hope for a tree,
When it is cut down, that it will sprout again,
And its shoots will not fail.
Though its roots grow old in the ground,
And its stump dies in the dry soil,
At the scent of water it will flourish
And put forth sprigs like a plant.
But man dies and lies prostrate.
Man expires, and where is he?
As water evaporates from the sea,
And a river becomes parched and dried up,
So man lies down and does not rise.
Until the heavens be no more,
He will not awake nor be aroused out of his sleep."
    (Job 14:1-12)

Job becomes very pessimistic. He considers that life is short, trials are great, death is sure. None of us gets through unscathed. He employs seven pictures to describe his life—a withering flower (verse 2), a shifting shadow (verse 2), a hardworking laborer (verse 6), a chopped-down tree (verse 7), evaporating water (verse 11), a dried-up river (verse 11), and a falling mountain (verse 18).

Like a frail flower that grows and soon withers, so is a man's life. He is here today, gone tomorrow. Like a moving shadow, so a man's life is temporary and easily moved. Like a hired man toiling and groaning, so a man longs for his due rest and reward. Unlike a tree that is cut off but grows back, humans have no hope that life will continue the same after death. Like evaporating water, a human life ascends upward to the heavens at death. Like a dried-up river, a human life is empty and dry at the end.

> "But the falling mountain crumbles away,
> And the rock moves from its place;
> Water wears away stones,
> Its torrents wash away the dust of the earth;
> So Thou dost destroy man's hope." (Job 14:18-19)

Finally, Job compares himself to a towering mountain—tall, strong, erect, highly visible, admired by all. However, an underground river flows and causes the inside of the mountain to erode and be eaten away, stripping away its foundation. Externally, the mountain appears strong and immovable; internally, it is eroding and soon to collapse.

Job says, "My life appears to be strong to all who look at me. Like a mountain, I am highly visible and looked up to by others. But on the inside, I'm dying. My faith is eroding and I am about to collapse. I will collapse in death very soon."

Let me ask you this: If someone brought a scathing criticism against you and you knew you were only going to live for another forty-eight hours, would you really care? No. Not if you knew your life was so short-lived.

Because Job sees the shortness of his life, it helps him endure present criticism.

> "Oh that Thou wouldst hide me in Sheol,
> That Thou wouldst conceal me until Thy wrath returns to Thee,
> That Thou wouldst set a limit for me and remember me!
> If a man dies, will he live again?
> All the days of my struggle I will wait,
> Until my change comes.
> Thou wilt call, and I will answer Thee;
> Thou wilt long for the work of Thy hands.
> For now Thou dost number my steps,
> Thou dost not observe my sin.
> My transgression is sealed up in a bag,
> And Thou dost wrap up my iniquity." (Job 14:13-17)

IT'S NOT THE CRITIC WHO COUNTS

It's not easy to respond to criticism, is it?

Sometimes the criticism we receive is right on target. When it finds the mark, one measure of our maturity is to listen to it, accept it, and not allow our pride to dismiss it.

But there are other times when the criticism misses the mark. If you become involved in the Kingdom of God, you're going to be subjected to criticism. Count on it. If you attempt to do what's right, you're going to face criticism head on.

The following quote is attributed to Theodore Roosevelt: "It's not the critic who counts. Not the one who points out how the strong man stumbles, or how the doer of deeds might have done it better. The credit belongs to the man who is actually in the arena, whose face is marred with sweat and dust and blood. Who strives valiantly. Who errs and comes up short again and again and again. Who knows the great enthusiasms, the great devotions, and spends himself in a worthy cause. Who, if he fails, at least he fails while daring great things. That his place may never be with those cold and timid souls who know neither victory nor defeat."

Just remember that truth the next time you are facing criticism. Most critics are sideline quarterbacks who never know victory or defeat. Most have never been in the game as you have. When your face is bloody, beaten, and full of sweat from the blows of life, just remember that it's because you have been in the arena making a difference.

You may be wondering, "Why am I being attacked so hard by my critics?" Just remember Job. If you're in the arena of life, beaten and bloodied by critics, follow his example. Study the criticism carefully. Speak to your critics openly. Seek to please God ultimately. Search your heart honestly.

Hang tough!

CHAPTER 8

THERE'S HOPE
AT THE END OF YOUR ROPE

▼

O ctober 23, 1990. Could I ever forget that day?
    I was studying in my office when the phone call came.
    Anne, my wife, could barely speak. She was at our pediatrician's
office with our eight-day-old son, John.

With a desperate urgency, she said, "Come now! John has turned
blue. We're rushing him to the hospital under oxygen." The starkness
of her voice jerked me to attention.

"What's wrong?"

"I don't know. Just come as soon as you can!"

I bolted out of my office, jumped in my car, and flew to the doctor's office. My mind was racing feverishly. "God, what are You doing?
You *just* gave John to us. You're not going to take him back, are You?"

As I pulled up to the doctor's office, Anne and a nurse came running out the front door with John cradled in their arms. His tiny face
was under an oxygen mask.

The three jumped into my car and I sped to the hospital. I screeched
to the front curb. The nurse jumped out with John and sprinted through
the hospital's front doors. I followed, carrying his oxygen tank on
wheels. Anne, only eight days post-op, trailed behind us.

131

Running through the lobby, we went up the back elevator to the Children's Critical Care Unit on the fifth floor. A team of nurses was ready with an oxygen hood—a small plastic dome that would fit over John's head for breathing.

Instantly, every kind of monitor and gadget imaginable was hooked up to our little John. A needle protruded out of his head. An IV was stuck in his foot. Electrodes were fastened onto his chest and head.

John looked so helpless. He was too innocent and defenseless to go through this. He struggled to get loose but couldn't. He screamed at the top of his lungs for relief.

I became so ill at this pathetic sight that I had to leave the room. It was too much to bear.

Anne followed me out to the hall. Still without explanation, I frantically pressed, "What on earth is going on?"

Anne recounted for me that, earlier in the day, she was watching John under his Bili-lite without any clothes on. John had come home from the hospital with yellow jaundice and had to be under a home Bili-lite. John was holding his breath for long periods of time, not breathing for as long as eighteen to twenty seconds. Then he would gasp frantically to catch his breath.

Anne called our pediatrician and he said, "Bring John over here immediately."

At the doctor's office, John was closely examined and found to have a fever—very unusual for a baby eight days old. It was a red flag that *something* was not right. Possibly spinal meningitis. Possibly worse.

Sensing trouble, our doctor did a spinal tap on John in his office—and he stopped breathing. John turned blue!

All this led to the mad dash to the hospital.

Anne and I pulled an all-night vigil in John's hospital room, waiting up around the clock with his nurse. It was the longest night of our lives.

The next morning, the doctors began a battery of tests. We anxiously awaited the results of each round. Would our baby live? If so, for how long? What kind of limitations would he suffer?

I slipped away down the hall, to a quiet, secluded waiting room to be alone with God. I poured out my heart, "God, what is going on? God, why is this happening? God, please do something!" We soon learned that John had apnea, a mysterious breathing disorder that causes certain babies to stop breathing. The dysfunction is also called SIDS, or sudden infant death syndrome.

After several days, John was released and went home with a monitor attached around his chest. Whenever John would stop breathing for fifteen seconds, the monitor alarm would sound and we would come running to shake him and restart his breathing.

That alarm sounded like an air-raid siren to be heard for miles around. No terror compares with being dead asleep and hearing that shrill alarm going off. When the monitor would blast at night, Anne and I would bolt out of bed, our hearts pounding hard, and run to John's side and shake his little body until he would start breathing.

We lived this way for the next eleven months. One of us had to always be at his side, or we had to arrange for a CPR-trained person to be with him. We couldn't take him out of the house for the winter months. Needless to say, our lifestyles were dramatically changed.

How's John doing now, you ask? He couldn't be any healthier, thank you. He's as strong as an ox. Very healthy. Good-looking. A future Heisman Trophy winner in the making. The total package.

God certainly taught me a lot through this time. Again, it was another of those breaking points in my life. It was a time in which God took me down several notches in order to remake me into Christ's image.

More than anything else, I was reminded that I'm not in control. God is. I know that theologically, but living it practically is another matter.

It's hard for someone like myself—a goal-oriented, take-charge, in-control, storm-the-hill kind of person—to be out of control and have nothing to do but pray and trust God. Now, that cuts against my entire personality design.

When I went into that room to pray that day, my nerves were worn thin. I was stripped of my power. Just barely hanging on. By a thread. I had nowhere to turn but to God. To trust Him when I was at the end of my rope. But He was silent. It was eleven months before we could be sure John was okay. Eleven months! And all the while we were just hanging on.

JOB'S FRIENDS: ROUND TWO

That's exactly where Job finds himself. Hanging on by a thread. His health and wealth have been taken. His children's lives and his wife's support have been taken. Now, even his friends are a major discouragement. Job is barely hanging on. His hope is all but gone.

He cries out for help from above. But there is no answer. Only silence. We come to the second round of dialogues between Job and his friends. Job is at the end of his rope. In his desperation, he comes to a turning point; he discovers there's still hope; he comes to a breakthrough in his faith. He is encouraged to hang in there with God.

Let's set the scene. Round one is complete and the second round of conversations between Job and his friends begins. While Job had been answering his friends, they were busy reloading, putting more ammo in their guns. Instead of listening to Job, they've been waiting for him to stop talking so they can fire back bullets. They're not comforting him nor sympathizing with him like true friends. The only thing on their minds is trying to win theological points with Job.

Eliphaz, Bildad, and Zophar are like theological buzzards circling overhead. They see Job dying in a pile and are ready to swoop down and pick his carcass clean.

YOU DESERVE TO SUFFER!

The first buzzard to descend upon Job is Eliphaz. He is well-named because his name means "God dispenses." Specifically, it means God dispenses judgment. How would you like to have a friend named "God dispenses judgment"? Or maybe you're married to one.

Eliphaz is the theologian. The philosopher. He's actually the most considerate of the three, but that's not saying much. I call him Eliphaz the Exterminator because he's like your local pest controller, all squeaky-clean, well-dressed, and polite—but deadly! His comments, whether he realizes it or not, are like the exterminator's poison, killing Job's spirit. Bug off, Eliphaz.

To summarize his whole argument, Eliphaz tells Job, "You deserve to suffer. If you're suffering, it has to be because you've sinned against God. You are reaping what you've sown." In his first speech (Job 4–5), Eliphaz spoke politely and indirectly about Job's sin. Now, however, Eliphaz speaks more pointedly to Job. Here's what he says:

> Then Eliphaz the Temanite responded,
> "Should a wise man answer with windy knowledge,
> And fill himself with the east wind?
> Should he argue with useless talk,
> Or with words which are not profitable?
> Indeed, you do away with reverence,
> And hinder meditation before God.

For your guilt teaches your mouth,
And you choose the language of the crafty.
Your own mouth condemns you, and not I;
And your own lips testify against you." (Job 15:1-6)

Eliphaz accuses Job of being a lot of hot air who speaks irreverently of God. Talk about irrational. Eliphaz is a role-model Pharisee before the Pharisees were even invented! He completely ignores the possibility that Job could be telling the truth about his innocence. He's ruled out any opinion except his own. If he wants your opinion, he'll give it to you. While he stops short of condemning Job, his language belies his lack of sympathy for Job.

"Were you the first man to be born,
Or were you brought forth before the hills?
Do you hear the secret counsel of God,
And limit wisdom to yourself?
What do you know that we do not know?
What do you understand that we do not?
Both the gray-haired and the aged are among us,
Older than your father.
Are the consolations of God too small for you,
Even the word spoken gently with you?
Why does your heart carry you away?
And why do your eyes flash,
That you should turn your spirit against God,
And allow such words to go out of your mouth?
What is man, that he should be pure,
Or he who is born of a woman, that he should be righteous?
Behold, He puts no trust in His holy ones,
And the heavens are not pure in His sight;
How much less one who is detestable and corrupt,
Man, who drinks iniquity like water!" (Job 15:7-16)

Eliphaz rebukes Job for letting his emotions get the better of him, rather than using logical thought or the wisdom of the ages. This is one of Eliphaz's strongest statements yet on the depravity of man. Man is too vile to stand before God, Eliphaz argues. At this point he's right. Man *is* impure and born unrighteous (too bad Eliphaz doesn't seem to realize that this truth affects him, too). This is why a person must be born *again* to enter the Kingdom of God.

If God does not trust His angels—referring to "His holy ones" who reside in "the heavens"—how much less can God trust sinful man? Think about it, Job! Because fallen man is born with a radically depraved heart, he guzzles sin like water. The image of Job as the depraved man is correct, but not unique to Job. All men have sinned and have fallen short of the glory of God. Eliphaz continues his error in assuming that Job's sin nature is the cause of his suffering.

> "I will tell you, listen to me;
> And what I have seen I will also declare;
> What wise men have told,
> And have not concealed from their fathers,
> To whom alone the land was given,
> And no alien passed among them." (Job 15:17-19)

Appealing to the past tradition of the ancients, Eliphaz bolsters his argument. He will now debate Job's contention that wicked men prosper in this life. No way! Look at the wicked man.

> "The wicked man writhes in pain all his days,
> And numbered are the years stored up for the ruthless.
> Sounds of terror are in his ears,
> While at peace the destroyer comes upon him.
> He does not believe that he will return from darkness,
> And he is destined for the sword.
> He wanders about for food, saying, 'Where is it?'
> He knows that a day of darkness is at hand.
> Distress and anguish terrify him,
> They overpower him like a king ready for the attack,
> Because he has stretched out his hand against God,
> And conducts himself arrogantly against the Almighty.
> He rushes headlong at Him
> With his massive shield.
> For he has covered his face with his fat,
> And made his thighs heavy with flesh.
> And he has lived in desolate cities,

In houses no one would inhabit,
Which are destined to become ruins.
He will not become rich, nor will his wealth endure;
And his grain will not bend down to the ground.
He will not escape from darkness;
The flame will wither his shoots,
And by the breath of His mouth he will go away.
Let him not trust in emptiness, deceiving himself;
For emptiness will be his reward.
It will be accomplished before his time,
And his palm branch will not be green.
He will drop off his unripe grape like the vine,
And will cast off his flower like the olive tree.
For the company of the godless is barren,
And fire consumes the tents of the corrupt.
They conceive mischief and bring forth iniquity,
And their mind prepares deception." (Job 15:20-35)

Here are the terrible troubles that come upon the wicked. They don't prosper; they are punished. See the wicked writhing in pain, cut off from life, destroyed, starving for food, attacked by God, alone and forsaken, bankrupt, and ruined. Again, the implication is that Job is suffering such devastation because he has sinned against God.

GO AHEAD, MAKE MY DAY!

Again, Job rejects Eliphaz's advice. He fights fire with fire, responding in like manner. Job tells his friends that not he, but they, are full of hot air.

Then Job answered,
"I have heard many such things;
Sorry comforters are you all.
Is there no limit to windy words?
Or what plagues you that you answer?
I too could speak like you,
If I were in your place.
I could compose words against you,
And shake my head at you.
I could strengthen you with my mouth,
And the solace of my lips could lessen your pain." (Job 16:1-5)

Job further describes his crisis situation. He sees himself as the object of God's wrath. He pictures God as a savage beast, hunting him down, and tearing him apart limb from limb. Our suffering can give us a distorted view of God, can't it?

> "If I speak, my pain is not lessened,
> And if I hold back, what has left me?
> But now He has exhausted me;
> Thou hast laid waste all my company.
> And Thou hast shriveled me up,
> It has become a witness;
> And my leanness rises up against me,
> It testifies to my face.
> His anger has torn me and hunted me down,
> He has gnashed at me with His teeth;
> My adversary glares at me." (Job 16:6-9)

Then, he refers to his three friends as an opposing army who mistreated him and roughed him up, all at God's whim. With *friends* like these, who needs enemies?

> "They have gaped at me with their mouth,
> They have slapped me on the cheek with contempt;
> They have massed themselves against me.
> God hands me over to ruffians,
> And tosses me into the hands of the wicked."
>   (Job 16:10-11)

Worse, Job says God is using him for target practice. Mercilessly, God, like a warrior crashing through a wall, has filled Job's belly with deadly arrows of wrath and judgment. With a *God* like this, who needs enemies?

> "I was at ease, but He shattered me,
> And He has grasped me by the neck and shaken me to pieces;
> He has also set me up as His target.
> His arrows surround me.
> Without mercy he splits my kidneys open;

He pours out my gall on the ground.
He breaks through me with breach after breach;
He runs at me like a warrior."
    (Job 16:12-14)

Consequently, Job has covered himself with sackcloth, a symbol of mourning. You can just picture him as a raging bull whose energy is spent lying on its side with its horn buried in the sand, its lungs heaving for air, its desire to fight almost gone.

"I have sewed sackcloth over my skin,
And thrust my horn in the dust.
My face is flushed from weeping,
And deep darkness is on my eyelids,
Although there is no violence in my hands,
And my prayer is pure." (Job 16:15-17)

At a breaking point, Job pours out his heart to God in prayer. He claims to be blameless of any wrongdoing deserving such judgment.

"O earth, do not cover my blood,
And let there be no resting place for my cry.
Even now, behold, my witness is in heaven,
And my advocate is on high.
My friends are my scoffers;
My eye weeps to God.
O that a man might plead with God
As a man with his neighbor!
For when a few years are past,
I shall go the way of no return.
My spirit is broken, my days are extinguished,
The grave is ready for me.
Surely mockers are with me,
And my eye gazes on their provocation." (Job 16:18–17:2)

Job now asks God to give a pledge that no one will take further advantage of him. He wants a guarantee from God that He recognizes Job's innocence.

"Lay down, now, a pledge for me with Thyself;
Who is there that will be my guarantor?
For Thou hast kept their heart from understanding;
Therefore Thou wilt not exalt them.
He who informs against friends for a share of the spoil,
The eyes of his children also shall languish." (Job 17:3-5)

But God has not posted such bond. Instead, Job believes that God has made him the laughingstock of his peers. A joke. An object of scorn.

"But He has made me a byword of the people,
And I am one at whom men spit.
My eye has also grown dim because of grief,
And all my members are as a shadow.
The upright shall be appalled at this,
And the innocent shall stir up himself against the godless.
Nevertheless the righteous shall hold to his way,
And he who has clean hands shall grow stronger and stronger."
    (Job 17:6-9)

Job sees his only hope to be the grave. At this point, death appears to be the only way to escape this injustice and pain.

"But come again all of you now,
For I do not find a wise man among you.
My days are past, my plans are torn apart,
Even the wishes of my heart.
They make night into day, saying,
'The light is near,' in the presence of darkness.
If I look for Sheol as my home,
I make my bed in the darkness;
If I call to the pit, 'You are my father';
To the worm, 'my mother and my sister';
Where now is my hope?
And who regards my hope?
Will it go down with me to Sheol?
Shall we together go down into the dust?" (Job 17:10-16)

YOU'RE BEYOND HELP!

Without allowing Job one moment to catch his breath, Bildad immediately steps up to bat and speaks again in Job 18. You remember him: Bildad the Brutal. His name means "son of contention," and that he is. He lives for an argument. What Eliphaz started, Bildad now keeps alive.

Bildad is angry that Job doesn't answer him with kindness and courtesy. He is impatient with Job's mindless babbling. Here's what he says.

Then Bildad the Shuhite responded,
"How long will you hunt for words?
Show understanding and then we can talk.
Why are we regarded as beasts,
As stupid in your eyes?
O you who tear yourself in your anger—
For your sake is the earth to be abandoned,
Or the rock to be moved from its place?" (Job 18:1-4)

Then Bildad describes the fate of the wicked. Each is like a captured criminal, trapped by the cords of God's judgment. Notice the words *trap, net, webbing, snare,* and *noose,* which all picture being caught and punished by God's judgment.

"For he is thrown into the net by his own feet,
And he steps on the webbing.
A snare seizes him by the heel,
And a trap snaps shut on him.
A noose for him is hidden in the ground,
And a trap for him on the path.
All around terrors frighten him,
And harry him at every step.
His strength is famished,
And calamity is ready at his side.
His skin is devoured by disease,
The first-born of death devours his limbs.
He is torn from the security of his tent,
And they march him before the king of terrors.
There dwells in his tent nothing of his;

Brimstone is scattered on his habitation."
(Job 18:8-15)

Bildad is telling Job, "You can't get away with it. You're just like an animal that will be hunted down. You may have prospered for a while, but God's after you. God is tracking you down. You're just like a criminal that's going to be captured. A fugitive that will finally be taken in by God.

Can't you just see an animal running through the forest? All of a sudden, his foot steps into a trap. SNAP! It closes and he's taken up—he's caught. Bildad says, "Job, that's you. You're just like a trapped animal. The noose of God's judgment is waiting for you. God has laid a trap for you. You've stepped into God's judgment, Job, because of the wicked way that you've lived."

Next Bildad pictures the wicked as a tree uprooted. Dead. Cut down. Shriveled up. Unproductive.

"His roots are dried below,
And his branch is cut off above.
Memory of him perishes from the earth,
And he has no name abroad.
He is driven from light into darkness,
And chased from the inhabited world.
He has no offspring or posterity among his people,
Nor any survivor where he sojourned.
Those in the west are appalled at his fate,
And those in the east are seized with horror.
Surely such are the dwellings of the wicked,
And this is the place of him who does not know God."
    (Job 18:16-21)

Bildad reasons that this is Job's life. Because he had lost his wealth, children, and health, he obviously was judged by God. In fact, he says that Job didn't even know God. All this calamity couldn't happen to a true believer. No way!

I SHALL SEE GOD!

Job has been accosted by his friends like an enemy would be attacked by an armed army. As he responds, his faith rises above their "below-the-belt" attack. His spirit suddenly rises. Like an emotional roller coaster, Job first swings low and then rides high in this reply to Bildad.

First, Job languishes about how long he would have to endure these callous counselors.

> Then Job responded,
> "How long will you torment me,
> And crush me with words?
> These ten times you have insulted me,
> You are not ashamed to wrong me.
> Even if I have truly erred,
> My error lodges with me.
> If indeed you vaunt yourselves against me,
> And prove my disgrace to me." (Job 19:1-5)

Then, Job turns his attention to God and bemoans the treatment he has suffered at God's hands. "God has wronged me!" he cries out. "Intentional foul!"

> "Know then that God has wronged me,
> And has closed His net around me.
> Behold, I cry, 'Violence!' but I get no answer;
> I shout for help, but there is no justice.
> He has walled up my way so that I cannot pass;
> And He has put darkness on my paths.
> He has stripped my honor from me,
> And removed the crown from my head.
> He breaks me down on every side, and I am gone;
> And He has uprooted my hope like a tree.
> He has also kindled His anger against me,
> And considered me as His enemy.
> His troops come together,
> And build up their way against me,
> And camp around my tent." (Job 19:6-12)

What a picture Job paints of God's anger toward him! "God doesn't listen to me. He has given up on me! He has restricted my travel, stripped my honor, uprooted my hope, and attacked my comfort! I am God's enemy!"

Furthermore, Job accuses God of running off his family, friends, servants, and associates. He feels he is persecuted for his faith. Persecuted by *God*!

> "He has removed my brothers far from me,
> And my acquaintances are completely estranged from me.
> My relatives have failed,
> And my intimate friends have forgotten me.
> Those who live in my house and my maids consider me a
>   stranger.
> I am a foreigner in their sight.
> I call to my servant, but he does not answer,
> I have to implore him with my mouth.
> My breath is offensive to my wife,
> And I am loathsome to my own brothers.
> Even young children despise me;
> I rise up and they speak against me.
> All my associates abhor me,
> And those I love have turned against me.
> My bone clings to my skin and my flesh,
> And I have escaped only by the skin of my teeth.
> Pity me, pity me, O you my friends,
> For the hand of God has struck me.
> Why do you persecute me as God does,
> And are not satisfied with my flesh?" (Job 19:13-22)

Suddenly, Job's emotional roller coaster shoots back up. As quickly as his confidence fell, now his faith rallies and rises again.

> "Oh that my words were written!
> Oh that they were inscribed in a book!
> That with an iron stylus and lead
> They were engraved in the rock forever!" (Job 19:23-24)

Job wishes that his case could be written in a book. Then anyone who reads it would see that he suffered unjustly. Job's response in the midst of this Satanic attack becomes, I believe, a major turning point for Job's faith. I want us to focus on three or four verses. They are found in Job's second response to Bildad. These words contain an outstanding and extraordinary statement of deep faith in God—indeed, one of the greatest statements of faith in all the Bible.

"And as for me, I know that my Redeemer lives,
And at the last He will take His stand on the earth.
Even after my skin is destroyed,
Yet from my flesh I shall see God;
Whom I myself shall behold,
And whom my eyes shall see and not another.
My heart faints within me." (Job 19:25-27)

Here is hope when you're at the end of your rope. Here is the hope that Job found that enabled him to endure and persevere and hang in there. It's your hope and my hope as well.

You see, hope is not wishful thinking. We say "I hope it doesn't rain tomorrow" as a wishful thought. But that's not how the Bible uses the word *hope*. Leon Morris says hope is always something yet in the future but completely certain. That's why the second coming of Christ is called the blessed hope. It's not, "Oh, I just hope He might come back." It's, "I'm certain that He's coming back." Hope is a mighty force in my heart that fills me with strength in the present.

So, Job has a steadfast conviction. He speaks emphatically, with great certainty. Here is his hope: "I know that my Redeemer lives."

God Will Make Everything Right

First of all, Job addresses God as "my Redeemer." He obviously has a personal relationship with his Redeemer, who is God. "God is alive and ready to come to my aid. He lives to help me. He lives to defend me. That is my hope."

Let's open up this word *redeemer*. It is the Hebrew word *goel*, which referred to a person's nearest male relative who assumed the responsibility to come to the aid of a family member in distress. That's what a redeemer was. An uncle, a brother, a cousin, a second cousin. It was your closest male relative who would come to your aid in times of unusual need.

Let me give you a couple of examples from Scripture. First, a redeemer could buy back a relative's lost property that had passed into another's hands. He would reclaim and restore lost property. If a wife's husband died, she might lose the family farm to someone else in the community. She would be left without any financial provision. Legally, under the Mosaic Law (Leviticus 25:23-25), her closest male relative could come to her aid, buy back that family estate, and give it back to the distressed widow. It was the law. So, this person was a defender of the oppressed.

Second, a redeemer was someone who could avenge a slain relative by killing his or her murderer. This one was called the "kinsman-redeemer." For example, if my brother was murdered, under the Mosaic Law, I would have the right to pursue that murderer, put him to death, and see that justice was served.

You will recall there were certain cities of refuge to which a murderer could run and escape his blood avenger. But the picture here is of a kinsman-redeemer who would come to right such wrong that was suffered.

Third, a redeemer was someone who would buy a close relative out of slavery. If you got in debt back in Job's day (which is amazing because they didn't even have credit cards), the only way to get out of debt would have been to sell yourself to your creditor, become that person's slave, and try to work yourself out of debt. But once you got into that position, your creditor was allowed to set the terms, and it could take years and years for you to get out of debt. (Sound familiar?) The debt-holder had the right to enslave the debtor. In such a time of desperate need, a redeemer could come to your defense and pay off your debt so you would be freed from bondage to the debt-holder.

Fourth, as the term is used in the Old Testament, a redeemer had the right to defend a close relative's cause in a lawsuit. For example, if someone were to press charges against me and I had to go into a courtroom and defend myself, my redeemer, my closest male relative, could come, stand beside me, and plead my case. As my advocate, he could represent me in court. (Hopefully, we'd win!)

Fifth, a redeemer could marry a near relative's childless widow. That was the case in the Old Testament book of Ruth. The redeemer could step in if the husband had died and left a widow in distress, without any means of taking care of herself. The redeemer would step in, marry her to provide for her, and take care of her.

That's the word that Job uses. I hope I haven't lost you in talking about that. But for us who speak the English language, we just read the word *redeemer*, and it doesn't carry the punch that it did for those in this early time who read Hebrew.

A redeemer was a vindicator of one unjustly wronged. He was a defender of the oppressed. A champion of the suffering. An advocate of one unjustly accused. If you were ever wronged, a redeemer would come and stand beside you as your champion and advocate. He would be on your team and pull you through to see that you were done right. He was the cavalry riding to your rescue.

This is the turning point for Job. He sees that God is on *his* side. He sees that God will stand beside him and with him. No matter who opposes him. He sees that God will make right every wrong that he has suffered in his life. God will do the same for you and me.

Did you hear that?

God will right every wrong that we unjustly suffer.

And this is the hope Job sees. "As for me, I know that my Redeemer lives and *at the last*, He will take His stand on the earth." Hope deals with the future. At the end of time, God is going to stand on the earth. This refers to the second coming of Jesus Christ.

Job says, "I can go through this trial and suffering because I know that God is my Avenger and Advocate. At the end of the age, God will have the final say about my life. He will have the final word. He will stand on this earth and will defend me of all the false accusations that have been made against me."

In the ancient courtroom, the one who spoke last was always the winner. In other words, he had the *final say* on the case, and the judge would grant him victory.

What Job is saying is, "No matter what men may say against me, no matter what this world may do to me, I know that at the end of time, God will have the final say. God will defend me. He will vindicate me. God will reward me."

I Shall See God!

When Job says, "Even after my skin is destroyed," he's referring to death. Literally, the phrase means to peel off one layer at a time. It pictures the disease that Job is going through. He says, "My skin is flaking off one layer at a time." He says, "Even after I die, yet from my flesh I shall see God."

My friend, that's a bold statement of faith. Job didn't have the Scriptures to read as we do. There wasn't a book in the Bible written yet. Yet his faith in God was strong! He says, "I know after I die from my own flesh, I will see God. And when I see God, He will make everything right in that day." That's incredible! It is an inference to the final resurrection of the body from the grave. He says his skin is destroyed, yet in his flesh, he will see God.

Job says, "God's not talking to me now. I don't hear God. I'm calling out, I'm hanging on to the end of my rope and God's not saying a thing. But at the end when God sets his feet on the earth, then I'm going to see God face to face."

In that day, my friend, God is going to make every wrong right. You may be going through all kinds of suffering and trials, but He will make it right.

I was thinking about that as I was writing this chapter. Who knows how much you have suffered unjustly? You may have suffered sexual abuse as a child. Unjust suffering. God's going to make that right, one day. You may have gone through divorce. Forsaken by your spouse. You've suffered unjustly. Listen, at the end of the age when Jesus comes back, He's going to make it all right. Others of you have been singled out at work for being a Christian, or for whatever reason, and promotion has escaped you. God is going to make it right at the end of the age.

Think about it.

You will see God. Though there will be millions of people surrounding the throne, you will gaze intently upon your Redeemer who, in that day, will reward you for all suffering that you endured unjustly. What a day that will be!

This Hope Is Overwhelming!

Job says, "My heart faints within me." Job is overwhelmed at this thought. He is emotionally exhausted. He is consumed and spent by this great thought: that his Redeemer will reward him one day.

In this statement, Job is saying, "In my lifetime, I may never escape suffering. But that's okay. Because at the end of time, I will see God, and He will reward me."

I don't know what your trial might be. I don't know what suffering you're going through. And it might be just a foreshadowing of what you'll yet have to endure during your time on this earth. But there will be an end to it.

On that final day, God will reward us for enduring and hanging tough during our suffering. You see, Jesus had to become man in order to become our Redeemer. A kinsman-redeemer was the closest relative. That's why Jesus Christ became flesh and blood—so that He might become our eldest Brother and closest to us, our Champion and Advocate to defend us when we are wronged.

I love this story about Henry C. Morrison. Henry Morrison was a great missionary who, with his wife, served on the mission field in Africa for over forty years. They toiled and served back before there were fax machines like we have now, where you can fax a prayer request back and forth. When you went to Africa to serve the Lord back then, you went to Africa and you stayed there for forty years.

At the end of his stay, it came time to come back to the States. Henry and his wife were on a steamer coming back to America. They were wondering, "Would anyone even remember us? Would anyone still recall us?" They had totally supported themselves overseas.

Unknown to Henry Morrison and his wife, on board this steamer was the President of the United States, Teddy Roosevelt. He had gone to Africa for a big-game hunting safari. He was returning to the States.

As the steamer pulled into New York Harbor, Henry Morrison went to the edge of the ship to see whether anyone had come to welcome him home from serving the Lord for forty years in Africa.

As he looked at the harbor, he was astounded at what he saw. Thousands of people had turned out. The Marine Band was there playing "Hail to the Chief." There were signs and banners and billboards. Henry's heart just leaped out of his chest. He said, "Sweetheart, they've remembered us!"

As the ship pulled into the harbor, Henry prepared to deboard. He looked back and there came the royal entourage escorting Teddy Roosevelt off the ship. As he was ready to receive his acclaim, only then did he notice that all the hoopla was for the President of the United States.

As Teddy Roosevelt got off the steamer, a ticker-tape parade followed. Henry and his wife were left standing in the confetti and the debris. Henry was so downcast. They went to their hotel room. Henry sat on the edge of his bed and said, "Sweetheart, it just doesn't seem right. We've served the Lord so faithfully for these forty years. We've served in total anonymity, but we've been faithful to God. And Teddy Roosevelt goes to Africa for two weeks and shoots some elephants that they have set up to run in front of him, and the whole world turns out to applaud him. You know, it just doesn't seem right that we would come home and not have the kind of reward and applause that we really deserve."

Henry's wife looked up at him and said, "Henry, you know you're not home yet. You're not home yet. Because when you do come home, that's when the reward and the applause will be given from Heaven."

That's exactly where Job is. As he's going through his suffering and discouragement, he's hanging by the end of his rope. And he looks up and he sees his Redeemer. He sees that God is alive and still on His throne, and at the end of time, God's going to have the final word. God's going to have the final say. When Jesus comes back (Job didn't know this about the Second Coming at this point, but we do), He's going to land back on this planet and reward us for our faithfulness in suffering for His name's sake—that which He ordained, sovereignly.

THE WICKED DO PROSPER

Following a rebuttal from Zophar—the gist of his argument being that the wicked's prosperity is short-lived—Job again answers his friends. As he speaks, he moves to counter and correct their false views of God and life. First, Job appeals for a hearing. He demands their attention. He gets "in their faith."

> Then Job answered,
> "Listen carefully to my speech,
> And let this be your way of consolation.
> Bear with me that I may speak;
> Then after I have spoken, you may mock.
> As for me, is my complaint to man?
> And why should I not be impatient?
> Look at me, and be astonished,
> And put your hand over your mouth.
> Even when I remember, I am disturbed,
> And horror takes hold of my flesh." (Job 21:1-6)

Second, Job contends that, contrary to what they have said, wicked men do live in prosperity. Just look around. Their lives are long and prosperous. Their children are safe. Their houses safe. Their businesses prosperous. Their hearts singing. Then they die.

> "Why do the wicked still live,
> Continue on, also become very powerful?
> Their descendants are established with them in their sight,
> And their offspring before their eyes,
> Their houses are safe from fear,

Neither is the rod of God on them.
His ox mates without fail;
His cow calves and does not abort.
They send forth their little ones like the flock.
And their children skip about.
They sing to the timbrel and harp
And rejoice at the sound of the flute.
They spend their days in prosperity,
And suddenly they go down to Sheol."
     (Job 21:7-13)

All this despite rejecting God!

"And they say to God,
'Depart from us!
We do not even desire the knowledge of Thy ways.
Who is the Almighty, that we should serve Him,
And what would we gain if we entreat Him?'
Behold, their prosperity is not in their hand;
The counsel of the wicked is far from me." (Job 21:14-16)

How rarely does the wicked man suffer in this world. When at the height of his success, rarely is he suddenly judged and toppled into the gutter.

"How often is the lamp of the wicked put out,
Or does their calamity fall on them?
Does God apportion destruction in His anger?
Are they as straw before the wind,
And like chaff which the storm carries away?
You say, 'God stores away a man's iniquity for his sons.'
Let God repay him so that he may know it.
Let his own eyes see his decay,
And let him drink of the wrath of the Almighty.
For what does he care for his household after him,
When the number of his months is cut off?
Can anyone teach God knowledge,
In that He judges those on high?" (Job 21:17-22)

Instead, some of the wicked die happy and the righteous often die bitter. Prior to death, a man's character cannot be determined by his position in life. Only God can judge men properly.

> "One dies in his full strength,
> Being wholly at ease and satisfied;
> His sides are filled out with fat,
> And the marrow of his bones is moist,
> While another dies with a bitter soul,
> Never even tasting anything good.
> Together they lie down in the dust,
> And worms cover them." (Job 21:23-26)

In conclusion, Job acknowledges his friends' conspiracy to assault his character. He anticipates their rebuttal to his line of reasoning and lays out their return argument. Job's friends say the wicked are reserved for calamity. But if they would ask travelers who have seen the world, those travelers would agree with Job.

> "Behold, I know your thoughts,
> And the plans by which you would wrong me.
> For you say, 'Where is the house of the nobleman,
> And where is the tent, the dwelling places of the wicked?'
> Have you not asked wayfaring men,
> And do you not recognize their witness?
> For the wicked is reserved for the day of calamity;
> They will be led forth at the day of fury." (Job 21:27-30)

The wicked man continues on in his sinful ways unconfronted. Even in death, he is honored by those who attend his funeral.

> "Who will confront him with his actions,
> And who will repay him for what he has done?
> While he is carried to the grave,
> Men will keep watch over his tomb.
> The clods of the valley will gently cover him;
> Moreover, all men will follow after him,
> While countless ones go before him." (Job 21:31-33)

In light of this, his friends' comfort was of no help to Job. None at all. He sees through their arguments and recognizes the falsehood with which they speak.

"How then will you vainly comfort me,
For your answers remain full of falsehood?" (Job 21:34)

So where will Job find hope? Not in listening to the poisoned counsel of his well-meaning friends. But in looking to his Redeemer, who will make everything right on the Final Day.

His hope is yet future: it is in God.

LOOK, THERE'S HOPE!

A couple of years ago, Anne and I were in Dallas seeing her parents. Anne's mom was there for a cancer checkup, having made remarkable progress. James and Andrew, my twin sons, were just little babies at the time.

We were driving back from Dallas late at night after seeing her folks. We used to drive an old diesel station wagon that you could hear for miles around. That diesel engine clanked louder than a dozen loose golf balls in a clothes dryer.

We were coming back on the interstate, somewhere between Texarkana and Little Rock. The boys were asleep. Anne was half asleep (she never goes to sleep when I'm driving).

We were out in the middle of nowhere on Interstate 30. It was so dark that night that you couldn't see two feet in front of you without the headlights. As we were driving along, all of a sudden I felt a loss of power. I thought maybe the engine had just missed a bit. I looked up in the rear-view mirror and there were clouds of smoke coming out of the back of our car. Well, if you know me and my familiarity with cars, you'd know how hopeless this was!

I said, "Sweetheart, look!" Anne turned around and looked at the trail of smoke behind us, as the car literally began to coast. Cruising up a hill, I began to think, *What are we going to do? It's almost midnight. We have a diesel car. Nobody works on diesel cars. Do I pull over to the side and walk for help? But it'll be miles to the next stop. And if I left them stranded on the side of the road, will I come back and find that someone has taken them? Maybe I'll just take Anne and the boys. But the boys aren't even walking yet, and I don't know how far Anne and*

I can go carrying both of the kids. Or, maybe we'll just have to sit in the car and wait for someone to help us. Of course, we could wait until the Second Coming before somebody would help us. What would we do?

As we coasted up to the ridge, I said, "Sweetheart, I'm just going to have to pull over. We can't go any farther, and I don't know what we're going to do."

Then I looked up and saw a sight. I still can't believe the sight I saw. Just over the ridge, there was a large sign with one word on it. "Hope." And there was an arrow pointing off to the exit ramp. And I said, "Sweetheart, look, *there's hope.*"

By this point we were barely rolling forward. You could hear the knocking of metal against metal in the engine. We coasted to the top of the exit ramp.

Two signs were turned on. One was a Chevrolet dealership. It was the only one within a hundred miles that worked on diesel cars. And right across the highway was the second lighted sign—a Holiday Inn. Those were the only lights on in town. I said, "Sweetheart, *there's hope.*"

It was Hope, Arkansas.

Listen, when you're at the end of your rope, there's still hope. No matter how impossible the situation seems—no matter how dark the night—there's always hope.

You may be spewing smoke out the back end of your life and have lost all power to go on. You may be just coasting, barely rolling forward. I want you to know *there's hope.*

Are you at the end of your rope? Remember, *there's hope.* He will pull you through.

CHAPTER 9

COME IN OUT OF THE PAIN

▼

I need to catch my breath. Can we stop and rest for just a minute? We have now reached the halfway mark of Job's trials. And I'm worn out.

I know how you feel. I'm feeling it, too. These middle chapters of Job are intense. Draining. Heavy. Oppressive. Depressing. Anguishing.

If you're like me, you may be tempted to hit the fast-forward button and speed ahead to the end of the book. Maybe you're wondering, "Can't we just zoom ahead to the happy ending?"

Unfortunately, we can't. It wouldn't be true to Scripture. And it wouldn't be true to life. Let's face it, life is full of trials. All kinds of trials. Trials that won't go away. Trials that won't let up. Trials that suck your every ounce of strength. Trials that knock you down, flat on your back.

Maybe that's why you're reading this book—because that's where you are. Smack-dab in the middle of the darkest trial of your life. Caught in the squeeze. Barely hanging on. About to lose your grip. Searching for answers. Filled with despair. And no fast-forward button in sight.

Maybe you have a life-threatening disease and are facing major surgery. You'd love to fast-forward to a happy ending, but you can't.

Your life is stuck on regular speed, and you're having to live out every dreaded scene. The doctors. The treatment. The hospital stay. The early retirement. The whole nine yards.

Maybe you're in a financial *crunch*. Make that a *crisis*. No, make that a *catastrophe*. The bottom has fallen out and there's no relief in sight. You're going to have to go through it all. The bankers. The creditors. The lawyers. The court hearings. The IRS. The whole mess.

Life is like that. Suffering is not an elective. It's a core course in the university of life. Sure, we'd love to fast-forward through our trials and get to the happy ending. But we can't. We have to face them head on. One day at a time.

If you're tempted to zoom ahead to the end of *this* book . . . don't! Hang in there with me. We want to walk with Job every step of the way. We'll eventually get to the happy ending, but we learn more about faith and trusting God here—in the midst of his pain—than in reading the last chapter where Job is without a problem.

So, have you caught your breath yet?

Great! Let's get back to Job. We're at the halfway mark. If this book were a golf course, we just made the turn and are teeing off the back nine.

We have come to Job 22, as we begin this, the third and final dialogue between Job and his buddies—Eliphaz, Bildad, and Zophar. You remember them—the Crude, the Bad, and the Ugly. Here they come again. If short visits make long friends, then long visits make short friends. Just ask Job.

GET RIGHT OR GET LEFT!

First up is Eliphaz. Of the three, he's the philosopher. Mr. Theologian. Dr. "Know-It-All." Just what you *don't* need when you're down and hurting.

Today, we could call him Eliphaz the Egghead. He probably wore thick glasses, had six pens in his front pocket, and hiked his pants up under his armpits. Had he been on board the Titanic, Eliphaz would have lectured the captain about his driving rather than helping rescue drowning people. Pharisees are like that.

Eliphaz's life philosophy is simple. Only the wicked suffer. If you are suffering, it's very simple. It's because of sin in your life. The bigger your sin, the more you suffer. So, Job must be a gigantic sinner. Just look at his suffering.

Getting more perturbed by the minute, Eliphaz finally loses his cool. He blows his stack, erupts like Mount St. Helens, and spews out white-hot lava all over Job.

In his first two addresses, Eliphaz indirectly implied that Job was suffering because of his sin. Now, Eliphaz directly accuses Job of sin. He pulls no punches. In fact, he hits below the belt.

Here's how *not* to be a friend or counselor. Here are five mistakes to avoid like the plague in counseling.

Don't Play Holy Spirit

First, Eliphaz points a fiery finger at Job and directly condemns him of sin. Pointblank, the accuser says, "You have sinned!" Diplomacy has been called the art of saying "nice little doggie" until you have time to locate a rock. Well, Eliphaz has put his hand on a large rock and hurls it at Job's head.

> Then Eliphaz the Temanite responded,
> "Can a vigorous man be of use to God,
> Or a wise man be useful to himself?
> Is there any pleasure to the Almighty if you are righteous,
> Or profit if you make your ways perfect?
> Is it because of your reverence that He reproves you?
> That He enters into judgment against you?
> Is not your wickedness great,
> And your iniquities without end?
> For you have taken pledges of your brothers without cause,
> And stripped men naked.
> To the weary you have given no water to drink,
> And from the hungry you have withheld bread.
> But the earth belongs to the mighty man,
> And the honorable man dwells in it.
> You have sent widows away empty,
> And the strength of the orphans has been crushed.
> Therefore snares surround you,
> And sudden dread terrifies you,
> Or darkness, so that you cannot see,
> And an abundance of water covers you."
> (Job 22:1-11)

Who needs the Holy Spirit when you have Eliphaz, right? He has come into the world to convict Job of sin, righteousness, and judgment. Know anyone like that?

Eliphaz indicts Job with an array of charges. Taking pledges from his brothers. Foreclosing on the poor. Withholding water from the weary. Rejecting widows. Crushing orphans. This is getting real nasty!

The image Eliphaz paints here is striking because of its complete lack of evidence. In accusing Job of taking pledges and having "stripped men naked," he raises the most heinous of charges. It's the image of taking a man's clothing in pledge for a debt and then foreclosing on him, leaving the debtor naked against the cold of the night.

Further, he calls Job the "mighty man" and "the honorable man," indicting him for living too well while others suffer. The image is that of the arrogant rich man living off his vast estate while others suffer in poverty, and ignoring the wayfarer who passes by—grossly offensive crimes in Job's day.

What's most incredible about these charges is that they are all false. Fabricated. Concocted. Job has not treated people this way. Eliphaz has no such evidence. He's using intimidation tactics, trying to manipulate Job. He throws the book at him, hoping that some charge—*any* charge—will stick.

Do you recognize the hiss in Eliphaz's voice? It's the voice of the Serpent again. From the pit, the Devil is speaking through Eliphaz. Satan, the "accuser of our brethren" (Revelation 12:10), is constantly accusing us of wrongdoing. He will even conjure up charges. Anything to heap coals of false guilt upon our heads and incapacitate us.

We must learn an important lesson here. We must carefully distinguish between the conviction of the Spirit and the accusation of Satan. There is a difference.

The Holy Spirit convicts us of specific sin. He will do so until we confess it. The Spirit of God is like a concerned physician probing an injury until he puts his finger on the exact bone that needs mending. Once He finds it, he pushes on it inflicting a sharp pain of conviction. And He does so until we deal with it together. Once we have confessed our sin, the Holy Spirit restores peace and joy to our hearts. Then He will no longer convict us about that specific sin. Because it is forgiven.

On the other hand, Satan is a grave digger. He uncovers all kinds of dirt from our past and throws a barrage of sins at us. Sins we have committed but not confessed. Sins we have committed but *already* confessed. Even sins we *haven't* committed. Anything to heap guilt upon our heads.

It's the last two where Satan does his most devilish destruction. He majors on sin that does *not* need our attention. After we confess our sin, Satan still haunts us with guilt. Or he will make up charges to press against us.

The Devil is like a dishonest car mechanic. Even if he can't find something that needs fixing, he'll nevertheless tell us something needs to be fixed. In our naiveté, we pay for things to be fixed in our lives that aren't even broken.

Learn this. The difference between Holy Spirit conviction and Satanic accusation is the difference between a rifle and a shotgun. The Holy Spirit directly targets individual sin that must be confessed. He is clear, specific, and true. When the Spirit convicts us, we won't have any questions about our need to confess. But Satan uses a shotgun approach, firing buckshot at any- and everything. He is vague, generic, and false. When he's doing his dirty work we'll feel confused and guilty, but unclear on what to do. Don't let him use this tactic on you!

Eliphaz uses the shotgun approach with Job. He tries to pin all kinds of vague and unmerited charges on Job, hoping that one will stick. Guess who has Eliphaz in his fiendish grip?

Have you someone like that in your life? Someone who thinks his or her primary ministry is to point out all your mistakes? A nagging spouse. A critical boss. A perfectionist parent. A demanding teacher. A jealous colleague. No matter what you do, it's never good enough. Such people make very little positive contribution to your life. Like the Evil One wielding a sledgehammer, this person blasts away and tears down. But never builds up.

Have you allowed an Eliphaz in your life to heap guilt upon you? Such people bury us under the law and heap mountains of guilt upon us if we cower to their intimidation. They try to play Holy Spirit in our lives, but bring Satanic accusation instead.

Don't Judge Another's Heart

Here's the second way Eliphaz blows it. He presumes to know Job's heart. He assumes to know what Job is thinking in the secret counsels of his mind. Worse, he speculates about what Job is thinking about God. A bit brash, wouldn't you say?

"Is not God in the height of heaven?
Look also at the distant stars, how high they are!
And you say, 'What does God know?
Can He judge through the thick darkness?
Clouds are a hiding place for Him, so that He cannot see;
And He walks on the vault of heaven.' " (Job 22:12-14)

Trying to shake Job's confidence, Eliphaz says, "Job, you think God is so exalted in Heaven that He can't look through the clouds and see your sin. But God does see your sin. So, come clean, Job." We could call this the Gestapo approach: "We have ways to make you talk."

Mind you, Job never said such a thing to God. Nor thought it. Nor verbalized it to Eliphaz. Yet Eliphaz falsely judges Job's heart and presumes to know what he is thinking.

The Apostle Paul refused to let others judge his heart. Standing up to the Corinthians' intimidation, he said,

To me it is a very small thing that I should be examined by
you, or by any human court; in fact, I do not even examine
myself. For I am conscious of nothing against myself, yet I
am not by this acquitted; but the one who examines me is the
Lord. Therefore do not go on passing judgment before the time,
but wait until the Lord comes who will both bring to light the
things hidden in the darkness and disclose the motives of men's
hearts; and then each man's praise will come to him from God.
(1 Corinthians 4:3-5)

Do you have someone like this in your life? Someone who says, "If I want your opinion, I'll give it to you"? These people are experts on what you are thinking or feeling. They try to control you by planting their thoughts into your mind and making you think it's your idea. In reality, it's nothing more than manipulative mind control. Beware!

Don't Project Your Own Baggage
Eliphaz continues his assault:

"Will you keep to the ancient path
Which wicked men have trod,

Who were snatched away before their time,
Whose foundations were washed away by a river?
They said to God, 'Depart from us!'
And 'What can the Almighty do to them?'
Yet He filled their houses with good things;
But the counsel of the wicked is far from me.
The righteous see and are glad,
And the innocent mock them,
Saying, 'Truly our adversaries are cut off,
And their abundance the fire has consumed.'" (Job 22:15-20)

Eliphaz's nastiness reaches a new low here. Sarcastically, he asks Job if he plans to continue going in the wrong direction—along the path of the wicked. He says this same path that Job is now traveling led to the drowning of an entire generation in Noah's day "by a river," a reference to the Flood. These people, who were destroyed by God's judgment, were filled with contempt for God's goodness, even ordering God to get out of their lives. Eliphaz says that this is Job's problem, too. What a cruel and unfounded comparison with Job!

"Job only pretends to have iniquity," says Eliphaz. He suggests that Job *says* he rejects the wicked and their path, when he actually holds to it.

Here is the third way Eliphaz crosses the line with Job. He tries to project his baggage onto his friend. These false charges against Job are more of a commentary on *Eliphaz* than they are on Job. They actually reflect Eliphaz's fractured relationship with God, not Job's. He has projected his own baggage—a faulty view of God—on to Job. Eliphaz sees God as so beyond humans that He has nothing to do with us except to judge. This errant view he accuses Job of comes from "the counsel of the wicked," which Eliphaz quickly and inadvertently tries to refute.

Finally, Eliphaz accuses Job of thinking he is above the law. He says Job travels the broad path of the wicked—the crowd who think they are beyond God's power to judge. He claims Job has disregard for God's goodness that once filled his house with good things. This is why Job now suffers and has lost everything—he is under God's judgment, while "the righteous" and "innocent" (Eliphaz and friends) watch gladly.

Do you see what's happening? It's actually Eliphaz who thinks he is above God's law. It's Eliphaz who assumes he's beyond the

Almighty's power to judge. It's Eliphaz whose heart is filled with self-righteousness. Not Job.

I've had this happen to me. Occasionally, a very abrasive person will confront me about being unloving. And do so in a very abrupt, unkind way. Immediately, I search my own heart to see if this is true. And sometimes what these people say is true and I have to repent. But many times, their attack is the result of their own frustrations. Actually, they lack patience and kindness themselves. And I'm left in the difficult position of having to defend my own integrity.

People will do the same to you. They will try to project their own baggage onto you. Don't let them. Hear what they say. Search your own heart. Discern if it is true. Like a man eating a fish dinner, eat the meat but spit out the bones. Accept what is true but spit out the rest. If what they say is true, then confess your sin and change. But if it's not, let them tote their own baggage.

Don't Force a Confession

Here's Eliphaz's fourth fault. He presses Job hard for a confession. Like a police officer who violates the Miranda rights of an arrested suspect, he tries to beat a confession out of Job. Eliphaz pushes Job around with high pressure, backroom tactics. Here's what Eliphaz says:

> "Yield now and be at peace with Him;
> Thereby good will come to you.
> Please receive instruction from His mouth,
> And establish His words in your heart.
> If you return to the Almighty, you will be restored;
> If you remove unrighteousness far from your tent,
> And place your gold in the dust,
> And the gold of Ophir among the stones of the brooks."
>   (Job 22:21-24)

Eliphaz comes on like a house on fire. He insists that Job repent—yield, receive, return, remove! These are four excellent synonyms for repentance. It is *yielding* to God, *receiving* His Word, *returning* to purity, and *removing* sin. Each word conveys a vital part of repentance. The only problem is that this advice does not apply to Job. Correct theology, but the wrong audience.

Eliphaz is saying, "Just admit it. Admit you've done something wrong. Pick a charge. Any charge. Just admit something. How about materialism (Eliphaz's accusation in referring to the 'gold of Ophir')?"

But Job's integrity won't allow him to admit to something he hasn't done. That would be dishonest toward him, toward others, and worse, toward God. Job must have been tempted to confess a wrongdoing just to create peace. Just to get Eliphaz off his back. Pragmatically, it would end the fuss. He could confess to wrongdoing to instigate a cease-fire. What a temptation.

But integrity demanded that he *not* confess sin that he had not committed.

Be honest. Have you husbands ever admitted to your wife a wrong-doing just to stop her tears? Even though you didn't do it. But you admitted to something, just to restore peace in the family. Have you ever taken the blame with your boss, just to repair a fractured situation and get back on his good side? But you didn't do it. Tempting, isn't it?

We must applaud Job for his honesty. He didn't buckle under Eliphaz's barrage of accusations. It would have been tempting to end this debate by confessing one of Eliphaz's charges. Just to get these guys off his back.

But he didn't. His integrity wouldn't allow it. Neither should ours.

Don't Promise a Quick Fix
Finally, Eliphaz provides the last-ditch effort of a desperate man. He tells Job that if he will just repent, everything will be great in his life. Eliphaz concludes:

"Then the Almighty will be your gold
And choice silver to you.
For then you will delight in the Almighty,
And lift up your face to God.
You will pray to Him, and He will hear you;
And you will pay your vows.
You will also decree a thing, and it will be established for you;
And light will shine on your ways.
When you are cast down, you will speak with confidence
And the humble person He will save.
He will deliver one who is not innocent,
And he will be delivered through the cleanness of your hands."
(Job 22:25-30)

Eliphaz says, "If you will just repent, then God will become as precious as gold to you. God will then answer your prayers. He will guide you into His perfect will. You can then be used to minister to others who have fallen. Just repent."

Some of this is true. But some is not. If we confess our sin, everything doesn't automatically become right. There are often consequences to sin that are irreversible, even if we do confess it.

Do you see what Eliphaz has shown us? He has shown us how *not* to counsel others. He's a role model for failure.

What do we learn from him? Don't play Holy Spirit. Don't judge others' hearts. Don't project your own baggage. Don't force a confession. Don't promise a quick fix.

Instead, allow God to use you to encourage, uplift, and if necessary, confront others. In *His* time. In *His* power. In *His* way. Not yours.

I WANT MY DAY IN COURT!

As in a fast-paced tennis match, the ball is back in Job's court. With blinding topspin. But instead of arguing with Eliphaz, Job does something very wise here. Don't miss it. Job ignores Eliphaz and speaks to the Lord. Job's dispute is not with men, but with God. So he pours out his heart to God—not Eliphaz—and asks two great questions that we ask when our life is in turmoil. Job asks, "God, where are You?" (Job 23) and "Why doesn't God do something?" (Job 24).

God, Where Are You?

We begin with the first of these two questions.

> Then Job replied,
> "Even today my complaint is rebellion;
> His hand is heavy despite my groaning.
> Oh that I knew where I might find Him,
> That I might come to His seat!
> I would present my case before Him
> And fill my mouth with arguments.
> I would learn the words which He would answer,
> And perceive what He would say to me.
> Would He contend with me by the greatness of His power?
> No, surely He would pay attention to me.

There the upright would reason with Him;
And I would be delivered forever from my Judge."
  (Job 23:1-7)

Job complains that God is hiding from him. So he pleads with God to meet him in court and have a fair trial. If Job could subpoena God, he would state his case, present his evidence, and God would acquit him. Surely. Job believes his arguments are so persuasive that God will see it too, and deliver him from this unfair treatment. So Job complains:

"Behold, I go forward but He is not there,
And backward, but I cannot perceive Him;
When He acts on the left, I cannot behold Him;
He turns on the right, I cannot see Him.
But He knows the way I take;
When He has tried me, I shall come forth as gold.
My foot has held fast to His path;
I have kept His way and not turned aside
I have not departed from the command of His lips;
I have treasured the words of His mouth more than my
  necessary food." (Job 23:8-12)

But here's the problem. No matter where Job searched, he couldn't find God. He searched forward and backward, left and right. No God anywhere. Job reasoned, "God knows the way I take—a path of righteousness. So He must be avoiding me so that the truth can't come out in court."

If Job could take God to court, he would emerge from the trial as good as gold. It would become obvious to all. Even to God. Job has held fast to the path of holiness. It would all come out on the witness stand. He would surely be acquitted.

Job is cracking a bit here. He fails to see that he is not being punished for any sin in his life. Instead, he is suffering because he has lived a righteous life. He just can't see this. He's starting to believe the critic's lie.

Behind every trial we face, God always has His eternal purpose. Every disappointment is a divine appointment. His plan is to bless us, not blast us. Not to crush us, but to make us into the image of Christ.

"But He is unique and who can turn Him?
And what His soul desires, that He does.
For He performs what is appointed for me,
And many such decrees are with Him.
Therefore, I would be dismayed at His presence;
When I consider, I am terrified of Him.
It is God who has made my heart faint,
And the Almighty who has dismayed me,
But I am not silenced by the darkness,
Nor deep gloom which covers me." (Job 23:13-17)

Job recognizes God is "unique." That means He is in a class by Himself. No one else is even in God's league. He is the only One who cannot be restrained. He sits in the heavens and "does whatever He pleases" (Psalm 115:3). Despite this incredible demand for a court hearing, Job finally comes to his senses and acknowledges that God will have His own way. He cannot be resisted. Job recognizes that all God's sovereign decrees will be performed in his life. Why argue with a God who cannot be overruled?

Suddenly the thought of appearing before God sinks in. Job becomes terrified at the thought of appearing before God. This breeds discouragement because now he feels "damned if I do and damned if I don't."

Maybe you have felt that way. Maybe you've thought, "It doesn't matter what I do." A marriage gone sour. A baby died in delivery. An engagement broken. A business deal that collapsed. You have cried out, "Lord, why have you done this to me? I have loved you. Why didn't this happen to somebody who doesn't even care about you? It doesn't matter what I do!"

God, Do Something!

Job looks up to Heaven with empty frustration and deep anguish over the injustices he sees in the world. Why does God allow wrong to go unpunished? Why does right go unrewarded? Why doesn't God punish evil?

Job appeals to God to set regular court dates to punish evildoers.

"Why are times not stored up by the Almighty,
And why do those who know Him not see His days?" (Job 24:1)

Job pleads with God to subpoena sinners and judge them. With mounting frustration, Job cites example after example of sinners who go unpunished.

"Some remove the landmarks;
They seize and devour flocks.
They drive away the donkeys of the orphans;
They take the widow's ox for a pledge.
They push the needy aside from the road;
The poor of the land are made to hide themselves altogether.
Behold, as wild donkeys in the wilderness
They go forth seeking food in their activity,
As bread for their children in the desert.
They harvest their fodder in the field,
And they glean the vineyard of the wicked.
They spend the night naked, without clothing,
And have no covering against the cold.
They are wet with the mountain rains,
And they hug the rock for want of a shelter.
Others snatch the orphan from the breast,
And against the poor they take a pledge.
They cause the poor to go about naked without clothing,
And they take away the sheaves from the hungry.
Within the walls they produce oil;
They tread wine presses but thirst.
From the city men groan,
And the souls of the wounded cry out;
Yet God does not pay attention to folly." (Job 24:2-12)

Here is a list of the wicked who go unpunished. This was the original cast of *Dirty, Rotten Scoundrels.* Thieves. Orphan-bashers. Widow-abusers. Leeches on society. Con men. Exploiters. All the things Job's critics falsely accused him of. Yet, God seems oblivious to these atrocities, even the folly of Job being falsely accused.

Job gropes for answers. "Why do *they* go unpunished while I suffer?"

Admit it. It's not just Job who wrestles with injustice in the world. We *all* do. We all struggle with it. Why do criminals go unpunished? Why do the innocent suffer? Why do bad things happen to good people?

At some point, we all cry out from the depths of our souls, "God, do something!" Every time I watch the evening news, I silently scream for God to punish evildoers. I want God to make this world right. Job, I hear you!

Job sinks deeper into perplexity.

"Others have been with those who rebel against the light;
They do not want to know its ways,
Nor abide in its paths.
The murderer arises at dawn;
He kills the poor and the needy,
And at night he is as a thief.
And the eye of the adulterer waits for the twilight,
Saying, 'No eye will see me.'
And he disguises his face.
In the dark they dig into houses,
They shut themselves up by day;
They do not know the light.
For the morning is the same to him as thick darkness,
For he is familiar with the terrors of thick darkness."
      (Job 24:13-17)

Job asks the tough questions. Why do murderers go free? Why do the thieves go uncaught? Why do adulterers go undetected? Why do robbers go unprosecuted? Why, God?

Like a pendulum swinging back to the center, Job now balances his thinking. In a sudden shift from one extreme back to the middle, Job recognizes that wicked men will be judged in the end. They will eventually die and perish in hell.

"They are insignificant on the surface of the water;
Their portion is cursed on the earth.
They do not turn toward the vineyards.
Drought and heat consume the snow waters,
So does Sheol those who have sinned.
A mother will forget him;
The worm feeds sweetly till he is remembered no more.
And wickedness will be broken like a tree.
He wrongs the barren woman,

And does no good for the widow.
But He drags off the valiant by His power;
He rises, but no one has assurance of life.
He provides them with security, and they are supported;
And His eyes are on their ways.
They are exalted a little while, then they are gone;
Moreover, they are brought low and like everything gathered up;
Even like the heads of grain they are cut off." (Job 24:18-24)

Yes, God provides the wicked with some comforts. The rain falls
on the just and the unjust. But be assured that God records their every
wicked deed. Though temporarily comforted, they will be ultimately
judged. There is a payday some day.

"Now if it is not so, who can prove me a liar,
And make my speech worthless?" (Job 24:25)

Growing more confident in his own arguments, Job challenges
Eliphaz to dispute him if his words are not true. "Put up or shut up!"

YOU MAGGOT!
Bildad now speaks for the third and final time. Zophar is so frustrated
that his arguments are rebutted that he remains quiet and refuses to
speak to Job this last time. He sulks silently while Bildad speaks.

What Bildad says is noticeably short and brief. Perhaps he has
run out of arguments. Perhaps Job's responses are too overpowering.
Regardless, Bildad is at the end of his rope.

Then Bildad the Shuhite answered,
"Dominion and awe belong to Him
Who establishes peace in His heights.
Is there any number to His troops?
And upon whom does His light not rise?
How then can a man be just with God?
Or how can he be clean who is born of woman?" (Job 25:1-4)

In his last hurrah, Bildad makes two final points with Job. One,
God is sovereign; two, man is sinful. Bildad argues that an infinite
gap exists between a holy God and His sinful creation. There's no way

that Job, a sinful man, can stand before a holy God. Much less argue with Him.

No argument here, Bildad. Job believes God *is* absolutely sovereign and man is utterly depraved. As the One who establishes moral order in the universe, God commands His angelic army. So great are His soldiers that they cannot even be numbered. As the sun rises over the earth, so does God's sovereignty extend over all His creation. What makes Job think he could argue with this Despot?

"If even the moon has no brightness
And the stars are not pure in His sight,
How much less man, that maggot,
And the son of man, that worm!" (Job 25:5-6)

Further describing man's depravity, Bildad calls man a maggot and a worm. Feeding on filth. Crawling in the dirt. Worthless. Insignificant. Less than nothing. He argues, "If even the bright moon and the shining stars are dark and dreary in comparison to God's glory, how insignificant must man be. How could Job, lowly as he is, expect to argue his case before a majestic God?

Bildad's theology is all wrong. Humans are not maggots! Man is not a worm. He is God's creation, uniquely bearing the image of God. Sin has caused man's fall, resulting in depravity and the ruin of God's image in him (see Romans 3:10-18). Salvation is a renewal of the image of God in us (Colossians 3:10). You see, God's image in humans has not been altogether blotted out, only marred by sin. Consequently, fallen man is not a maggot, lower than the lowest of animals; rather, humans are still God's special creation, corrupted by iniquity, but nevertheless bearing God's image.

Job, then, is not worthless, as Bildad charges, but of great value to his Maker. Ray Stedman writes,

The Scriptures never treat man like a worm. God's view of man is that though he has turned his back upon the light and plunged himself into darkness and is reaping the result of his own iniquity, God never treats him like a worm. He treats him like a deeply loved and valuable individual to whom He is ready to commit himself in order to redeem him. This much is true: only when a man admits he cannot help himself, that he is indeed a wretched person, can he be helped. But God never treats him like a worm. Bildad here reflects a narrow theology that does not fit the facts.[1]

Bildad forgets that this same argument applies to himself. The same gulf exists between God and Bildad. He, too, does *not* have God figured out.

Whenever you point an accusing finger at someone else, there are always four fingers pointing back at yourself. Like a true-blue Pharisee, Bildad fails to practice what he preaches. He refuses to take a dose of his own medicine.

There's a lesson here for us. When accepting counsel and advice from others, consider their lives. Is there a consistency of life and advice about them? Any humility? Do they model the message? Do they admit their own shortcomings? If not, then they are probably wrong.

THANKS FOR NOTHING!

With biting sarcasm, Job answers Bildad. Personally, I can't really blame him. Sarcasm isn't necessarily wrong. God Himself will speak to Job with extreme sarcasm. Job's three friends won't listen to a gentle answer, so they need strong words with some sting. Job loads up his words with sarcasm.

> Then Job responded,
> "What a help you are to the weak!
> How you have saved the arm without strength!
> What counsel you have given to one without wisdom!
> What helpful insight you have abundantly provided!
> To whom have you uttered words?
> And whose spirit was expressed through you?" (Job 26:1-4)

With tongue in cheek, Job fires back, "What a help you have been to me." You can just see Job rolling his eyes as he says this. Obviously, they have been no help to him. Zero.

Job asks a penetrating question, "Whose spirit was expressed through you?" Good question! Was it God or Satan speaking through Bildad? Was Bildad a voice from Heaven or hell?

It definitely was not the Holy Spirit speaking through Bildad. That leaves only one option. The fact is, a sinister spirit was speaking through

Bildad. A dark, devilish demon had been hurling fiery darts at Job via Bildad. Earlier, God told Satan, "Job won't curse Me." But Satan countered, "Yes, he will." So Satan fired all the artillery of hell at Job to cause him to curse God. When the loss of family, fortune, and health did not cause Job to turn against God, the Evil One attacked Job through his friends. In reality, these three counselors were mouthpieces for Satan, sent to subvert Job's faith.

We must be careful to whom we listen. Even our closest friends can become brokers of the Devil's trash, dumping their lies at our feet. With spiritual discernment, we must carefully weigh and evaluate the advice we receive. Always ask yourself, "Was that the Holy Spirit speaking? Or a demon spirit?" Too often, we are like naive children picking up dirty food off the floor and plopping it into our mouths. With gross gullibility, we accept the Devil's lies believing it is God's wisdom. Believer, beware!

Likewise, we must be careful what counsel we give to others. We, too, will either be a mouthpiece for God or for Satan. Our lives must be yielded to God and filled with His Spirit if we are to give wise guidance to others.

After his sarcastic barbs, Job concludes with a statement about God's greatness. Bildad claimed that God was sovereign, but Job stated that God is far more sovereign than Bildad realized.

> "The departed spirits tremble
> Under the waters and their inhabitants.
> Naked is Sheol before Him
> And Abaddon has no covering.
> He stretches out the north over empty space,
> And hangs the earth on nothing.
> He wraps up the waters in His clouds;
> And the cloud does not burst under them.
> He obscures the face of the full moon,
> And spreads His cloud over it.
> He has inscribed a circle on the surface of the waters,
> At the boundary of light and darkness.
> The pillars of heaven tremble,
> And are amazed at His rebuke.
> He quieted the sea with His power,
> And by His understanding He shattered Rahab.

By His breath the heavens are cleared;
His hand has pierced the fleeing serpent." (Job 26:5-13)

After death, God determines the eternal destiny of every man and woman. Whether that departed spirit goes to Sheol (Abaddon) or Heaven, God sees and controls every person's destiny. Heaven and hell are in His hands to give or withhold.

God is sovereign over all creation. His absolute control extends to every realm. He governs the outer space, the earth, the clouds, the moon, the ocean, light, darkness, the mountains, the sea, and the heavens. Everything.

How much more the souls of men!

It is before this awesome God that we will all one day bow and await the verdict of His court. Only faith in Jesus Christ will usher us into His glorious presence to live forever.

In conclusion, Job says:

"Behold these are the fringes of His ways;
And how faint a word we hear of Him!
But His mighty thunder, who can understand?" (Job 26:14)

God is beyond our comprehension, explains Job. What little we know of Him. Finite man cannot intelligently grasp an infinite God. It is impossible for us to understand the extent of His reign.

TRUST HIS INSTRUMENTS IN THE STORM

Dr. Edwin Lutzer, the pastor of the famous Moody Memorial Church in downtown Chicago, tells the story of flying on a commercial air flight. Seated next to him was a man who used to be a commercial airline pilot, but now flies his own smaller plane. The two became engaged in a conversation about the safety of flying.

The pilot said, "Many people think these huge jets are built more safely and, therefore, are safer to fly than smaller planes. People think that because there are more crashes with smaller planes than with commercial jets.

"But," he said, "that's not true. The reason why so many lighter planes crash is not because of bad equipment. It's because of inexperienced pilots flying the little planes."

Lutzer replied, "Tell me more."

"The error of inexperienced pilots is that they refuse to believe their instruments," the pilot said. "In a storm, they trust their instincts rather than their navigation instruments. That's where they get in trouble.

"For example, they are absolutely convinced that the altitude of the plane is increasing when it's not. There is an internal mechanism that tells them the altitude. But, when the altitude is not increasing, they often choose to disbelieve the instruments and adjust the plane according to their senses. They think that the plane is turning or banking when it's actually not. When the pilot ignores his readings and adjusts the plane according to his intuition, it is sure to crash."

Then he said, "There wouldn't be as many light planes that crash if pilots would blindly and devotedly believe their instrument panels rather than accepting what they think their senses are telling them."

Lutzer shook the man's hand and said, "I want to thank you for that sermon illustration."

The point is obvious. The application clear. In life's storms, many a Christian has trusted his or her feelings rather than the truth of God's Word. Whenever that occurs, we too are sure to crash.

There wouldn't be as many lives that crash if we ceased accepting direction from our natural senses and began reading with our super-natural senses. If we read the discouraging circumstances of life—the people who do us in, the job that doesn't work out, and the other struggles that seem to engulf us—we will surely crash. But if we would keep our eyes on Jesus Christ and stay grounded in His Word, then we will make it safely through the storm.

Maybe you are flying through a storm presently. Maybe you're in a tailspin. The winds of adversity may be blowing strongly against you and it seems like your life is out of control.

Don't listen to your feelings. Feelings are fickle. They will fail us. But the instrument panel of God's Word is *always* correct. It is *always* true.

Will you listen to your feelings, or to God's Word? Will you fly by intuition, or by divine revelation? That is the choice each of us must make.

Your emotions may tell you that your circumstances are out of control. Don't listen to them. Believe God's Word, which says—to the contrary—that He is absolutely in control.

God has a purpose in leading you into the storm. He has power to preserve you through the storm. And He has a plan to eventually lead you out of the storm.

Put your eyes on Christ. Trust His Word. His instrument panel is *always* correct. Trust Him.

NOTE

1. Ray Stedman, *Expository Studies in Job* (Dallas, TX: Word Books, 1981), pages 103-104.

CHAPTER 10

IT'S TIME
TO TAKE INVENTORY

▼

I have a favorite men's clothing store where I buy all my clothes.
Anyone who knows me well is aware of this quirk.

I'm what you call a conservative dresser. I sleep in pajamas
that have cuffs. If a tie wasn't chartered by some English prep school at
least a millennium ago, I won't wear it. I wear only dark, three-button
suits. The first time I set foot on campus at Reformed Theological Seminary, the professors thought I was a Mormon missionary.

Twice a year, my favorite haberdasher puts a sign in the storefront
window that reads "Closed for Inventory." The door is locked. The
window blinds are pulled. The store is shut down tighter than a drum.
The customer parking lot is empty. The outside sign is turned off. The
store looks lifeless. Like a ghost town.

Inside is another story. Inside, employees are frantically working like a colony of ants. The owners are pacing up and down aisles
with clipboards, checking off their merchandise. Salesmen are counting
suits. Stacking trousers. Sorting ties. Itemizing sweaters. Writing off
damaged goods.

For these men, this is the busiest day of the year. Don't call in sick
on Inventory Day. Not if you want to keep your job. This is important.

Critically important.

Sure, there's money in the cash register. Yes, there's money in the bank. But are they *making* money? They can't know until they take inventory and find out where they stand. How much inventory is in the showroom? How much is on the shelf? What about the stockroom?

If you've ever been in business, you know how imperative it is to know where you stand. Bottom line, where do I stand? If you're going to balance the books, you've got to temporarily shut down and take inventory. If you don't close down your business, you'll be out of business. Chapter eleven. Ancient history. Nobody likes taking inventory. It's tedious. It's time-consuming. You've got to shut down your whole business and put a "Closed for Inventory" sign on your door. There's no immediate reward. Make a sale and the cash register rings. But take inventory and no money exchanges hands. Only meticulous bean counting.

What is true in the business world is also true in the spiritual world. In both worlds, there must be a time to take inventory. A time to close for internal auditing. In our spiritual lives, we must periodically shut down and examine ourselves.

Recently, I went through such a time of thorough, intense self-evaluation. It was a needed time to take inventory. A time to take stock. I walked through the warehouses of my life and audited my heart. I itemized my priorities. Let me tell you, it was most challenging, but very needed.

As I turned the searchlight inward, I evaluated my strengths. I considered my weaknesses. I audited my giftedness. I tallied my limitations. I surveyed every pocket of my life. I wrote off the areas of past failure.

This was no easy process. It required a time of heart-searching evaluation. Assessing goals. Itemizing relationships. Clearing out sins. Writing off failures. Rearranging priorities. The process was well worth it. Taking inventory put me in a much better position to love and serve God.

Maybe it's time for you to take inventory as well. You knew I was going to say that, didn't you? Just as with my life, it's critically important for you, too, to take inventory.

When is the last time you audited your life? When's the last time you took inventory of your heart? When did you last audit your spiritual disciplines? When did you last evaluate how you are using your spiritual gifts? Have you recently assessed the use of your time? Have you accounted for how you treat other people? We need to add up how we use our money. We need to examine how we use our tongues.

It's not easy. It's tedious. It's time-consuming. Maybe even painful. You'll have to momentarily shut down your business. But the results will put you in much better position to love and serve God.

As we follow Job's experience, it's now time for him to take inventory. After hearing from his three friends, Job stops to conduct an internal audit. He pauses to take personal inventory, making a careful evaluation of where he is spiritually.

As we observe Job's life, we discover some basic principles on how to take inventory of our lives. The life not worth examining is not worth living. Taking inventory is necessary for staying on track spiritually. Taking stock is critical if we are to grow in our faith.

One benefit of a trial is it can cause us to look inward and take inventory—something we might not otherwise do. Job's trial has driven him to the point of internal investigation. It can do the same for you and me. Here are five key principles from Job's life on taking personal inventory.

TAKE A HARD, HONEST LOOK AT YOURSELF
We must take a hard, honest look at ourselves. We must be willing to look under the hood and undergo a checkup. Job did.

> Then Job continued his discourse and said,
> "As God lives, who has taken away my right,
> And the Almighty, who has embittered my soul,
> For as long as life is in me,
> And the breath of God is in my nostrils,
> My lips certainly will not speak unjustly,
> Nor will my tongue mutter deceit.
> Far be it from me that I should declare you right;
> Till I die I will not put away my integrity from me.
> I hold fast my righteousness and will not let it go.
> My heart does not reproach any of my days." (Job 27:1-6)

Job begins by saying "as God lives." In so doing, he is taking an oath. The most solemn oath that someone can take. When Job says, "as God lives," he is inviting God to kill him if what he says is not true.

Now that's taking a hard, serious look! What Job says about himself is as certain, Job says, as the fact that God lives.

As Job looks at his own life—his character, his conduct, his conversations—he says honestly, before God, that he desires to live with personal integrity.

With God as his witness, Job says his tongue has not spoken unjustly. Nor has he sacrificed his integrity. He held fast his righteousness. His heart has not reproached him. Everything under his spiritual hood is humming.

In reality, only God can properly assess our hearts. We must yield our lives to Him as we look inward. Only then can we see what is there.

Our hearts are so deceitful we cannot begin to accurately gauge our inner life. Jeremiah 17:9 says,

> "The heart is more deceitful than all else
> And is desperately sick;
> Who can understand it?"

Surely not us.

Only God can properly look into our souls, turn on the searchlight, and reveal what is there. That is why David wrote,

> Search me, O God, and know my heart;
> Try me and know my anxious thoughts;
> And see if there be any hurtful way in me. (Psalm 139:23-24)

David realizes that if he is to take a hard, honest look at his life, God must be the One who searches and reveals what is there. Elsewhere, David said,

> Examine me, O LORD, and try me;
> Test my mind and my heart. (Psalm 26:2)

In other words, "God, I invite You to turn on the searchlight and reveal where I am in my relationship with You."

It's the same with you and me. Only God Himself can reveal to us what's really in our hearts. Without His help, we are like blind men trying to find the noonday sun.

For the remainder of Job 27, Job will distance himself from his "friends," whom he believes God will judge. Categorically, Job says he does not believe that his life belongs in the camp of the wicked. What his friends have been saying to him does not match up with the hard, honest look that he is taking of his life.

> "May my enemy be as the wicked,
> And my opponent as the unjust.
> For what is the hope of the godless when he is cut off,
> When God requires his life?
> Will God hear his cry,
> When distress comes upon him?
> Will he take delight in the Almighty,
> Will he call on God at all times?
> I will instruct you in the power of God;
> What is with the Almighty I will not conceal.
> Behold, all of you have seen it;
> Why then do you act foolishly?" (Job 27:7-12)

As you see, Job is in the awkward position of having to defend himself. Honestly, before God, Job says, "I do not believe what my friends have said about me is true."

Here's the next key principle.

USE WISDOM, NOT COMMON SENSE

We must use wisdom, not common sense, to evaluate our lives. As we look inward, we need God-given wisdom with which to see. Not natural eyes. We need to see *as* God sees if we are to see *what* God sees. This requires divine wisdom.

What is wisdom? Wisdom is the spiritual insight that allows the proper application of biblical truth. It's one thing to know truth, but something else entirely to know how it applies to our lives. Knowledge is the understanding of truth; wisdom is the proper application of truth. Wisdom is seeing ourselves for who we are and applying God's truth accordingly. So, wisdom is absolutely essential if we are to properly evaluate and take spiritual inventory.

We all know we can see something in our lives so often that it soon becomes invisible to us. Especially our faults. We need supernatural insight to see what naturally escapes our sight. In these verses, Job compares his search for wisdom with the search for gold or silver, both valuable commodities.

"Surely there is a mine for silver,
And a place where they refine gold.
Iron is taken from the dust,
And from rock copper is smelted.
Man puts an end to darkness,
And to the farthest limit he searches out
The rock in gloom and deep shadow.
He sinks a shaft far from habitation,
Forgotten by the foot;
They hang and swing to and fro far from men.
The earth, from it comes food,
And underneath it is turned up as fire.
Its rocks are the source of sapphires,
And its dust contains gold.
The path no bird of prey knows,
Nor has the falcon's eye caught sight of it.
The proud beasts have not trodden it,
Nor has the fierce lion passed over it.
He puts his hand on the flint;
He overturns the mountains at the base.
He hews out channels through the rocks;
And his eye sees anything precious.
He dams up the streams from flowing;
And what is hidden he brings out to the light." (Job 28:1-11)

Here is a remarkable account of an early mining business. A shaft has been dug down deep into the earth. A man has been lowered in a basket that is attached to a rope and let down deep, deep, deep into this mining shaft. He is swinging back and forth in the basket, suspended by the rope, in pursuit of precious gems and metals.

The Source of Spiritual Wisdom
Although such ingenuity may uncover earthly commodities, man in his own efforts cannot discover spiritual wisdom. Wisdom must be supernaturally given by God from above. It is not discovered by digging down, but by looking up. Neither can wisdom be bought, says Job.

"But where can wisdom be found?
And where is the place of understanding?

Man does not know its value,
Nor is it found in the land of the living.
The deep says, 'It is not in me';
And the sea says, 'It is not with me.'
Pure gold cannot be given in exchange for it,
Nor can silver be weighed as its price.
It cannot be valued in the gold of Ophir,
In precious onyx, or sapphire.
Gold or glass cannot equal it,
Nor can it be exchanged for articles of fine gold.
Coral and crystal are not to be mentioned;
And the acquisition of wisdom is above that of pearls.
The topaz of Ethiopia cannot equal it,
Nor can it be valued in pure gold.
Where then does wisdom come from?
And where is the place of understanding?
Thus it is hidden from the eyes of all living,
And concealed from the birds of the sky.
Abaddon and Death say,
'With our ears we have heard a report of it.'" (Job 28:12-22)

How can Job find God's insight to evaluate his life? It cannot be purchased by silver or gold or onyx or sapphire. If so, the rich would be the wisest people on the earth. Neither can coral, crystal, pearls, or topaz buy it. Wisdom is far too valuable. Neither an ascension into the heights of the clouds, nor a descent into the depths of death can reveal wisdom. Only God can reveal wisdom.

Here is the conclusion to which Job comes. Because only God possesses wisdom, only God can give wisdom. Wisdom is the result of pursuing the knowledge of God.

"God understands its [wisdom's] way;
And He knows its place.
For He looks to the ends of the earth,
And sees everything under the heavens.
When He imparted weight to the wind,
And meted out the waters by measure,
When He set a limit for the rain,
And a course for the thunderbolt,

Then He saw it and declared it;
He established it and also searched it out." (Job 28:23-27)

Think about it! The very wisdom that God employed to create the world with beauty and balance is available to you and me. God's wisdom—which perfectly created the wind and the rain that control the thunderbolts and the seas—can likewise create beauty and balance in our lives, too. How then do we receive the wisdom that leads to spiritual insight and successful living?

"And to man He said, 'Behold, the fear of the Lord, that is
    wisdom;
And to depart from evil is understanding.'" (Job 28:28)

Wisdom is the result of fearing God. Solomon wrote, "The fear of the LORD is the beginning of wisdom" (Proverbs 9:10). We could easily misunderstand what it means to fear God, so let's walk carefully.

What It Means to Fear God

Fearing God does *not* mean to cower before Him like a young boy cowering when he sees the neighborhood bully walking down the block. It means to be filled with reverence, awe, and respect for God. It means to honor God with highest esteem. To take Him very seriously.

Fearing God means to realize that God is my Creator and I am accountable to Him alone. It means to remember that I am on His earth, breathing His air. To believe that all of my days here are in His hands. To know He controls my eternal destiny. That is the fear of God.

Fearing God means to humble myself before Him and give Him the control of my life. It means to bow before Him with loving trust. Then—and only then—do I receive the wisdom that enables me to see myself as God sees me.

Do you fear God? When was the last time you were in awe of God? If you are to have God-given wisdom to see your life with spiritual insight, you and I must fear God.

Here's the next principle.

AUDIT YOUR PERSONAL ASSETS

Job assesses his assets and determines what positive things God has done in his life. He now looks back over his life and recounts what great things God has done on his behalf. In chapter 29, Job recalls that he has been blessed with God's favor (verses 2-6), man's respect (verses 7-11), and personal godliness (12-16).

> And Job again took up his discourse and said,
> "Oh that I were as in months gone by,
> As in the days when God watched over me;
> When His lamp shone over my head,
> And by His light I walked through darkness;
> As I was in the prime of my days,
> When the friendship of God was over my tent;
> When the Almighty was yet with me,
> And my children were around me;
> When my steps were bathed in butter,
> And the rock poured out for me streams of oil!" (Job 29:1-6)

Retracing his steps, Job longs for past days when it was so readily apparent that God's good hand was upon him. He remembers the days when his path was bathed in butter—meaning that his path was greased with an abundance of God's blessing. He considers how he was once respected and esteemed by the influential people of his day.

> "When I went out to the gate of the city,
> When I took my seat in the square;
> The young men saw me and hid themselves,
> And the old men arose and stood.
> The princes stopped talking,
> And put their hands on their mouths;
> The voice of the nobles was hushed,
> And their tongue stuck to their palate.
> For when the ear heard, it called me blessed;
> And when the eye saw, it gave witness of me." (Job 29:7-11)

These words describe Job's onetime honored position in the community. With great influence, he stood at the gate, the most visible place in the city. It was here that legal matters were settled and business was conducted. It was here that the most mature men sat and were honored. Job previously occupied such an important place that the young men were quiet when he spoke, drinking in his every word. You've heard

that when E. F. Hutton speaks, people listen. That was Job! When he
spoke, the ancient world listened. He was the ultimate mentor. Even
nobles and princes would come to sit at Job's feet.

"Because I delivered the poor who cried for help,
And the orphan who had no helper.
The blessing of the one ready to perish came upon me,
And I made the widow's heart sing for joy.
I put on righteousness, and it clothed me;
My justice was like a robe and a turban.
I was eyes to the blind,
And feet to the lame.
I was a father to the needy,
And I investigated the case which I did not know.
And I broke the jaws of the wicked,
And snatched the prey from his teeth." (Job 29:12-17)

What a man is Job! He helped the poor. Befriended orphans. Comforted widows. Guided the blind. Carried the crippled. Defended the
innocent. Snatched innocent victims from sure death at the hands of the
wicked. Naturally, Job assumed that his life would continue in unbroken
strength and success until he died.

"Then I thought, 'I shall die in my nest,
And I shall multiply my days as the sand.
My root is spread out to the waters,
And dew lies all night on my branch.
My glory is ever new with me,
And my bow is renewed in my hand.'" (Job 29:18-20)

Admittedly, Job was the most respected man in town. Admired.
Honored. Revered. He assumed, prior to his tragedy, that he would die
with his children surrounding him ("in my nest"), after a long life of sta-
bility (the "root"), prosperity ("dew"), an enviable reputation ("glory"),
and strength (the "bow").

"To me they listened and waited,
And kept silent for my counsel.
After my words they did not speak again,

And my speech dropped on them.
And they waited for me as for the rain,
And opened their mouth as for the spring rain.
I smiled on them when they did not believe,
And the light of my face they did not cast down.
I chose a way for them and sat as chief,
And dwelt as a king among the troops,
As one who comforted the mourners." (Job 29:21-25)

Job is not bragging here. Nor being arrogant. He is simply being honest and declaring what God has done in his life. Just stating the facts.

Let's do the same. Let us give the glory to God for what His grace has done in our lives. May we praise Him for those areas where He has brought about spiritual maturity. May we offer thanks for how He has worked in our hearts to help others, to be a servant, and to be involved in His work.

Why don't you audit your assets right now and list three areas where God has been at work in your life recently.

Now, here's the next key to a helpful inventory.

ITEMIZE YOUR PERSONAL LOSSES

Job itemizes his losses. He adds up not only his gains, but also his pains. He audits his losses so they could be written off the books. Far too often, we try to carry forward our losses like a ball and chain, rather than erasing them from the books.

"But now those younger than I mock me,
Whose fathers I disdained to put with the dogs of my flock.
Indeed, what good was the strength of their hands to me?
Vigor had perished from them.
From want and famine they are gaunt
Who gnaw the dry ground by night in waste and desolation,
Who pluck mallow by the bushes,
And whose food is the root of the broom shrub.
They are driven from the community;
They shout against them as against a thief,
So that they dwell in dreadful valleys,
In holes of the earth and of the rocks.

Among the bushes they cry out;
Under the nettles they are gathered together.
Fools, even those without a name,
They were scourged from the land." (Job 30:1-8)

"But now" marks a great contrast from what preceded! While the previous chapter detailed what good God had done in Job's life, he now talks about what losses he has suffered.

Where Job was once revered by his peers, he is now mocked. He has forfeited their respect and honor. Where the younger men were once silent in Job's presence, they now mock and belittle him.

Job describes these young men as urchins whose fathers weren't worthy of running with the dogs of his flock! This was a deep insult to them, since in Job's day dogs were considered the lowest of animals, but it shows how deep was Job's humiliation at being scorned by them. Job's description pictures these low-bred rascals as the scum of the earth:

- Useless and weak (30:2).
- Gaunt from famine and scavenging the ground for food (30:3).
- Surviving on mallow—a bitter diet that would only be eaten by the poor (30:4).
- Driven from the community like thieves (30:5).
- Living in caves (holes in the earth) and dry riverbeds (wadis) or under thornbushes (30:6-7).
- So foolish in their behavior they didn't deserve names but should be run out of town ("scourged from the land") (30:8).

How humiliating for Job! Even the scourges of his day considered him lower than themselves!

"And now I have become their taunt,
I have even become a byword to them.
They abhor me and stand aloof from me,
And they do not refrain from spitting at my face." (Job 30:9-10)

Understandably, this taunting has deeply wounded Job. Their sharp words have cut into his wounded heart, afflicting his soul.

"And now my soul is poured out within me;
Days of affliction have seized me.
At night it pierces my bones within me,
And my gnawing pains take no rest.
By a great force my garment is distorted;
It binds me about as the collar of my coat.
He has cast me into the mire,
And I have become like dust and ashes." (Job 30:16-19)

Adding insult to injury, Job's cry to God receives no answer. Only silence. As is our natural tendency, Job misinterprets God's silence as lack of concern and indifference. Job assumes that God's silence means God's displeasure. God once seemed so close, but now He seems so distant and uncaring.

"I cry out to Thee for help, but Thou dost not answer me;
I stand up, and Thou dost turn Thy attention against me.
Thou hast become cruel to me;
With the might of Thy hand Thou dost persecute me.
Thou dost lift me up to the wind and cause me to ride;
And Thou dost dissolve me in a storm.
For I know that Thou wilt bring me to death
And to the house of meeting for all living." (Job 30:20-23)

Unraveling further, Job now says God is persecuting him. In reality, it is not God who is attacking Job, but Satan. It is Satan who has launched his fiery arsenal at Job, not God. Yet in the dark night of adversity, it is hard to discern the origin of missiles.

Job cries out that this torture goes on day after day.

Job feels that he has become a brother to jackals and a companion of ostriches. Both animals known for their lonely, whining cry. As others hear Job cry out, he sounds eerie and weird to those around him.

"Yet does not one in a heap of ruins stretch out his hand,
Or in his disaster therefore cry out for help?
Have I not wept for the one whose life is hard?
Was not my soul grieved for the needy?
When I expected good, then evil came;
When I waited for light, then darkness came.

I am seething within, and cannot relax;
Days of affliction confront me.
I go about mourning without comfort;
I stand up in the assembly and cry out for help.
I have become a brother to jackals,
And a companion of ostriches.
My skin turns black on me,
And my bones burn with fever.
Therefore my harp is turned to mourning,
And my flute to the sound of those who weep." (Job 30:24-31)

So there's the record. Job has lost the respect of his peers. He has lost the comfort of God. He has lost the answers to his prayers. He has lost his personal health. That's quite a loss.

What about your losses? You will need to itemize them. Confess them to God, write them off the books, and move on. Don't dwell on the past. Cut your losses. It's like that coffee mug that says, "Get Over It!"

Finally, here's the last principle:

DON'T LET ANY AREA GO UNCHECKED

Job evaluates every area of his life. He leaves no stone unturned. He doesn't let any area escape his scrutiny. As Job concludes his internal audit, he leaves no area of his life unexamined. Here are the major departments Job audited.

His Thought Life

First, Job looks into the secret, unseen recesses of his own heart. Specifically, he looks for sexual purity in his thought life. Talk about tackling a tough area right off the bat! Job does not claim to be sinless, but he has declared war on lust in his heart. He has made a binding commitment not to allow his eyes to look on a woman and fantasize, causing his heart to be sexually aroused.

"I have made a covenant with my eyes;
How then could I gaze at a virgin?
And what is the portion of God from above
Or the heritage of the Almighty from on high?
Is it not calamity to the unjust,

And disaster to those who work iniquity?
Does He not see my ways,
And number all my steps?" (Job 31:1-4)

Job says he had made a covenant with his eyes. This means he made a prior commitment that he would not gaze upon another woman and allow his thoughts to cross the line of propriety. That's how serious Job was about living a holy life.

What about you? Only one person can inventory this secret part of your life. This is the closed vault of your life. Is it pure? Is your mind closed to pornography? Do you resist looking at other men or women?

His Ethical Life
Second, Job examines his professional life at the office. Bottom line, he looks for honesty in his business dealings. Again, this is a painfully practical area.

"If I have walked with falsehood,
And my foot has hastened after deceit
Let Him weigh me with accurate scales,
And let God know my integrity.
If my step has turned from the way,
Or my heart followed my eyes,
Or if any spot has stuck to my hands,
Let me sow and another eat,
And let my crops be uprooted." (Job 31:5-8)

What about your ethics? Have you padded your expense account? Have you failed to report all your income to the IRS? Is your word your bond?

His Home Life
Third, Job looks at his marriage and home life. He claims that he has been faithful to his wife. He has kept his marriage vows. Fidelity is his standard.

"If my heart has been enticed by a woman,
Or I have lurked at my neighbor's doorway,

> May my wife grind for another,
> And let others kneel down over her.
> For that would be a lustful crime;
> Moreover, it would be an iniquity punishable by judges.
> For it would be fire that consumes Abaddon,
> And would uproot all my increase." (Job 31:9-12)

What's your standard? Is it forsaking all others? There's an old saying: When the cat's away, the mice will play. When you're not with the one you love, do you love the one you're with?

His Work Life

Fourth, Job looks to see how he has treated those who work for him. Has he treated his servants fairly? Yes. They register not a complaint against him. Job considers those who work for him to have been made by God and deserving of equitable treatment.

> "If I have despised the claim of my male or female slaves
> When they filed a complaint against me,
> What then could I do when God arises,
> And when He calls me to account, what will I answer Him?
> Did not He who made me in the womb make him,
> And the same one fashion us in the womb?" (Job 31:13-15)

Can you say that you treat your secretary fairly? Do you treat your employees with compassion? Would they say the same? Could those who work for you raise a complaint against you? How about those you work *for*?

His Community Life

Fifth, Job looks at his life to see how he helps widows, orphans, and the poor. How does he treat those less fortunate than he is? Job examines his life to see if he has extended charity to the orphans and the poor.

> "If I have kept the poor from their desire,
> Or have caused the eyes of the widow to fail,
> Or have eaten my morsel alone,
> And the orphan has not shared it

(But from my youth he grew up with me as with a father,
And from infancy I guided her),
If I have seen anyone perish for lack of clothing,
Or that the needy had no covering,
If his loins have not thanked me,
And if he has not been warmed with the fleece of my sheep,
If I have lifted up my hand against the orphan,
Because I saw I had support in the gate,
Let my shoulder fall from the socket,
And my arm be broken off at the elbow.
For calamity from God is a terror to me
And because of His majesty I can do nothing." (Job 31:16-23)

The charge had been brought against Job by Bildad that he had been unkind to the underprivileged. But Job's evaluation revealed the contrary. He had consistently acted with charity toward those who are helpless. He shared his resources with the poor and had been very generous with what God gave him.

What about you? Do you reach out to widows? Do you help orphans? Do you give to the poor? A real part of our Christian faith is how we treat those who are destitute.

His Financial Life

Sixth, Job investigates his attitude toward money. Did becoming rich cause him to stop loving God? Was materialism or idolatry to be found in his heart? Greed? Covetousness?

"If I have put my confidence in gold,
And called fine gold my trust,
If I have gloated because my wealth was great,
And because my hand had secured so much." (Job 31:24-25)

God increased Job's wealth, but he did not gloat over his success. He recognized that all his wealth came from God. Job knew that God had given him the ability to make money. So he held his possessions with an open hand. He did not worship his money, but kept a singleness of heart toward God.

What is your attitude toward money? Do you hold your money with an open hand? Are you gripped with a passion to have more of it? Do you live for it?

His Spiritual Life

Seventh, Job looks into his heart to see where his loyalty was. Whom did he worship? Who was his God?

> "If I have looked at the sun when it shone,
> Or the moon going in splendor,
> And my heart became secretly enticed,
> And my hand threw a kiss from my mouth,
> That too would have been an iniquity calling for judgment,
> For I would have denied God above." (Job 31:26-28)

Had he worshiped false gods? Did he worship the stars like other pagans in the land? Did he worship the moon and the sun? To the contrary, Job worshiped the one true God. He worshiped the Creator of the stars, not the stars. Resisting all forms of primitive idolatry, Job remained true in his devotion to God.

His Social Life

Eighth, Job examines the use of his tongue. Had he gloated over his enemies? Had he cursed others? Had he used his tongue for good?

> "Have I rejoiced at the extinction of my enemy,
> Or exulted when evil befell him?
> No, I have not allowed my mouth to sin
> By asking for his life in a curse.
> Have the men of my tent not said,
> 'Who can find one who has not been satisfied with his meat'?
> The alien has not lodged outside,
> For I have opened my doors to the traveler." (Job 31:29-32)

Job is an incredible man. He's not on an ego trip. What Job has expressed here is a private soliloquy. He's not standing on the street corner saying this to everyone. He is alone with God. He is no longer addressing his friends. This is between Job and God.

Job takes a hard, honest look at his life. He uses wisdom, not common sense, to help him see. He assesses his assets. He identifies his losses. He carefully looks at each area of his life. Throughout this internal investigation, Job has not tried to cover his transgressions as Adam did. Job has dealt openly with God and not tried to hide any sin.

> "Have I covered my transgressions like Adam,
> By hiding my iniquity in my bosom,
> Because I feared the great multitude,
> And the contempt of families terrified me,
> And kept silent and did not go out of doors?" (Job 31:33-34)

Finally, Job endorses every word of his oath as true. "Here is my signature," he says. He puts his John Hancock on this verbal document.

> "Oh that I had one to hear me!
> Behold, here is my signature;
> Let the Almighty answer me!
> And the indictment which my adversary has written,
> Surely I would carry it on my shoulder;
> I would bind it to myself like a crown.
> I would declare to Him the number of my steps;
> Like a prince I would approach Him." (Job 31:35-37)

His Stewardship Life

If all this introspection is not enough, Job suddenly remembers one more area of his life that he has not yet inspected. Job examines whether he has been a good steward of the land and money God gave him. He opens that area of his life up for divine investigation as well.

> "If my land cries out against me,
> And its furrows weep together;
> If I have eaten its fruit without money,
> Or have caused its owners to lose their lives,
> Let briars grow instead of wheat,
> And stinkweed instead of barley." (Job 31:35-40)

Job says that if he has not been a faithful steward of the land and resources that God has given him, then He should cause stinkweed to grow all over his land and curse it.

What has God entrusted to your care? What material resources?

What spiritual gifts and ministry opportunities? What family responsibilities? What witnessing opportunities? Have you been a faithful steward of these entrustments?

Chapter 31 concludes, "The words of Job are ended" (verse 40). These will be the final words that Job will say until the very end.

HAVE YOU TAKEN INVENTORY RECENTLY?

Let me ask you a question. Where are you in your walk with the Lord? There is an ebb and flow about our spiritual life. It is never stagnant, but constantly changing. Where are you?

Have you taken inventory recently? Have you taken a hard, honest look at your life lately? Have you used the eyes of wisdom to assess your assets and identify your losses? Have you been careful to look into every area of your life?

It's time to take inventory.

Dr. Ray Stedman told the following story about Dr. Harry Ironside. At approximately age thirteen, young Ironside was employed by a cobbler named Dan. Harry's responsibility at work was to take the pelts used in making shoes out of a vat and place them on an anvil. This meant beating the water out of them with a wooden mallet.

This process was very time-consuming. It was work that was best described as drudgery. And, as a thirteen-year-old boy, Dr. Ironside couldn't recommend it to anyone.

One day, young Harry Ironside was walking down the street. He looked in the window of another cobbler shop. He saw that cobbler take a pelt out of the vat and simply shake the water out of it. He then laid it over his lap and cut out a shoe. This competitor completely neglected the tedious work of beating the water out.

Harry was most intrigued by this. So he walked into the cobbler shop and asked the owner, "Mister, how come you don't beat the water out of your pelts like Dan down the street? I work for Dan and he makes me work long and hard to pound the water out."

The cobbler answered, "Well, that process is very time-consuming. Also, the shoes made like this don't last as long, so my customers will come back to buy shoes more often."

To the young mind of a thirteen-year-old, that sounded like pretty sound logic—especially to one with a sore right arm from pounding the water out.

Harry walked straight to talk to Dan about this. He told him what the cobbler down the street had told him. Then he asked Dan, "Why do you have me go to such trouble of pounding the water out of the pelts?"

Dan took his apron off and hung it on the nail in the wall. He said, "Harry, I need to talk to you." So they sat down together.

"Harry, I'm a Christian," Dan explained. "I know that one day I will stand before the Lord at the judgment seat of Christ. There, every pair of shoes that I have ever made will be in a large pile. In that day, there will be no time constraints. There will be no lines, no people waiting. At that time, the Lord and I will go over every pair of shoes that I have ever made.

"Jesus will say, 'Dan, you brought your stitches too close to the sole, here. We'll have to discard this pair.'

"Then, 'This pair, the nails are just right. Good work! We'll put this pair over here on this stack.' Or 'Here's one that's made perfectly. We'll put it on the right side.'

"Then he'll pick up another pair. He will say, 'Dan, you brought your stitches too close to the edge of your sole here. We'll have to discard that pair.'"

That story illustrates why it is so important for us to take inventory of our lives today. One day—on that final day—we will stand before the Lord and He will evaluate the work we've done for Him. There at the judgment seat of Christ, He will sort through our lives.

He will put all our good works—those things built with gold, silver, and precious stones—into one stack. We will be rewarded for those efforts.

Then He will put into another stack all our worthless works—those things built with wood, hay, and stubble. Our Lord will subsequently burn up and consume those works, and there will be no reward.

Because of this coming day, it is most important that each of us evaluate his life today. Right now counts forever! We must take inventory today and make necessary corrections because there is coming that final day when Christ will audit our lives.

Evaluation and corrections made today will bring our Lord's pleasure and approval in that day.

Let's prepare for that day today. Like Job, why don't you examine your life? You'll be glad you did.

It's time to take inventory!

CHAPTER 11

PUTTING THE PIECES
BACK TOGETHER

▼

Wᵉ've all had them. "Chance meetings." "Coincidental encounters." In reality, they are divine appointments orchestrated by the invisible hand of God's providence designed to bring someone across our path who will help get us back on track.

They are not encounters that we engineer or contrive. God, by His sovereign will, brings just the *right person* across our path to help us. This person comes at just the *right time*. With just the *right word*. To guide us back in the *right direction*.

Sometimes this unexpected divine appointment occurs in a restaurant, an airport, or a shopping mall. Sometimes it occurs in a home, or an office. Sometimes it occurs on the golf course or at a retreat. Wherever, they are orchestrated by God for our good.

One of these "chance encounters" occurred recently to help bring clarity back to my life vision. I found myself sitting in the majestic Smoky Mountains outside Asheville, North Carolina, last summer. I was attending The Cove, the Billy Graham Conference Center, for a time of much needed spiritual renewal. The fact is, I was emotionally burned out and spiritually depleted, in need of rest and revival.

Originally, I had signed up for the conference because Ray Stedman was to teach. But Dr. Stedman became terribly ill, later to die. Dr. Johnny Miller, who was to co-teach the conference, was now thrust into the role of teaching all the sessions.

There's no doubt in my mind that this entire conference was for me. Everyone else was sitting in on what God wanted to say to me personally.

At dinner one evening, I "happened" to be seated between Johnny Miller and his wife. It was a divine appointment.

Dr. Miller and I set up a time to visit privately together. I'll never forget sitting on the back veranda of The Cove's conference center, leaning back in a rocking chair, listening to his words of counsel, as I stared out with misty eyes across the cloud-filled valleys of the Smokies.

What he shared with me that day was exactly what I needed. It was the *right word*. At the *right time*. To point me back in the *right direction*.

His words put my life back into focus. I could suddenly see again. The obscuring clouds began to lift. The path became clear again. The direction was again revealed. I could now see an opening to chip my ball back onto the fairway.

This was God's ordained means for getting me back on track. A divine appointment. Not a vision in the sky. Not a voice from above. But God speaking to me through another person—a godly believer full of wisdom and insight.

Why do I mention this? Because Job is about to experience the same. Unsolicited and unsought by Job, God will bring the *right person* into his life, who will help him refocus on God and recapture the eternal perspective he needs.

His name is Elihu. He will bring to Job the *right word*. At the *right time*. To point him back in the *right direction*.

What Elihu will do for Job is help him reestablish a proper view of God. That's what was lacking in Job's life. A right view of God.

Life can be so confusing. Sometimes the pieces just don't seem to fit. We cannot understand why something has happened. That's when we need to see God again for who He is. Only then will the big picture come back into focus.

That is what Elihu will do for Job. Job has been unable to put all the pieces together. But like a skilled counselor, Elihu will help Job see God again.

A MAN NAMED ELIHU

We are now introduced to a new voice. It is the voice of a young man. A bystander who has been overhearing this debate between Job and his friends. Having listened to and analyzed the arguments, Elihu will now speak and accurately put his finger on the problem: Job must recapture a right view of God.

Where Eliphaz, Bildad, and Zophar failed, Elihu will succeed in helping point Job in the right direction. In the end, God will rebuke Eliphaz, Bildad, and Zophar, but not Elihu, because his assessment is on target. Job will not rebut Elihu. His silence indicates that Elihu's words are correct. As Job listened silently, so we, too, should listen carefully to Elihu's counsel.

An overview of Elihu's message will be helpful. Elihu will speak four times to Job. Each is designed to correct Job's wrong picture of God. Elihu will say the following: (1) God is not silent (Job 33), (2) God is not unjust (Job 34), (3) God is not uncaring (Job 35), and (4) God is not powerless (Job 36–37). Each of these truths is necessary to have a right, balanced, and complete view of God.

Before Elihu launches his discourses, he will introduce himself to Job and his friends. As he does, feel for the emotion of his voice.

> Then these three men ceased answering Job, because he was
> righteous in his own eyes. But the anger of Elihu the son of
> Barachel the Buzite, of the family of Ram burned; against Job
> his anger burned, because he justified himself before God. And
> his anger burned against his three friends because they had
> found no answer, and yet had condemned Job. (Job 32:1-3)

Elihu is angered at both sides. He is angry with Job because Job has developed a self-righteous attitude. But he is also angry with Eliphaz, Bildad, and Zophar because they have misrepresented God. Like a steaming teakettle on a hot stove, Elihu's pent-up anger seethes with deep passion and intensity.

> So Elihu the son of Barachel the Buzite spoke out and said,
> "I am young in years and you are old;
> Therefore I was shy and afraid to tell you what I think.
> I thought age should speak,
> And increased years should teach wisdom.

But it is a spirit in man,
And the breath of the Almighty gives them understanding.
The abundant in years may not be wise,
Nor may elders understand justice.
So I say, 'Listen to me,
I too will tell what I think.' " (Job 32:6-10)

Young Elihu has been silent to this point and, out of respect for his elders, has allowed them to speak first. Those mature in years are known for their wisdom. Now Elihu feels compelled to speak and set matters right. He pleads for a hearing with Job and his three friends.

True wisdom is God-given, not learned from experience over years. As James tells us, "If any of you lacks wisdom, let him ask of God, who gives to all men generously and without reproach, and it will be given to him" (James 1:5).

"Behold, I waited for your words,
I listened to your reasonings,
While you pondered what to say.
I even paid close attention to you,
Indeed, there was no one who refuted Job,
Not one of you who answered his words.
Do not say,
'We have found wisdom;
God will rout him, not man.'
For he has not arranged his words against me;
Nor will I reply to him with your arguments." (Job 32:11-14)

Elihu says, "I paid close attention to you men, and I don't think you properly refuted Job. Not one of you answered his words." That was certainly true. They were so busy reloading their guns after they spoke that they never heard what he said.

We can be that way, can't we, when we're talking to somebody? The whole time they are talking to us, we're thinking about what we're going to say next.

"They are dismayed, they answer no more;
Words have failed them.

And shall I wait, because they do not speak,
Because they stop and answer no more?
I too will answer my share,
I also will tell my opinion.
For I am full of words;
The spirit within me constrains me." (Job 32:15-18)

Elihu says the three friends are dismayed, worn down, and tired.
They have nothing more to say. But he has something to say.

"Behold, my belly is like unvented wine,
Like new wineskins it is about to burst.
Let me speak that I may get relief;
Let me open my lips and answer.
Let me now be partial to no one;
Nor flatter any man.
For I do not know how to flatter,
Else my Maker would soon take me away." (Job 32:19-22)

Elihu feels very strongly about what he has to say. God has been
getting a bum rap through these discussions. So, filled with a godly
jealousy, Elihu wants to put God in the right light.

Having now completed his introductory remarks, Elihu will speak
to Job in four separate messages. Each message is an important piece to
the puzzle that reestablishes a right view of God. Here's the first one.

GOD IS NOT SILENT!

Job has been saying that God is *not* speaking to him. But Elihu says that
God *has* been speaking. He says that Job's suffering is God speaking
to him. However, Job's pain is not God speaking as Job's friends were
saying ("You are a sinner"). Instead, God is saying something entirely
different.

First, Elihu politely asks for a hearing with Job. No use talking if
no one is listening, right? He promises to speak with honesty, humility,
and courtesy.

"However now, Job, please hear my speech,
And listen to all my words.

Behold now, I open my mouth,
My tongue in my mouth speaks.
My words are from the uprightness of my heart;
And my lips speak knowledge sincerely.
The Spirit of God has made me,
And the breath of the Almighty gives me life.
Refute me if you can;
Array yourselves before me, take your stand.
Behold, I belong to God like you;
I too have been formed out of the clay.
Behold, no fear of me should terrify you,
Nor should my pressure weigh heavily on you." (Job 33:1-7)

Second, Elihu begins to analyze what Job has said. He quotes Job, indicating he had been carefully listening to Job's words. Here are Job's words quoted back to him by Elihu.

"Surely you have spoken in my hearing,
And I have heard the sound of your words:
'I am pure, without transgression;
I am innocent and there is no guilt in me.
Behold, He invents pretexts against me;
He counts me as His enemy.
He puts my feet in the stocks;
He watches all my paths.'" (Job 33:8-11)

Job has claimed that God mistreated him for no reason. Arbitrarily. Capriciously. Job firmly believes he is innocent and that God has invented charges against him. He feels that God is treating him like one of His enemies, not one of His children.

Elihu directly confronts Job and says, "You're wrong, buddy. God is infinitely greater than man. So stop your complaining."

"Behold, let me tell you, you are not right in this,
For God is greater than man.
Why do you complain against Him,
That He does not give an account of all His doings?
Indeed God speaks once,
Or twice, yet no one notices it." (Job 33:12-14)

Elihu says that God is beyond us, infinitely greater than our ability to grasp and understand. So be careful before you complain against God. It may be out of ignorance.

Job has contended that God will not answer him. But Elihu responds that God has been speaking to him. The problem is, Job just hasn't been listening.

He Speaks Through Our Dreams
Elihu now reveals how God would speak to Job. First, in a dream.

> "In a dream, a vision of the night,
> When sound sleep falls on men,
> While they slumber in their beds,
> Then He opens the ears of men,
> And seals their instruction,
> That He may turn man aside from his conduct,
> And keep man from pride;
> He keeps back his soul from the pit,
> And his life from passing over into Sheol."
>   (Job 33:15-18)

To keep a man from destroying himself, God sends him a terrifying dream to turn him back from the pit of destruction. I'm not saying that we should begin analyzing our dreams, but many times they are the expression of our subconscious. What we are thinking about will show up in our dreams. In our dreams God may speak a word of warning to us.

He Speaks Through Our Pain
Another way God speaks to us is in our pain. Lovingly, God chastens us to turn us away from sin.

> "Man is also chastened with pain on his bed,
> And with unceasing complaint in his bones;
> So that his life loathes bread,
> And his soul favorite food.
> His flesh wastes away from sight,
> And his bones which were not seen stick out.
> Then his soul draws near to the pit,

And his life to those who bring death."
(Job 33:19-22)

C. S. Lewis wrote, "God whispers to us in our pleasures, speaks in our consciences, but shouts in our pains. It is His megaphone to rouse a deaf world."

I agree. God sure gets my attention with pain. We see life in a far different perspective when we are hurting. Our values and priorities change instantly.

What does God say to us in our pain? He reveals to us what is really important in life. There is nothing like pain to teach us what is of eternal value in this world.

He Speaks Through Others

God speaks to us a third way—through angels, who are God's messengers sent with God's message.

"If there is an angel as mediator for him,
One out of a thousand,
To remind a man what is right for him,
Then let him be gracious to him, and say,
'Deliver him from going down to the pit,
I have found a ransom';
Let his flesh become fresher than in youth,
Let him return to the days of his youthful vigor;
Then he will pray to God, and He will accept him,
That he may see His face with joy,
And He may restore His righteousness to man." (Job 33:23-26)

God has numerous angels to instruct His saints. The word *angel* can mean a heavenly being, or a human messenger who is like a counselor, sent to represent God to man. Elihu is such a mediator through whom God is speaking to Job. Job should accept Elihu's message and pray to God, then God would reveal Himself to Job and restore him.

"He will sing to men and say,
'I have sinned and perverted what is right,
And it is not proper for me.

He [God] has redeemed my soul from going to the pit,
And my life shall see the light.' "
(Job 33:27-28)

God is saying to Job through Elihu, "Job, if you would pray to God and repent of your bitterness, then you would have a dynamic testimony to sing before your peers."

"Behold, God does all these oftentimes with men,
To bring back his soul from the pit,
That he may be enlightened with the light of life."
(Job 33:29-30)

Elihu says that God does speak to us in each of those ways to enlighten us. God *is* speaking. He is not silent.

"Pay attention, O Job, listen to me;
Keep silent and let me speak.
Then if you have anything to say, answer me;
Speak, for I desire to justify you.
If not, listen to me;
Keep silent, and I will teach you wisdom." (Job 33:31-33)

Can you think of how God has dramatically spoken to you in your life? How has God used suffering as a wake-up call? How has He spoken to you through others?

That's the first piece to the puzzle. God is not silent.

GOD IS NOT UNJUST!

Here is Elihu's second speech. It is a rebuttal of Job's contention that God is unfair. As Job looked at life, he concluded that there is no profit to loving and obeying God. "Look what it's brought me. Only suffering and heartache." So, Elihu responds to this charge.

Again, Elihu invites Job and his three friends to listen to his argument.

Then Elihu continued and said,
"Hear my words, you wise men,
And listen to me,

You who know.
For the ear tests words,
As the palate tastes food.
Let us choose for ourselves what is right;
Let us know among ourselves what is good." (Job 34:1-4)

Elihu now quotes what Job said about God.

"For Job has said, 'I am righteous,
But God has taken away my right;
Should I lie concerning my right?
My wound is incurable, though I am without transgression.'
What man is like Job,
Who drinks up derision like water,
Who goes in company with the workers of iniquity,
And walks with wicked men?
For he has said, 'It profits a man nothing
When he is pleased with God.' " (Job 34:5-9)

Job has contended all along that he is righteous. He has been wounded incurably, even though he is without sin. What profit is there in serving God if suffering is the reward? Job claims that God has sentenced an innocent man.

At this point, Job is dangerously close to buying into Satan's lies. The Devil said Job wouldn't worship God if He took away Job's material prosperity. Job is almost at that point. He is almost ready to throw in the towel. "Why bother worshiping God if this is what it brings me?"

He Always Does Right

Elihu will now rebut Job. Elihu states that God cannot be unjust. He is always true to His character. God always acts in accordance to His nature.

"Therefore, listen to me, you men of understanding.
Far be it from God to do wickedness,
And from the Almighty to do wrong.
For He pays a man according to his work,
And makes him find it according to his way.

> Surely, God will not act wickedly,
> And the Almighty will not pervert justice."
>   (Job 34:10-12)

God will judge the wicked no matter how long it may take. He may not settle his accounts immediately, but one day He will do it. There will be a Payday someday. God will one day give the unrighteous what he deserves.

Then Elihu contended that God is beyond accountability to anyone. He is the sovereign Authority over all the universe and answerable to no one.

> "Who gave Him authority over the earth?
> And who has laid on Him the whole world?
> If He should determine to do so,
> If He should gather to Himself His spirit and His breath,
> All flesh would perish together,
> And man would return to dust." (Job 34:13-15)

Job has been bellyaching and saying, "Where is God?" Elihu says, "God is here. If God were to withdraw Himself for one second from our lives, we would all perish! God alone has the power to continue or withdraw a man's life."

Next, Elihu declares that God is the impartial Ruler of the universe. He judges mighty kings and the wealthy without any partiality.

> "But if you have understanding, hear this;
> Listen to the sound of my words.
> Shall one who hates justice rule?
> And will you condemn a righteous mighty one,
> Who says to a king, 'Worthless one,'
> To nobles, 'Wicked ones';
> Who shows no partiality to princes,
> Nor regards the rich above the poor,
> For they all are the work of His hands?
> In a moment they die, and at midnight
> People are shaken and pass away,
> And the mighty are taken away without a hand."
>   (Job 34:16-20)

Men are partial and play favorites. But God doesn't. Men flatter kings to keep them happy, but God will judge a king when he's wrong. God has the power to judge a king whom men tremble before.

Then, Elihu extols God as the omniscient Judge who sees all the steps of man. God need not investigate a case before He judges because He sees even in the dark all the ways of man.

> "For His eyes are upon the ways of a man,
> And He sees all his steps.
> There is no darkness or deep shadow
> Where the workers of iniquity may hide themselves.
> For He does not need to consider a man further,
> That he should go before God in judgment.
> He breaks in pieces mighty men without inquiry,
> And sets others in their place.
> Therefore He knows their works." (Job 34:21-25)

Nothing escapes the all-seeing gaze of God. He sees the heart and understands all man's ways. Don't think just because God has not yet judged the wicked that He is blind to their iniquity. In reality, God sees all their sin!

> "And He overthrows them in the night,
> And they are crushed.
> He strikes them like the wicked
> In a public place,
> Because they turned aside from following Him,
> And had no regard for any of His ways;
> So that they caused the cry of the poor to come to Him,
> And that He might hear the cry of the afflicted—
> When He keeps quiet, who then can condemn?
> And when He hides His face, who then can behold Him,
> That is, in regard to both nation and man?—
> So that godless men should not rule,
> Nor be snares of the people." (Job 34:25-30)

Finally, Elihu argues that God is the absolute Executor of the universe who will overthrow the wicked when they least suspect it. Whether at night when they cannot see, or in a public place in broad daylight,

God will eventually strike with judgment all who disobey Him.

God is the CEO of the galaxy. If God chooses to remain silent and not explain what He is doing, who can charge God with wrongdoing? Just because He has not explained His actions to us does not mean that God does not have His reasons.

Elihu now applies all this to Job. Job may ask God why he is suffering, but he may not ask God to act as he thinks He should.

> "For has anyone said to God,
> 'I have borne chastisement;
> I will not offend anymore;
> Teach Thou me what I do not see;
> If I have done iniquity,
> I will do it no more'?
> Shall He recompense on your terms, because you have
>   rejected it?
> For you must choose, and not I;
> Therefore declare what you know." (Job 34:31-33)

Demanding that God explain Himself to Job is crossing the line. He may ask God to reveal his sin, but not demand an explanation as if God were accountable to Job. That's going too far. In conclusion, Elihu quotes Job's three friends, who have said that Job speaks without understanding.

> "Men of understanding will say to me,
> And a wise man who hears me,
> 'Job speaks without knowledge,
> And his words are without wisdom.
> Job ought to be tried to the limit,
> Because he answers like wicked men.
> For he adds rebellion to his sin;
> He claps his hands among us,
> And multiplies his words against God.'" (Job 34:34-37)

They feel like Job ought to be prosecuted to the fullest extent of the law for speaking like a wicked man. Job has added a rebellious attitude to whatever sin he first committed to get into this mess.

Such is the reality of life. We suffer and become discouraged, causing us to lose sight of God. When life seems unfair, it causes us to question God's goodness.

But God is fair. God does reward us for our pain. His reward may come in this lifetime. Or it may come in that final day. We must always remember that we're not home yet. God will reward us, just not yet.

Remember, you're not home yet.

GOD IS NOT UNCARING

Elihu now begins his third speech and declares to Job that God is not distant in our suffering. No, God is right here with us in our pain. God may feel very distant when we hurt, but in reality, that's when He is the closest.

Do you see the first two pieces? God is not silent. God is not unjust. Here's the third piece to the puzzle.

Once again, Elihu begins by quoting Job. He certainly has been listening carefully to what Job was saying. That's more than we can say for Job's other friends.

> Then Elihu continued and said,
> "Do you think this is according to justice?
> Do you say, 'My righteousness is more than God's'?
> For you say, 'What advantage will it be to You?
> What profit shall I have, more than if I had sinned?'"
> (Job 35:1-3)

Elihu restates Job's contention that living righteously profits nothing. It appears there is no reward for the righteous.

Elihu will now correct Job and his friends' misunderstanding about God.

> "I will answer you,
> And your friends with you.
> Look at the heavens and see;
> And behold the clouds—they are higher than you.
> If you have sinned, what do you accomplish against Him?
> And if your transgressions are many, what do you do to Him?
> If you are righteous, what do you give to Him?
> Or what does He receive from your hand?
> Your wickedness is for a man like yourself,
> And your righteousness is for a son of man." (Job 35:4-8)

Elihu points to the clouds hovering overhead. "Do you see those clouds floating above? They are out of your reach. So is God. He is far above you and beyond your grasp."

God said through Isaiah the prophet,

"For My thoughts are not your thoughts,
Neither are your ways My ways," declares the LORD.
"For as the heavens are higher than the earth,
So are My ways higher than your ways,
And My thoughts than your thoughts." (Isaiah 55:8-9)

Whether man sins or is righteous, God is not affected by man's actions. God exists above our lives. Our actions affect us and our fellow man. But they won't change God.

He Is with Us

Now Elihu moves into the main point of the third speech. God is not distant when we suffer. He is with us.

"Because of the multitude of oppressions they cry out;
They cry for help because of the arm of the mighty.
But no one says, 'Where is God my Maker,
Who gives songs in the night,
Who teaches us more than the beasts of the earth,
And makes us wiser than the birds of the heavens?'"
     (Job 35:9-11)

When we are suffering, we cry out to God for help. At such a time, no one can say, "God is not there for me." No one can say, "Where is God, my Maker?" because God will never leave us. In our darkest hour, God's presence gives us a song in the night. God gives His peace and comfort to us, which is greater than the pain of our suffering. In our time of greatest need, God is right there with us.

Maybe you're at that place in your life now. Maybe you want things to work out in a particular area. Maybe you want your relationship with your spouse to work out. Maybe you want your career to work out. Maybe you want your children's lives to work out. While you are waiting, remember that God is there with you. He gives His peace and comfort. We must simply wait on Him.

In a man's dream, he had a vision of walking through life on a sandy beach with Jesus by his side. As he looked back at the footprints in the sand, he noticed that at the troublesome spots of his life only one set of footprints marked the sand. The man asked Jesus where the Lord had been during those troublesome times. Jesus replied, "That single set of footprints is mine. Then I was carrying you and your burden."

He Hears Us

Elihu continues his discourse, addressing whose prayer God does, and does not, answer.

> "There they cry out, but He does not answer
> Because of the pride of evil men.
> Surely God will not listen to an empty cry,
> Nor will the Almighty regard it." (Job 35:12-13)

The only time God does not answer is when our hearts are proud and lifted up. It's not until we come to the end of ourselves that we cry out to God in true faith. God doesn't answer the proud.

> "How much less when you say you do not behold Him,
> The case is before Him, and you must wait for Him!
> And now, because He has not visited in His anger,
> Nor has He acknowledged transgression well,
> So Job opens his mouth emptily;
> He multiplies words without knowledge." (Job 35:14-16)

Elihu refers to Job's words about wanting to present his case before God. He says, "Job, wait on God. He hears you and He is reaching out to you. He will give you songs in the night. Just wait on His perfect timing."

We have seen the first three pieces of the puzzle: God is not silent; God is not unjust; God is not distant. Now, here's the fourth.

GOD IS NOT POWERLESS!

In Elihu's fourth and final speech, he extols the greatness of God's power in creation. God is not impotent! He is mightily running the universe. Nothing is out of control!

Then Elihu continued and said,
"Wait for me a little, and I will show you
That there is yet more to be said in God's behalf.
I will fetch my knowledge from afar,
And I will ascribe righteousness to my Maker.
For truly my words are not false;
One who is perfect in knowledge is with you."
        (Job 36:1-4)

His Power over Humankind

Elihu claims to be speaking with God's authority. First, he declares that God is almighty and powerful.

"Behold, God is mighty but does not despise any;
He is mighty in strength of understanding.
He does not keep the wicked alive,
But gives justice to the afflicted.
He does not withdraw His eyes from the righteous;
But with kings on the throne
He has seated them forever, and they are exalted.
And if they are bound in fetters,
And are caught in the cords of affliction,
Then he declares to them their work
And their transgressions, that they have magnified themselves.
And He opens their ear to instruction,
And commands that they return from evil."
        (Job 36:5-10)

God is powerful to judge the wicked and help the afflicted. He does not misuse His power. He uses His power to reward the righteous and punish sinners.

"If they hear and serve Him,
They shall end their days in prosperity,
And their years in pleasures.
But if they do not hear, they shall perish by the sword,
And they shall die without knowledge." (Job 36:11-12)

There are two responses to suffering for the righteous. Either obey God's Word and enjoy prosperity, or disobey and perish.

"But the godless in heart lay up anger;
They do not cry for help when He binds them.
They die in youth,
And their life perishes among the cult prostitutes.
He delivers the afflicted in their affliction,
And opens their ear in time of oppression.
Then indeed, He enticed you from the mouth of distress,
Instead of it, a broad place with no constraint;
And that which was set on your table was full of fatness."
    (Job 36:13-16)

When the godless perish, it is not for lack of power on God's part to save them. Rather, it's because they refuse to yield to God and cry out to Him for help. But God powerfully delivers the godly because they hear and respond to the voice of God in their suffering.

"But you were full of judgment on the wicked;
Judgment and justice take hold of you.
Beware lest wrath entice you to scoffing;
And do not let the greatness of the ransom turn you aside.
Will your riches keep you from distress,
Or all the forces of your strength?
Do not long for the night,
When people vanish in their place.
Be careful, do not turn to evil;
For you have preferred this to affliction.
Behold, God is exalted in His power;
Who is a teacher like Him?
Who has appointed Him His way,
And who has said, 'Thou hast done wrong'?" (Job 36:17-23)

Elihu now applies this teaching about God's power to Job. These verses are a strong warning to Job not to forsake God's way and turn to evil. He should be careful not to sin by complaining.

"Remember that you should exalt His work,
Of which men have sung.
All men have seen it;

Man beholds from afar.
Behold, God is exalted, and we do not know Him;
The number of His years is unsearchable." (Job 36:24-26)

Elihu tells Job that he should praise God for His great works. He should magnify God's name, not criticize Him, for His majestic deeds. Exalt Him!

His Power over Nature
Elihu describes God's great power as seen in an autumn storm.

"For He draws up the drops of water,
They distill rain from the mist,
Which the clouds pour down,
They drip upon man abundantly.
Can anyone understand the spreading of the clouds,
The thundering of His pavilion?
Behold, He spreads His lightning about Him,
And He covers the depths of the sea.
For by these He judges peoples;
He gives food in abundance.
He covers His hands with the lightning,
And commands it to strike the mark.
Its noise declares His presence;
The cattle also, concerning what is coming up." (Job 36:27-33)

God's mighty power is seen in evaporation and rain, in clouds and thunder, in lightning on the flooding sea. All these works in nature display God's power and greatness. He uses these powers both for blessing and judgment. Elihu says, "Job, you need to see that God is absolutely in control of all His universe. God sovereignly reigns on His throne."

Elihu then gives a graphic description of an electrical storm. It is possible that a thunderstorm actually did begin to break out as Elihu was speaking to Job. Perhaps Elihu uses it as an example of God's mighty power.

"At this also my heart trembles,
And leaps from its place.

Listen closely to the thunder of His voice,
And the rumbling that goes out from His mouth.
Under the whole heaven He lets it loose,
And His lightning to the ends of the earth.
After it, a voice roars;
He thunders with His majestic voice;
And He does not restrain the lightnings when His voice is
    heard.
God thunders with His voice wondrously,
Doing great things which we cannot comprehend." (Job 37:1-5)

This electrical summer storm is awesome and terrifying. Thunder is roaring. Lightning is cracking. The sky is illuminated. This whole scene is frightening and terrifying.

God is like this. Awe-inspiring and powerful. He cannot be controlled by man. Threatening and terrifying. That is God.

"For to the snow He says, 'Fall on the earth,'
And to the downpour and the rain, 'Be strong.'
He seals the hand of every man,
That all men may know His work.
Then the beast goes into its lair,
And remains in its den.
Out of the south comes the storm,
And out of the north the cold.
From the breath of God ice is made,
And the expanse of the waters is frozen." (Job 37:6-10)

Elihu now describes a winter storm. God commands it. He tells the snow and ice to come. Man is helpless when it comes, completely at God's mercy.

"Also with moisture He loads the thick cloud;
He disperses the cloud of His lightning.
And it changes direction, turning around by His guidance,
That it may do whatever He commands it
On the face of the inhabited earth.
Whether for correction, or for His world,
Or for lovingkindness, He causes it to happen." (Job 37:11-13)

Next, Elihu says that God also directs the tornadoes and whirl-winds. He controls all the elements of nature that can render man powerless.

> "Listen to this, O Job,
> Stand and consider the wonders of God.
> Do you know how God establishes them,
> And makes the lightning of His cloud to shine?
> Do you know about the layers of the thick clouds,
> The wonders of one perfect in knowledge,
> You whose garments are hot,
> When the land is still because of the south wind?
> Can you, with Him, spread out the skies,
> Strong as a molten mirror?
> Teach us what we shall say to Him;
> We cannot arrange our case because of darkness.
> Shall it be told Him that I would speak?
> Or should a man say that he would be swallowed up?"
>   (Job 37:14-20)

Elihu challenges Job to carefully consider God's power over nature. Man cannot grasp how inscrutable are God's ways. It is a mystery to man. Neither can man understand how God is using His power to affect man's daily life.

Job cannot understand God's power over the clouds and the snow, the ice and the thunderstorm. Neither can he understand God's control over his life. Job cannot explain them. He cannot duplicate them. He cannot command them.

> "And now men do not see the light which is bright in the skies;
> But the wind has passed and cleared them.
> Out of the north comes golden splendor;
> Around God is awesome majesty.
> The Almighty—we cannot find Him;
> He is exalted in power;
> And He will not do violence to justice and abundant
>   righteousness.
> Therefore men fear Him;
> He does not regard any who are wise of heart." (Job 37:21-24)

Elihu says, "Job, trust that God will do what is right in your life. Don't pretend that you have the answers. If you do, God will disregard you. Instead, fear God and hold Him in reverential awe. God will honor you and make it right."

Do you see the four truths that Elihu has said to Job? He said God restores us with our suffering. God rewards us for our suffering. God reaches out to us in our suffering. And God reigns over us in our suffering.

Elihu brings to Job a totally different perspective on his sufferings. Job's friends told him that he is suffering because he had committed some grievous sin in his life. But Elihu says, "Oh no, it's not because you have sinned. It's in order to keep you from sinning further and to draw you closer to your God and to teach you how God is sovereignly in control over the affairs of your life, and to show you how God does reward the righteous."

CHAPTER 12

SPEECHLESS, SPITLESS, AND ALL SHOOK UP

▼

N ever before had a Senate hearing drawn the attention that the Clarence Thomas hearing drew. Never.

It was live. High drama. Pure human interest. The Big Shootout at the D.C. Corral.

The Clarence Thomas confirmation hearings started out innocently enough. Until the last-minute testimony of Anita Hill. Instantly, the focus shifted to the alleged moral turpitude of Judge Thomas.

One of the highest judges in the land suddenly found himself accused of sexual harassment. The charge was blatantly serious: the judge was unfit to sit on the bench.

Never mind that evidence was lacking. Witnesses were absent. Groundless charges were flying. Emotions were riding high.

As the entire nation watched, there sat the Senate Judiciary Committee presiding over the interrogation. Never mind that there sat Senator Joseph Biden, the chairman, who himself had been charged with plagiarism. Never mind that there sat Senator Teddy Kennedy, whose own morality relating to sexual harassment could be seriously questioned. Never mind.

The fact is that the judge who had been nominated to sit on the highest court of the land—the Supreme Court—was undergoing an unparalleled character assassination with unsubstantiated innuendos. This eleventh-hour attack was threatening to ruin his life and keep him off the Supreme Court.

Judge Clarence Thomas found himself in the awkward and embarrassing position of having to defend himself. Awkward, but necessary.

The issue was critical. Was the judge morally competent to sit on the Supreme Court? That was the issue.

Eventually, Judge Thomas was cleared of wrongdoing. The judge was found to be competent to sit on the judge's bench in the highest court of the land.

Take the emotion of that Senate hearing and multiply it a billion times and it only begins to scratch the surface of the universal drama between God and Job. Job has charged THE Supreme Court Judge of Heaven and earth with being unfit to sit upon His throne.

The issue at stake is the Judge's competency to rule the universe. Specifically, the Judge's competency to rule Job's life. Not to mention your life and mine.

Is God qualified to preside over all creation? That is the issue.

The Creator has been challenged by His creature. God, the Judge of all the universe, has been charged with wrongdoing and now must defend Himself. But rather than take the witness stand, God puts Job, the plaintiff, on the stand and examines him.

No other witness is brought forward. No other evidence is submitted. No other prosecutors cross-examine. God takes control of the entire court scene. He will ask Job over seventy—not seven, but seventy-plus—questions.

What follows is the longest conversation in the Bible in which God speaks. If you can learn about someone by his words, there is much for us to learn about God here.

JOB TAKES THE WITNESS STAND

God now breaks His long silence and speaks to Job. Directly. Audibly. Powerfully.

> Then the LORD answered Job out of the whirlwind and said,
> "Who is this that darkens counsel
> By words without knowledge?
> Now gird up your loins like a man,

And I will ask you, and you instruct Me!"
(Job 38:1-3)

A fierce whirlwind blows across the landscape. God once spoke to Moses from a burning bush. He now speaks to Job from a turbulent twister. Like a mighty storm, the voice of God thunders. This is no still, quiet voice, but God speaking with the force of a tornado.

God challenges Job, "Gird up your loins!" This was a military command that meant to get ready for battle. God says, "Get your helmet on and buckle up because you and I are fixing to go one on one."

That reminds me of a story told about Muhammad Ali, the undisputed heavyweight champion of the world. Ali was on an airplane that was preparing to take off. Proclaiming himself the greatest, the champ was walking up and down the aisle and signing autographs.

A stewardess approached the champ and asked him to sit down and buckle his seat belt.

Not wanting to be told what to do, Ali said, "Superman don't need no seat belt."

To which the stewardess replied, stone-faced, "Yeah, and Superman don't need no *airplane* either. Now, sit down and buckle up."

That is precisely what God is saying to Job. "Sit down and buckle up! I've got some questions to ask you."

Surprisingly, God will answer not one of Job's objections about His fairness. Instead, God will do the examining. He will ask Job ten questions concerning the physical creation. If Job could not understand the workings of God's physical creation, how could he possibly understand the far more profound workings of God in the moral order.

Again, don't miss the biting sarcasm behind these questions. If this weren't so serious, it would be hilariously funny.

Who Made the Earth?
First, God quizzes Job about the planet earth.

"Where were you when I laid the foundation of the earth!
Tell Me, if you have understanding,
Who set its measurements, since you know?
Or who stretched the line on it?
On what were its bases sunk?
Or who laid its cornerstone,

When the morning stars sang together,
And all the sons of God shouted for joy?" (Job 38:4-7)

The Creator is pictured as a builder who surveys the land, marks off the site, pours the foundation, and erects the building. With a deliberate jab, God scratches His head and says, "Job, you'll have to help me. I forgot where you were when I created the world." His question was designed to expose Job's ignorance and impotence. Obviously, Job was not on the scene when God created the earth.

The implication is clear. Since Job was not present at creation, he knows nothing about how God created the earth. Therefore, how could he possibly know much about God's moral government? If Job is ignorant of the planet earth, how could he possibly understand the invisible, spiritual world? It is an argument from the lesser to the greater. If Job could not explain creation, how could he possibly explain God?

"Earth to Job, earth to Job." No answer.

Who Enclosed the Sea?

Second, God examines Job about the ocean.

"Or who enclosed the sea with doors,
When, bursting forth, it went out from the womb;
When I made a cloud its garment,
And thick darkness its swaddling band,
And I placed boundaries on it,
And I set a bolt and doors,
And I said, 'Thus far you shall come, but no farther;
And here shall your proud waves stop'?" (Job 38:8-11)

Who established the coastlines and shorelines of the ocean? Who marked the boundaries of the sea? The Creator is pictured as a delivering mother who gives birth to the seas and then clothes the infant creation with clouds, darkness, and coastlines.

There is only silence from Job. Dead silence. If the ocean knows its place, so should man.

Job's feeling a little seasick. No answer.

Who Commands the Sun?

Third, God asks a few questions about the dawn.

"Have you ever in your life commanded the morning,
And caused the dawn to know its place;
That it might take hold of the ends of the earth,
And the wicked be shaken out of it?
It is changed like clay under the seal;
And they stand forth like a garment.
And from the wicked their light is withheld,
And the uplifted arm is broken." (Job 38:12-15)

Like a general commanding his troops, God orders the dawn to rise each morning. Something Job has never done. Because only the Creator can command the sun, why should Job, who can't command the sun, think he can command *God*?

The rising of the sun exposes evil deeds and restrains the criminal. So should Job be enlightened in his vicious attack upon God's fairness and justice.

Job's not feeling too bright. No answer.

Have You Explored the Underworld?
Fourth, God moves to the study of underground springs.

"Have you entered into the springs of the sea?
Or have you walked in the recesses of the deep?
Have the gates of death been revealed to you?
Or have you seen the gates of deep darkness?"
    (Job 38:16-17)

God questions Job about the subterranean waters below the earth's surface. "Job, do you understand the deep things under the earth? Have you gone down below the surface and searched out the underground springs that I have placed there? You haven't, have you, Job? It's all just a mystery to you, isn't it? Then, Job, how could I possibly explain to you what I am doing in your life? How could you possibly understand the deep, mysterious things of how I am working out My spiritual Kingdom. Job, if I were to explain to you why I was bringing you through this time of trial and suffering, it would be like trying to pour the Atlantic Ocean into a Dixie Cup. It just wouldn't fit."

Job could not see nor understand the deep things of the physical earth. So, how could he possibly understand the deep things of God?

This too deep for you, Job? No answer.

Who Orders the Light?

Fifth, God quizzes Job about the sun.

> "Where is the way to the dwelling of light?
> And darkness, where is its place,
> That you may take it to its territory,
> And that you may discern the paths to its home?
> You know, for you were born then,
> And the number of your days is great!" (Job 38:19-21)

Sarcastically, God questions Job about where the sun goes at night. Where does the darkness go during the day? Who turns on and off the universe's light switch? Surely Job must know because he was present at creation when God said "Let there be light."

If Job couldn't answer these basic questions, how could he presume to question God's running the universe? It's an argument from the lesser to the greater. If Job couldn't understand light, he must surely be in the dark about God.

Job's still in the dark and can't find the switch. No answer.

Who Sends Snow and Hail?

Sixth, God quizzes Job about the lower atmosphere.

> "Have you entered the storehouses of the snow,
> Or have you seen the storehouses of the hail,
> Which I have reserved for the time of distress,
> For the day of war and battle?
> Where is the way that the light is divided,
> Or the east wind scattered on the earth?" (Job 38:22-24)

Did Job understand the giant refrigerators in the sky where God keeps the snow and hail? How about where God keeps His lightning and winds? Did Job understand such mysteries?

No one completely understands such common occurrences as snow, much less commands them. Only God has that power.

If Job could not explain such common events in nature, how could he possibly explain God's working in providence? He couldn't.

Job's feeling a bit flaky now. All hail is breaking loose. No answer.

Who Sends the Rain and Lightning?
Seventh, God asks Job about a flood.

> "Who has cleft a channel for the flood,
> Or a way for the thunderbolt;
> To bring rain on a land without people,
> On a desert without a man in it,
> To satisfy the waste and desolate land,
> And to make the seeds of grass to sprout?
> Has the rain a father?
> Or who has begotten the drops of dew?" (Job 38:25-28)

Could Job tell the rain where and when to pour? Could he direct the lightning? Why does God send the rain in the desert to water flowers that no man can see? Why?

Then be silent, Job, until such questions can be answered. God rains because God reigns.

Job's all wet. No answer.

Who Makes Ice?
Eighth, God questions Job about ice.

> "From whose womb has come the ice?
> And the frost of heaven, who has given it birth?"
>   (Job 38:29)

How much does Job know about ice? Does he know how it is "born"? Until Job can grasp this simple truth, how can he expect to understand the deeper mysteries of divine providence?

Job's brain is iced over. No answer.

Who Directs the Planets?
Ninth, God explores the rotation of the planets.

"Can you bind the chains of the Pleiades,
Or loose the cords of Orion?
Can you lead forth a constellation in its season,
And guide the Bear with her satellites?
Do you know the ordinances of the heavens,
Or fix their rule over the earth?" (Job 38:31-33)

Did Job understand their movements? Could Job steer the planets across the skies? Of course not. Only God can control the planets high above. Similarly, only God can control the circumstances here below.

Job's looking a little "spaced out." No answer.

Who Forms the Clouds?
Finally, God quizzes Job about the clouds.

"Can you lift up your voice to the clouds,
So that an abundance of water may cover you?
Can you send forth lightnings that they may go
And say to you, 'Here we are'?
Who has put wisdom in the innermost being,
Or has given understanding to the mind?
Who can count the clouds by wisdom,
Or tip the water jars of the heavens,
When the dust hardens into a mass,
And the clods stick together?" (Job 38:34-38)

Could Job command the clouds? Could he direct the lightning bolt where to strike? Could he tell the clouds where to deposit their water? The answer is no. Only God controls nature. Likewise, only God is fit to control Job's life. Only God can command the storms of life to come. Only God can command the lightning of adversity to strike his life. Only God.

Job's thinking is a little foggy. No answer.

By this time, Job is wanting a reprieve. He has not answered one question. Not one. Zero. Not even a bonus question will help.

Scrawled in a nervous hand across a blackboard at Southern Methodist University during finals week was this message: "We have nothing to fear but F itself."

Job's worst fears have come true. He has scored an F in God's final exam thus far.

Before Job can catch his breath, God moves into another series of questions. These will deal with God's providential working in the animal kingdom. God doesn't let up.

"I'LL TAKE ANIMALS FOR 10"

God says, "Job, let's try you on another subject. You didn't score too well on this first category. Let's move to another category. How about 'Animals for 10'?"

God now questions Job in ten more areas, dealing with the animal world. The purpose is to show the limits of Job's knowledge. God is not searching for answers from Job. Instead, He is getting Job to realize God's power and sovereignty. Only when Job is humbled and silenced would he be able to learn from God.

Who Feeds the Lion?

First, God asks Job about the lion.

> "Can you hunt the prey for the lion,
> Or satisfy the appetite of the young lions,
> When they crouch in their dens,
> And lie in wait in their lair?" (Job 38:39-40)

Can Job care for the lion? Can he feed the young lions? Would he even know that they were hungry?

No. But God can feed them. His providence supervises all of creation and makes sure that all creatures are cared for.

"Job, have you ever seen the lions standing in a welfare line waiting to get their food? I can feed them, can't I?" The implication is clear. Then God can rule the moral order of the universe equally well.

Job, cat got your tongue? No answer.

Who Feeds the Raven?

Second, God quizzes Job about the raven.

> "Who prepares for the raven its nourishment,
> When its young cry to God,
> And wander about without food?" (Job 38:41)

Who teaches the raven to find the carcasses left behind by the lions? God taught the raven this. He put the instinct within them.

If God runs the animal kingdom with such precision, so too does He govern the spiritual world. The God who feeds the birds of the air cares for you and me.

Job feels like a birdbrain. No answer.

Who Delivers the Goats and Deer?
Third and fourth, God quizzes Job about the mountain goats and the deer.

> "Do you know the time the mountain goats give birth?
> Do you observe the calving of the deer?
> Can you count the months they fulfill,
> Or do you know the time they give birth?
> They kneel down, they bring forth their young,
> They get rid of their labor pains.
> Their offspring become strong, they grow up in the open field;
> They leave and do not return to them." (Job 39:1-4)

Does Job know about obstetrical care for the animals? Does he know about the gestation period for goats? Or how baby deer were born? Or how the mother knows when to send her young ones off to college?

Of course not. Job is totally ignorant of such divine workings. So too is he ignorant of much of God's divine workings in his life.

"Job, who delivers the baby animals? You or Me? If you don't understand how I work through pregnancy, labor, and delivery, how could you possibly understand this season of pain through which I am bringing you? It's all with a purpose. It's all a part of My master design. Just like the mountain calf and deer deliver at the end of the gestation time, so you will be delivered from your pain in due time."

Job's feeling like the goat of the game. No answer.

Who Made the Donkey Wild?
Fifth, God examines Job about the wild donkey.

> "Who sent out the wild donkey free?
> And who loosed the bonds of the swift donkey,
> To whom I gave the wilderness for a home,
> And the salt land for his dwelling place?

He scorns the tumult of the city,
The shoutings of the driver he does not hear.
He explores the mountains for his pasture,
And he searches after every green thing." (Job 39:5-8)

Who made the wild donkey to roam the wilderness wild? Who made the donkey to be undomesticated? Surely not Job. God did that. Job is impotent to control God's creation this way. He is therefore impotent to manipulate God with his demands.

God says, "Job, I know exactly what I am doing. Everyone has their assigned place. So why are you having trouble staying in your place?"

Nervously, Job clears his throat. In bewilderment, he shrugs his shoulders.

He's feeling like a jackass! No answer.

Who Made the Ox Wild?

Sixth, God asks Job about the wild ox.

"Will the wild ox consent to serve you?
Or will he spend the night at your manger?
Can you bind the wild ox in a furrow with ropes?
Or will he harrow the valleys after you?
Will you trust him because his strength is great
And leave your labor to him?
Will you have faith in him that he will return your grain,
And gather it from your threshing floor?" (Job 39:9-12)

This animal cannot be tamed by man. Certainly not by Job. This wild animal refuses to obey man's commands. It will not be housebroken. The ox has a mind all its own.

So, why should Job think he can tame God? Just like the wild ox, its Creator refuses to obey Job's commands. God is independent and autonomous. He has a mind and will all His own. Job should learn about God from His creation.

"What makes you think you can control Me when you can't even control the wild ox? I'm the One who created the wild ox!" God is revealing to Job that He is so much greater than he ever imagined. God is uncontrolled.

Job feels as dumb as an ox. No answer.

Who Made the Ostrich Strange?
Seventh, God examines Job about the ostrich.

> "The ostriches' wings flap joyously
> With the pinion and plumage of love
> For she abandons her eggs to the earth,
> And warms them in the dust,
> And she forgets that a foot may crush them,
> Or that a wild beast may trample them.
> She treats her young cruelly, as if they were not hers;
> Though her labor be in vain, she is unconcerned;
> Because God has made her forget wisdom,
> And has not given her a share of understanding.
> When she lifts herself on high,
> She laughs at the horse and his rider." (Job 39:13-18)

God points to the ostrich and says, "Explain this." The ostrich is a funny-looking bird. Strange. Foolish. Bizarre. Why did God create an animal that leaves her eggs unprotected and then forgets where she put them?

The point is, there will be parts of God's world that seem strange—like the ostrich—yet they are designed parts of God's wise plan. Life may seem strange—even bizarre—to Job, but it is a part of God's wise plan.

"Job, just as you can't understand the ostrich, how could you possibly understand the trials of your life?" It seems so foolish.

Look at the ostrich and learn. This bird lays its eggs and then seems to forget where she put them. Similarly, it may seem that God has forgotten where He placed Job. But not so. The God who created the ostrich is the God who created Job. Everything is going according to His master plan.

Job wishes he could stick his head in the sand. No answer.

Who Made the Horse Courageous?
Eighth, God questions Job about the horse. Who made this animal so courageous?

> "Do you give the horse his might?
> Do you clothe his neck with a mane?
> Do you make him leap like the locust?

His majestic snorting is terrible.
He paws in the valley, and rejoices in his strength;
He goes out to meet the weapons.
He laughs at fear and is not dismayed;
And he does not turn back from the sword.
The quiver rattles against him,
The flashing spear and javelin.
With shaking and rage he races over the ground;
And he does not stand still at the voice of the trumpet.
As often as the trumpet sounds he says, 'Aha!'
And he scents the battle from afar,
And thunder of the captains, and the war cry." (Job 39:19-25)

Who made the horse so eager to run into battle? Who gave the horse its kick and fury? Who made the horse to love to compete? Who made the horse to answer the trumpet call and gallop to the battlefield on the day of war? Not Job! It was God.

So God alone is qualified to govern the affairs of men. Not Job.

Job, are you a little "horse"? No answer?

Who Made the Hawk Soar?
Ninth, God tests Job about the hawk.

"Is it by your understanding that the hawk soars,
Stretching his wings toward the south?" (Job 39:26)

Who gave the hawk its migrating instinct to fly south? Who made the hawk to soar high above and glide so effortlessly? It was God—not Job—who made the hawk this way. Similarly, only God can help us soar above life's problems with grace.

Job wishes he could fly south. No answer.

Who Made the Eagle Nest on High?
Finally, God examines his critic about the eagle.

"Is it at your command that the eagle mounts up,
And makes his nest on high?
On the cliff he dwells and lodges,
Upon the rocky crag, an inaccessible place.

From there he spies out food;
He sees it from afar.
His young ones also suck up blood;
And where the slain are, there he is." (Job 39:27-30)

Who gave the eagle the instinct to build its nest high on the cliffs? Who made the eagle with such keen eyesight? Who made it with such fierce courage to find other animals to feed upon?

God did this. Similarly, just as the eagle can look down with keen eyesight, so does God, its Creator. God looks down from high above and sees all our lives with penetrating insight. He sees us and feeds us. He provides for all our needs. Job, look at the eagle and learn about God!

Job realizes that a turkey can't fly with the eagles. No answer.

The story is told about the college student who took a final exam at the end of the semester. When he received his exam, he was stunned. He didn't know the answer to any of the questions. Not one! This was devastating.

Attempting to win his professor's favor with humor, the student wrote at the top of the exam page, "Only *God* knows the answer to these questions. Merry Christmas!"

While at home during the Christmas break, the student received his exam in the mail, graded by the professor. At the top, it read, "Then *God* gets 100, and *you* get a 0. Happy New Year!"

Like that student, Job has now flunked God's exam. He has scored a big, fat zero. He has not answered one of the questions, because only God knows the answers.

God gets 100; Job gets a 0.

JOB, I'M WAITING!

Job sits in silence. He is blown away, overwhelmed, and stunned. Slam-dunked. But God doesn't let up. Not one bit. In fact, He pours it on even more. While Job is gasping for air, God reloads and fires again.

Then the LORD said to Job,
"Will the faultfinder contend with the Almighty?
Let him who reproves God answer it." (Job 40:1-2)

Using courtroom language, God calls upon Job to present his case. God has presented His case. Where is Job's case?

God says, "I'm waiting for an answer! Speak up, Job! How many of My questions have you gotten right? If you can't answer the ABC's about the physical world, how can you possibly think you know so much about My running of the spiritual world?"

> Then Job answered the LORD and said,
> "Behold, I am insignificant; what can I reply to Thee?
> I lay my hand on my mouth.
> Once I have spoken, and I will not answer;
> Even twice, and I will add no more."
>   (Job 40:3-5)

Devastated and humbled, Job says, "I have no right to open my mouth! God, You're in the Big Leagues and I'm just in T-Ball. I am nothing compared to You. I'm not going to say another word against You. The more I talk, the more I condemn myself." Job is still not brought to the point of repentance. He is silenced, but God must take him yet lower. Job must still come to the place where he fully repents before God.

JOB, COME SIT ON MY THRONE!

If possible, God now becomes even more sarcastic. If these next words were not in the Bible, I would be fearful of blasphemy. But these are God's words, not mine. God taunts Job to come sit on His throne and do a better job of being God.

> Then the LORD answered Job out of the storm, and said,
> "Now gird up your loins like a man;
> I will ask you, and you instruct Me.
> Will you really annul My judgment?
> Will you condemn Me that you may be justified?" (Job 40:6-8)

With divine ridicule, God mocks Job, "Strap it on! We're going at it again. Since you have scored so well on your exam, why don't you teach Me about life? I only created it. You instruct Me. Will you condemn Me in My own court?"

> "Or do you have an arm like God,
> And can you thunder with a voice like His?
> Adorn yourself with eminence and dignity;

And clothe yourself with honor and majesty.
Pour out the overflowings of your anger;
And look on everyone who is proud, and make him low.
Look on everyone who is proud, and humble him;
And tread down the wicked where they stand.
Hide them in the dust together;
Bind them in the hidden place.
Then I will also confess to you,
That your own right hand can save you." (Job 40:9-14)

God now escalates His sarcasm. He chides, "Are you as strong as God? Do you have the strength to judge sinners and sit on My throne? Let's see if you can act like Me. You say you can do a better job at being God than Me? Come on, Job! You can do a better job than I am doing running the universe. Come on!"

God is playing hardball with Job. And Job doesn't have a glove.

"Come on, Job. Put My crown on your big head. Sit upon My throne, Job. Clothe yourself with majesty, and I'll bow down and worship you."

God says, "Let's see if you can do a better job running the universe. Let's start with a couple problems that I have to deal with on a daily basis. Can you humble the proud? That's what I have to do on a daily basis. I spend my time humbling those who are proud (hint, hint!). Job, can you do that? If so, start with yourself. Then I will bow down and worship you."

Can You Capture the Hippopotamus?

God now returns to the natural world and parades two more animals before Job. The first is the Behemoth, which means "superbeast." Most Bible teachers believe that this animal is the hippopotamus. The hippo was a powerful force, especially in Job's day when men hunted with bows and arrows. God will ask Job if he thinks he can control this animal. If Job can't, then God will ask, "What makes you think you can control Me?"

"Behold now, Behemoth, which I made as well as you;
He eats grass like an ox.
Behold now, his strength in his loins,
And his power in the muscles of his belly.
He bends his tail like a cedar;
The sinews of his thighs are knit together.

His bones are tubes of bronze;
His limbs are like bars of iron.
He is the first of the ways of God;
Let his maker bring near his sword.
Surely the mountains bring him food,
And all the beasts of the field play there.
Under the lotus plants he lies down,
In the covert of the reeds and the marsh.
The lotus plants cover him with shade;
The willows of the brook surround him.
If a river rages, he is not alarmed;
He is confident, though the Jordan rushes to his mouth."
　　(Job 40:15-23)

The hippo has a powerful body, strong muscles, and steel-like bones. But man? He is frail and weak. The hippo swims in the river and nibbles upon plants, while man must work hard to eat. Even a raging river doesn't frighten this animal.

"Can anyone capture him when he is on watch,
With barbs can anyone pierce his nose?" (Job 40:24)

God asks, "Job, could you go fishing and catch a hippopotamus? Could you reel him in and bring him under your control? No, Job, you couldn't. So what makes you think you could do this to the Creator of that hippopotamus? You can't do anything with the hippopotamus, much less its Creator."

Can You Control the Crocodile?
Next, God brings a second animal before Job—Leviathan. Most believe this animal is a crocodile.

"Can you draw out Leviathan with a fishhook?
Or press down his tongue with a cord?
Can you put a rope in his nose?
Or pierce his jaw with a hook?" (Job 41:1-2)

Could you go fishing and catch a crocodile? Could you reel in a hungry croc? Not even Crocodile Dundee could do that.

"Will he make many supplications to you?
Or will he speak to you soft words?
Will he make a covenant with you?
Will you take him for a servant forever?
Will you play with him as with a bird?
Or will you bind him for your maidens?
Will the traders bargain over him?
Will they divide him among the merchants?
Can you fill his skin with harpoons,
Or his head with fishing spears?
Lay your hand on him;
Remember the battle; you will not do it again
Behold, your expectation is false;
Will you be laid low even at the sight of him?
No one is so fierce that he dares to arouse him;
Who then is he that can stand before Me?
Who has given to Me that I should repay him?
Whatever is under the whole heaven is Mine." (Job 41:3-11)

This is hilarious! God taunts Job and asks, "If you catch a crocodile, what would you do with it?" Could you make it pray to you? Could
you train it?

If Job can't subdue the crocodile, he surely can't subdue the croc's
Creator. No way.

With each quiz and question and penetrating interrogation, God is
bringing Job lower and lower and lower until he finally comes to the
very end of himself and can only look up and yield his life to God.

"I will not keep silence concerning his limbs,
Or his mighty strength, or his orderly frame.
Who can strip off his outer armor?
Who can come within his double mail?
Who can open the doors of his face?
Around his teeth there is terror.
His strong scales are his pride,
Shut up as with a tight seal.
One is so near to another,
That no air can come between them.
They are joined one to another;

They clasp each other and cannot be separated."
   (Job 41:12-17)

God gives a poetical description of this great creature. Mighty limbs. Fierce teeth. Strong jaws. Hard covering.

"His sneezes flash forth light,
And his eyes are like the eyelids of the morning.
Out of his mouth go burning torches;
Sparks of fire leap forth.
Out of his nostrils smoke goes forth,
As from a boiling pot and burning rushes.
His breath kindles coals,
And a flame goes forth from his mouth.
In his neck lodges strength,
And dismay leaps before him.
The folds of his flesh are joined together,
Firm on him and immovable.
His heart is as hard as a stone;
Even as hard as a lower millstone." (Job 41:18-24)

When the crocodile churns up river, it blows out water. The sun reflects upon the spray, and it could resemble fire and smoke from a dragon's mouth. His armor is so strong that he can go anywhere without fear.

"When he raises himself up, the mighty fear;
Because of the crashing they are bewildered.
The sword that reaches him cannot avail;
Nor the spear, the dart, or the javelin.
He regards iron as straw,
Bronze as rotten wood.
The arrow cannot make him flee;
Slingstones are turned into stubble for him.
Clubs are regarded as stubble;
He laughs at the rattling of the javelin.
His underparts are like sharp potsherds;
He spreads out like a threshing sledge on the mire.

He makes the depths boil like a pot;
He makes the sea like a jar of ointment.
Behind him he makes a wake to shine;
One would think the deep to be gray-haired.
Nothing on earth is like him,
One made without fear.
He looks on everything that is high;
He is king over all the sons of pride." (Job 41:25-34)

Here is a description of Leviathan—fierce anger and courage. People flee from him in fear, but he doesn't flee. The crocodile laughs at man's weapons. His underside is protected with an impregnable covering. He fears no enemy on land or in the water!

This brings God's science quiz to a conclusion.

Job's S.A.T. exam (the *S*overeign *A*lmighty's *T*est) is now concluded, and he has flunked miserably. Flunked is hardly strong enough. He hasn't even scored. He has made a big fat zero. Job bombed all seventy-seven questions. He couldn't answer even one.

How devastating!

Job is jolted by this assault of divine inquiry. He once thought he had *all* the answers. He now painfully realizes that he has *none* of the answers. In fact, he doesn't even know the questions. Much less the answers.

Why has God put Job through this painful exam? Quite simply, to reveal Himself to Job, and in the process, to put Job in his proper place. Through this interrogation, God has taught Job that He alone created everything—the heavens and the earth, and all that is in them—and He alone controls all that He created. He alone has the right to do with His own as He pleases. He is under no obligation to explain His actions to His creation. He alone is sovereign and unaccountable to anyone. Period. End of paragraph.

That's the lesson revealed by God to Job. In the absence of knowing why, Job needs only to know God. Only in seeing and knowing God will Job find the relief for which he is searching.

Job is so overwhelmed by this revelation of divine holiness and glory that he is now silent before God. He is too stunned to speak.

OVERWHELMED BY HIS GREATNESS

When was the last time you were overwhelmed by God?

Recently, I took my twin sons to Chicago, and while there we went to see the Sears Tower—the world's tallest building—which rises majestically above the downtown Chicago skyline. (We went to see Michael Jordan and the Chicago Bulls play the Charlotte Hornets, but we took in a little culture along the way.)

When we landed in Chicago, we went straight to the Sears Tower so that we could get an eagle's eye view of the city from the observation deck.

When we stepped out of the taxi, I stood on the sidewalk at the foot of the Sears Tower and instinctively looked up to try to see the top. As my eyes scanned up the side of the building, a few butterflies fluttered in my stomach. My head reared back. My neck arched upward, as I kept looking up and up and up, straining to see the top. The building just seemed to rise forever. The sight line disappeared into the lofty clouds overhead. I couldn't even see the top!

The clouds moving behind the tower gave an eerie illusion of the entire building moving. Suddenly, I felt incredibly dizzy. My head began to spin. My heart fluttered. My knees shook. Fear jerked a knot in my stomach. I was terrified of its imposing height. Intimidated. Overwhelmed.

My sons said, "Let's go up in it, Dad!"

"Wait a minute, guys," I replied. "Let's rest a second. I think we're all a little tired from the flight."

"No, Dad, let's go up right now," they chorused enthusiastically.

Back home in Little Rock, I couldn't wait to go to the top of this world-famous tower. But in its presence, I was scared to death!

There I was face-to-face with this eighth wonder of the world. It loomed 110 stories directly overhead. It's 76,000 tons of steel seemed to be ready to swallow my tiny frame. The 1,400 foot structure, 4.5 million gross square feet, 16,000 bronze-tinted windows, and 222,500 tons made me feel smaller than a speck of dust.

I was absolutely, completely, unequivocally horrified by the immense height of this towering structure.

No way I am going up into it! I thought.

Well, it took me a whole day to work up my courage. The next day we rode to the top—in a blowing snowstorm. What a father will do for his children!

Why do I share this story? Simply to illustrate this.

Earlier, Job couldn't wait to appear before God. He was eager to present his case in Heaven and press his arguments against God. But now, in God's presence, Job is reduced to his rightful place—a mere speck of God's own creation.

Job looks up and sees God—the sovereign Creator, the Judge of Heaven and earth—and is filled with holy fear. He now sees God for who He really is. In that revelation, he grows deeply in his personal knowledge of the Almighty. In that terrifying experience, he discovers that God is far greater than he ever imagined!

Job is now undone by the sheer magnitude of God's towering presence. He is awestruck. Stunned. Unnerved. Petrified. Paralyzed. Scared stiff. Suddenly, all his arguments are forgotten. His charges are dropped. Job has seen God, and everything else is put into proper perspective.

So it must be with us. Our souls must be gripped with holy awe for God. We must look up and see God in His unveiled, unrivaled holiness. Only then will we be able to pass through the dark night of the soul. Our faith will be strong only when our hearts are filled with a healthy fear of God.

That's where we must all find ourselves before God.

Speechless. Spitless. And all shook up.

CHAPTER 13

NOWHERE TO LOOK BUT UP

▼

As I think back over my life, one scene is indelibly etched upon my mind. I will never forget it.

As a young boy of five years old, I was in the backyard playing baseball by myself. I was running around an imaginary diamond, sliding into makeshift bases, signaling myself safe at home plate before an imaginary crowd. (I was a legend in my own mind!)

In the midst of this game, a bee started buzzing overhead and chasing me. I was terrified! So, I took off running to escape the bee and bolted up the back steps of our house. On the dead run, I hit the back door going full blast, assuming that the French-window–paned back door was unlocked.

It wasn't!

The door was locked tighter than a bank vault. I shoved my hand forward to push the glass door open, but the door didn't budge. My arm went crashing through the door and glass shattered everywhere. My wrist was deeply slashed and blood spewed everywhere. Mom and Dad were down in the basement and when they heard me screaming, they came running up the stairs in time to see blood gushing everywhere.

Dad scooped me up into his strong arms and carried me to our station wagon. I was scared to death as we made a mad dash to the hospital.

We ran through the doors and the next thing I knew, I was lying flat on my back in the emergency room. I cannot begin to tell you how terrified I was.

A flood of lights was shining down upon me as a team of nurses and doctors huddled over me. As I looked up, all I could see were the faces of total strangers staring down at me.

I tried to look over at my wrist, but a dividing curtain had been draped over my arm so I couldn't see them cleaning the glass out of my wound and beginning to stitch my lacerated wrist back up.

I struggled to get up off the table, but I couldn't. Two nurses were holding me down by my shoulders. The fact that I was pinned down and couldn't get up only added to my panic. I wrestled to get free but couldn't budge. I was trapped!

Then another head popped into view. I looked up and, peering out from behind the doctors' and nurses' heads was the most reassuring sight that I could possibly see. It was my dad's face. Amid the blinding lights and strange faces, I could now see my father's face!

As soon as I saw his face, my tense body relaxed. I became limp as a dishrag and lay still on the operating table. My wrist still hurt while they were cleaning out the glass from my wound, but I now knew everything would be okay. *Dad was there!* That was all I needed to assure me. As long as I could see my dad's face, I knew I'd be okay.

That's exactly where Job finds himself. Knocked down. Deeply hurt. Lying flat on his back. Looking up. Seeing the face of God. He now ceases to struggle.

Ever since Job's friends began accusing him of wrongdoing, he has been greatly panicked. Job has been frantic and in pain. But God now pins Job flat on his back, and he looks up into the face of God as never before. In that moment, Job knows everything is going to be okay.

Job sees God as the sovereign Creator of Heaven and earth. With a new awareness beyond his previous understanding, he realizes that God is greater than all his trials. God is above and beyond his ability to grasp.

God still hasn't told Job why he is suffering. Job doesn't have a clue why. All Job knows is that God is here. And that He is sufficient. It's a matter of trust. Job doesn't have to know *why*. All he needs to know is *who*.

Can you relate to this? Are you going through a trial and still struggling to see behind a curtain? Have you come to the place where you are knocked flat on your back and look up into the face of God? Do you see a sovereign God who is totally in control of all your circumstances?

Sure, God could explain everything to us of His workings behind the scenes of our trials. But we wouldn't be able to understand it. How can His infinite wisdom fit into our finite brains? All we need to know is that God is sovereignly in control of our lives and loves us very much.

Maybe you need to come to that place in your life. If so, I urge you to stop your squirming and simply look up. Look up and see the face of God. When there are no answers, there is still comfort for your troubled hearts. Peace is found in knowing the God who is there and who is sovereign. Strength is found in knowing the God who controls the universe.

As we come to the end of the book, Job now looks up and sees God in a new and fuller way. He now grasps that God is perfectly orchestrating all of the events of his life. He can trust God with his life. God is God.

Job is finally brought to the end of himself. That's good because the end of ourselves is the beginning of God. Notice Job's response of faith.

JOB'S RESPONSE

Job now humbles himself, opens his heart, and submits to God. This is one of the great confessions in all the Bible. Listen to Job's words of faith in God. Are these yours, too?

Recognize God's Sovereignty

First, Job recognized God's right to rule his life. So must we. God alone is sovereign. Job now accepts God's plan for his life, which includes suffering. None of God's plans can be overturned. Not by Satan. Not by man. Not by circumstances. Not by anything. God is absolutely sovereign.

> Then Job answered the LORD, and said,
> "I know that Thou canst do all things,
> And that no purpose of Thine can be thwarted." (Job 42:1-2)

God is God, whether we recognize it or not. So we might as well recognize it. He sits on His throne and does whatever He pleases.

Years later, Nebuchadnezzar, the Babylonian king, made the same declaration of God's sovereignty.

> "All the inhabitants of the earth are accounted as nothing,
> But He does according to His will in the host of heaven
> And among the inhabitants of earth;
> And no one can ward off His hand
> Or say to Him, 'What hast Thou done?' " (Daniel 4:35)

Man proposes, but God disposes.

Have you recognized God's sovereignty over your life? He chose you to be born in the family in which you were born. He gave you the parents He wanted. He had you born where He wanted. He had you born the gender you are. With the physical size, health, and appearance you have. It's all His right to choose. It's ours to accept.

Realize God's Inscrutability

Second, Job realized that God's ways are past finding out. They are inscrutable.

> "Who is this that hides counsel without knowledge?
> Therefore I have declared that which I did not understand."
>   (Job 42:3)

Job admits now that he spoke about divine things he didn't understand. He had spoken presumptuously about spiritual things beyond his comprehension. God is infinite. Our finite minds cannot fully grasp His infinite wisdom. We cannot fathom the deep things of God. He is past finding out.

We must live with divine mysteries in our Christian life. The lines of providence intersect far above our head. But what is darkness to our mind is sunshine to our heart. The Apostle Paul came to this very conclusion when he wrote, "Oh, the depth of the riches both of the wisdom and knowledge of God! How unsearchable are His judgments and unfathomable His ways! For who has known the mind of the Lord, or who became His counselor?" (Romans 11:33-34).

Appropriately, Jerry Bridges sounds a needed warning: "We need to be cautious of others who offer themselves as interpreters about the why and wherefore of all that is happening. Be wary of those who say,

'God let this happen so that you might learn such and such a lesson.'
The fact is, we do not *know* what God is doing through a particular set
of circumstances or events."[1]

Reflect on God's Superiority
Third, Job assumed a teachable spirit. No longer did he have all the answers.
Not after failing God's exam. Job is now ready to learn from God.

> "Hear, now, and I will speak;
> I will ask Thee, and do Thou instruct me." (Job 42:4)

Job now admits the bankruptcy of his own wisdom and insight. He
invites God to instruct him.

Suffering makes students of us all. Charles Spurgeon once said,
"The doorstep to the temple of wisdom is the knowledge of our own
ignorance." Job is standing at the very threshold now, ready to learn
life's most important lessons.

Refocus on God's Intimacy
Fourth, Job confessed that he now sees God and knows Him as never
before. No longer from a distance, Job now knows God face to face.

> "I have heard of Thee by the hearing of the ear;
> But now my eye sees Thee." (Job 42:5)

Job now sees God with the eyes of a renewed faith and with a
deeper spiritual understanding. Comparing his new awareness of God
with his previous experience is like comparing seeing with hearing. Job
now has a deeper insight into God's character. A more accurate view of
His attributes.

Christianity is a personal—and abiding—relationship with God
and Jesus Christ (John 17:3), a relationship in which we grow closer
to Him and know Him more fully. Is that true of your life? Are you
growing in your knowledge of God?

Job has been humbled. He has been knocked off his high horse and
is now prostrate before God. Humility is always the mark of godliness
and maturity.

Repent of All Sin
Finally, Job repented of the presumptuous words he spoke against God.

"Therefore I retract,
And I repent in dust and ashes." (Job 42:6)

Job's heart is painfully convicted of the audacious charges he leveled against God. He is convicted of his rebellious pride. Both his actions and attitudes were wrong!

Repenting in dust and ashes was a cultural sign of humility and grief. This external sign expresses the internal sorrow of his heart. Job is a broken man in deep turmoil over his sin.

One mark of a great person is not that he or she never sins. But that when the person does sin, he or she is sorrowful and broken over that sin. Vince Lombardi once said that a champion is not the team that never suffers defeat, but the team that bounces back after defeat! The same is true spiritually.

King David was a man after God's own heart, not because he never sinned. He was a godly man because when he sinned he was deeply broken over it and chose to turn back to God. That's the case with Job. Job sinned against God with prideful rebellion. But once God revealed his sin to him, Job was quick to repent.

What about you? Is your heart quick to repent when God points out your sin? Do you take full ownership of your sin by confessing it? Too many of us sin retail and want to confess it wholesale. We must humble ourselves and confess our sin.

I heard the story of two brothers who grew up on a farm. One went away to college to make a name for himself. He earned a law degree and quickly became a partner in a prominent law firm in the state capital. The other brother stayed on the family farm.

One day, the ambitious lawyer came and visited his brother, the farmer. Pompously, he asked, "Why don't you go out and make a name for yourself? Why don't you be somebody in this world so you can hold your head up high like me?"

The other brother pointed and said, "See that field of wheat out there? Look closely. Do you see it?"

"Yeah, what about it?"

"Notice carefully, those heads that are most mature and well-filled bend low to the ground. Only the *empty* heads stand up tall."

The point is clear. Empty heads stand tallest; mature hearts bend down low before God. We are never more like the Devil than when we are trying to elevate ourselves. And never more like Christ than when we humble ourselves.

Each of us must repent of the pride that elevates us. We must empty ourselves of self. We must clothe ourselves with humility. The Apostle Peter writes, "God is opposed to the proud, but gives grace to the humble" (1 Peter 5:5).

What a victory this is! God has won His wager with Satan. Job has worshiped God despite having his blessings removed. The Devil must now eat crow. He has lost the battle for Job's soul. Unknown to Job, God has won a great victory over Satan through his life. Job has brought glory to God by not cursing Him as Satan said he would. His faith in God, though weak, has remained true. The storm has passed.

A NEW BEGINNING

In the final scene, God restores all that was taken from Job's life. He restores it all twofold. God is a good God. He is a God of great mercy and grace. He more than made it up to Job. It was two steps backward, four steps forward.

Don't think God is some cosmic killjoy, making us squirm like worms in hot ashes. He isn't without feelings. Nor without pity. God couldn't hold back His love any longer and restored to Job all that he lost.

This same God will more than make up all your losses, too. The cross is a minus sign turned into a plus. It may happen in this lifetime. It may happen in the next life. But God will restore every loss. His grace is immeasurable; His mercy inexhaustible; His love inexpressible.

God Restored His Friends

God turns His attention to Job's three friends. You remember the "Three Amigos," don't you? Here they are one last time.

> It came about after the LORD had spoken these words to Job, that the LORD said to Eliphaz the Temanite, "My wrath is kindled against you and against your two friends, because you have not spoken of Me what is right as My servant Job has." (Job 42:7)

God addresses Eliphaz, the leader of this terrible trio. The Almighty was angry and thundered His displeasure. Their wrongdoing? They misrepresented God. They distorted who God is. No small offense.

How had they misrepresented God? These "Three Stooges" limited

God's sovereignty. They put God in a box. They claimed that human suffering must always be God's judgment for man's sin. Worse, they presumed to know why Job was suffering.

Wrong. Because God is sovereign, He freely acts in ways which we cannot predict or understand. God cannot be reduced to simplistic formulas and catchy clichés. They mouthed off things about God that were half-right, half-wrong. Suffering from diarrhea of the mouth, they claimed spiritual insight that none of them possessed.

> "Now therefore, take for yourselves seven bulls and seven rams, and go to My servant Job, and offer up a burnt offering for yourselves, and My servant Job will pray for you. For I will accept him so that I may not do with you according to your folly, because you have not spoken of Me what is right, as My servant Job has." (Job 42:8)

Here is the path leading to God's forgiveness. A blood sacrifice. The three counselors must offer seven bulls and seven rams. This large sacrifice indicates the magnitude of their sin. But it also points to the even greater magnitude of God's grace.

Acting as a priest, Job was to participate in their sacrifice, praying that God will accept them. In so doing, Job was to forgive those who had attacked and hurt him. Just as God has forgiven Job, so must Job forgive his friends.

This is our pattern for living. "Be kind to one another, tender-hearted, forgiving each other, just as God in Christ also has forgiven you" (Ephesians 4:32).

A man was telling a friend about an argument he'd had with his wife. He said, "Oh, I hate it. Every time we have an argument, she gets historical."

The friend replied, "You mean hysterical."

"No," he insisted, "I mean historical. Every time we argue, she drags up the past and gets historical."

Well, Job must not get historical with his three friends. He must forgive them of their past sins against him and move on. The past is past.

Is there someone you need to forgive? Are you harboring a grudge? Forgive that person and move on.

How did Job's three friends handle this? "So Eliphaz the Temanite and Bildad the Shuhite and Zophar the Naamathite went and did as the LORD told them; and the LORD accepted Job" (Job 42:9).

Swallowing their pride, the three friends obeyed God and offered these sacrifices. It was these sacrifices that prevented them from receiving what they deserved—the heavy hand of God's discipline. Instantly, God wiped the slate clean on the basis of this blood sacrifice. Job is now reconciled with his friends and vice versa.

God is in the business of forgiving sin. He can take all our sins and wipe our slate clean. Immediately, our past can be purged.

To repeat the words of the prophet:

"Come now, and let us reason together,"
Says the LORD,
"Though your sins are as scarlet,
They will be as white as snow;
Though they are red like crimson,
They will be like wool." (Isaiah 1:18)

A wealthy English merchant lived on the European continent. He was very eccentric and satisfied with only the best of everything.

So naturally, he had to drive a Rolls-Royce coupe. It was his pride and joy. But one day, after years of perfect service, he hit a deep pothole and his rear axle broke.

This Englishman shipped the car back to the Rolls-Royce plant and was surprised when the car was repaired overnight and returned to him without a bill. Although his warranty had run out, there was no charge. The car was fixed perfectly, all for free.

The owner called the company and inquired about the repair. The reply said, "We have absolutely no record of your Rolls-Royce axle ever breaking. There can be no charge."

The company's commitment to excellence would not permit a flaw to be made known. Therefore, they had repaired the injury immediately and without charge. As if nothing had ever gone wrong.

So it is with God's grace. When we confess our sin, Christ forgives us immediately and without charge. As if nothing had ever gone wrong.

God Restored His Fortune
And Job? What happened to him?

And the LORD restored the fortunes of Job when he prayed for
his friends, and the LORD increased all that Job had twofold.
Then all his brothers, and all his sisters, and all who had known
him before, came to him, and they ate bread with him in his
house; and they consoled him and comforted him for all the evil
that the LORD had brought on him. (Job 42:10-11)

When Job prayed for his friends, it was then that God restored his
lost fortune. Forgiving others opens up the floodgates of God's blessing
to pour into our own lives. The best way to get even is to forgive. Job's
brothers, sisters, and acquaintances rallied around him now. They ate
with him, consoled him, and comforted him for all the adversity he had
suffered.

And each one gave him one piece of money, and each a ring
of gold. And the LORD blessed the latter days of Job more than
his beginning, and he had 14,000 sheep, and 6,000 camels, and
1,000 yoke of oxen, and 1,000 female donkeys. (Job 42:11-12)

Job's family and friends brought him gifts of silver and gold. Then
God restored Job's livestock double what he had before. He started
with seven thousand sheep; now he has fourteen thousand. He started
with three thousand camels; now he has six thousand. He started with
five hundred oxen and five hundred donkeys; now he has a thousand
of each. God gave Job double everything he had to start with.

That is the grace of God. He longs to bless us to the extent we can
handle it. Job is a humble servant who can handle it.

God Restored His Family
God gave Job a new family as well.

And he had seven sons and three daughters. And he named
the first Jemimah, and the second Keziah, and the third Keren-
happuch. And in all the land no women were found so fair as
Job's daughters; and their father gave them inheritance among
their brothers. (Job 42:13-15)

God gave Job seven more sons and three more daughters. Maybe you
are thinking, "God has doubled everything but his sons and daughters. He

ended up with the same number of children with which he started."

Think about it this way. God did double his family. He now has ten children in Heaven and another ten on the earth. A total of twenty children. God did double his family.

Job named his three daughters Jemimah (meaning "dove"), Keziah ("perfume"), and Keren-happuch ("eye makeup"). Here is the fruit of Job's suffering. Peace like a dove, sweet fragrance like perfume, and beauty like eye makeup. Symbolically, God's peace, fragrance, and beauty is added to Job's life through his daughters.

In a move absolutely unheard of in the ancient world, Job is so moved that he includes his daughters in the family inheritance, which was usually given only to one's sons. These daughters shared alike in their father's inheritance. Why the inclusion? No doubt, Job now sees his children through new eyes. His gratitude is so great for his new family, he shares all he has with them.

God Restored His Future
The book concludes with these words: "And after this Job lived 140 years, and saw his sons, and his grandsons, four generations. And Job died, an old man and full of days" (Job 42:16-17).

If Job was 70 years old at this time, as we believe, God also doubled his years. Tradition says he lived to be 210 years old. That's 70 plus double that amount. And you thought you were getting old! He lived to see four generations—his children, grandchildren, great-grandchildren, and great-great-grandchildren. What a legacy!

This great man lived a full life and died immersed in God's blessing. He is a picture of piety, peace, and plenty.

LOOK UP AND TRUST HIM

As we conclude this book, I don't know what you are going through in your life. There's a good chance that you can relate to Job in his suffering and heartache.

If you are going through a trial, I want to encourage you. Look up to God. He is in total control of your life. He has your problems firmly in His loving hands. Just as He did for Job, He will bring you safely through.

I began this chapter telling you about a trial I experienced. What comfort and assurance looking up into my father's face brought to my troubled heart.

Maybe your life is so dark that you can't even see God's face. The night is too dark. The storm too fierce. Your faith too frail. Even if you can't see Him working, know that He is there for you.

The story is told of a young husband who lost his wife to cancer. He was left all alone in the world to raise their young daughter.

The father and daughter's first night alone in the big house was not an easy night. The dinner table was desperately lonely.

As bedtime came that evening, an electrical storm broke out. Lines were down and their house was suddenly without electricity. Dark. Still. Quiet. Empty.

When the daddy tucked the little girl into bed, the room was pitch dark.

"Daddy, are you there?"

"Yes, sweetheart. I'm here."

"Daddy, I can't see you."

"Sweetheart, I'm here. I'm talking with you, aren't I?"

"Daddy, I've never been this scared before."

"Sweetheart, I'm here. Trust me, everything's going to be okay."

With that word of assurance, the little girl put her head on the pillow and fell fast asleep.

The dad made the long, lonely walk down the hall to his own bedroom. The storm continued to blow and howl against the house. It was so dark he couldn't even see his hand in front of his face.

Lightning suddenly flashed across the sky, lighting up the bedroom momentarily. Then the darkness draped the room again like black velvet.

Getting into bed, the widower stared up at the ceiling. His heart felt like the room. Dark. Empty. Stormy.

He turned his broken heart toward Heaven. "Father, are You there?"

He felt the assurance of God, "Yes, son. I'm here."

"Father, I can't see You."

"My son, I'm here. I'm talking with you, aren't I?"

"Father, I've never been this scared before."

"Son, I'm here. Trust Me. Everything's going to be okay."

With that assurance of heart, the dad put his head on the pillow and fell fast asleep.

God is there for you, too. He is there and will never leave you. Never. He cares too much for you. Even if the night is dark and the storm is raging, know that God is there. He is there for *you*.

Will you trust Him? Even if you don't understand why, will you trust Him? Trust Him because you know that He knows why. Just look up and trust Him. When you are flat on your back, it's easier to look up and trust Him. What else could you do?

When all hell breaks loose, maybe you are doing something right. Just trust Him.

NOTE

1. Jerry Bridges, *Trusting God* (Colorado Springs, CO: NavPress, 1988), page 128.

AUTHOR

Dr. Steven J. Lawson is the Senior Pastor of The Bible Church of Little Rock, Arkansas. He has a B.B.A. from Texas Tech University, a Th.M. from Dallas Theological Seminary, and a D.Min. from Reformed Theological Seminary. A former sportswriter for the Texas Rangers and the Dallas Cowboys, he is also a featured speaker for the Billy Graham Evangelistic Association. Steve is the author of *Men Who Win: Pursuing the Ultimate Prize*, published by NavPress.

Steve and his wife, Anne, have four children.

For speaking information, cassette tapes, or other information about Steve Lawson's ministry, please contact:

The Bible Church of Little Rock
10618 Breckenridge Drive
Little Rock, AR 72211
(501)227-4980